Evaluating Teacher Effectiveness in ESL/EFL Contexts

Edited by

Christine Coombe
Mashael Al-Hamly
Peter Davidson
Salah Troudi

Ann Arbor

THE UNIVERSITY OF MICHIGAN PRESS

ACKNOWLEDGMENTS

This book is dedicated to colleagues and students at our respective institutions (Dubai Men's College, Kuwait University, Zayed University, and the University of Exeter). We are especially grateful to chapter authors. Without their important contributions this book would not have been possible. Special appreciation goes to Kelly Sippell, Acquisitions Editor at the University of Michigan Press, whose keen eye for detail and knowledge of the field helped immensely. Finally, to our families, who endured patiently the long periods of time spent on the production of this book, we are profoundly grateful for their support. Naturally, we are responsible for any errors or omissions contained in this book.

Grateful acknowledgment is made to the following publishers, organizations, and individuals for permission to reprint materials.

Copyright Clearance Center for Teachers of English to Speakers of Other Languages for Figure 5 of Domains in Teacher Education.

McGraw-Hill Education for Chart about the Materials and Domains from Chapter 8 of Volume 4 of *China TESOL Assessment Program.* Used with permission.

The Teacher Educator for the Diversity Responsive Assessment Tool from *The Teacher Educator,* Vol. 38, No. 4 by D. M. Sobel, S. V. Taylor, and R. E. Anderson. Copyright © 2003 by *The Teacher Educator.* Reprinted by permission.

Every effort has been made to contact the copyright holders for permission to reprint borrowed material. We regret any oversights that may have occurred and will rectify them in future printings of this book.

Copyright © by the University of Michigan 2007
All rights reserved
Published in the United States of America
The University of Michigan Press
Manufactured in the United States of America

♾ Printed on acid-free paper

2010	2009	2008	2007		4	3	2	1

ISBN-10: 0-472-03209-7
ISBN-13: 978-0-472-03209-9

Library of Congress Cataloging-in-Publication Data

Evaluating teacher effectiveness in ESL/EFL contexts / edited by Christine Coombe . . .
  [et al.].
    p.   cm.
  Includes bibliographical references and index.
  ISBN-13: 978-0-472-03209-9 (pbk. : alk. paper)
  ISBN-10: 0-472-03209-7 (pbk. : alk. paper)
    1. English language—Study and teaching—Foreign speakers—Evaluation. I. Coombe,
Christine A. (Christine Anne), 1962-

  PE1128.A2E828   2007
  428.2′4—dc22   2006052978

CONTENTS

INTRODUCTION

Essential to the improvement of teaching effectiveness is evaluation. When the evaluation of teacher performance is used to make high-stakes decisions (licensure, contract renewal, salary increase, etc.), it is more important than ever that the system used be valid, reliable, and non-threatening. Done properly, teacher evaluation not only helps teachers improve their performance but also provides them with much needed and appreciated information about all of the positive aspects of their classroom. However, educators often view evaluation as an attempt to find out what is wrong rather than an opportunity to find out what is right and how to encourage and reinforce positive aspects of the classroom. This book was written *by* language teachers *for* language teachers and administrators, with a view to encouraging readers to look closely at how they, as teachers, are being evaluated and how they are evaluating other teachers.

Evaluating Teacher Effectiveness in ESL/EFL Contexts reflects the growing interest in teacher evaluation and appraisal. This volume consists of fifteen chapters in which authors writing from their own unique and global perspectives examine a wide range of issues related to the evaluation of teacher effectiveness. One of our primary goals in putting this volume together was to showcase some of the interesting work that is being done throughout the world in the area of teacher evaluation and appraisal.

This book is organized into four parts. **Part 1, Standards in Teacher Evaluation,** presents two chapters designed to provide an introduction and background information to the establishment of standards for teacher assessment. Emphasis in this section is placed on what a qualified teacher must know and be able to do. These chapters contextualize and set the tone for the chapters in the rest of the volume.

McCloskey, Thornton, and Touba (Chapter 1) open the volume with a description of a three-year project on setting standards for newly qualified teachers of English in an Egyptian context. After establishing the need for standards that would define what a qualified teacher must know and be able to do, the chapter describes the process of goal-setting; standards development; validation, review, and revision of standards; awareness-raising and dissemination of standards; working toward official adoption of standards; putting standards to use in educational policy and processes; and recognizing how standards-setting can lead to the discovery of the need for further policy change. The chapter concludes by offering implications and recommendations to benefit future standards projects in other locations.

Burton (Chapter 2) makes a case for a broader description of responsibility, one that reduces teacher dependence on prescriptive curriculum resources and increases the possibility of professional fulfillment in practical ways. Working from a Thai TESOL case-study perspective, she argues that teachers should engage in the three main phases of curriculum activity: planning, implementing, and evaluating. Burton believes that teachers' engagement necessarily involves responsibility for decisions in these three curriculum phases and that it is practical for teachers to support their own professional renewal through critical adaptation and the use of existing curriculum and performance evaluation resources.

Part 2, Case Studies in Evaluating Teacher Effectiveness, presents six innovative and state-of-the-art case studies of successful teacher evaluation programs in five different countries.

Kaufman (Chapter 3) describes the design and implementation of a comprehensive assessment system for teachers that occurred in conjunction with National Council for Accreditation of Teacher Education (NCATE) accreditation at a North American university. This multidimensional assessment system, designed to be formative in nature and focus on enhancing learning and teaching, included the development of assessment instruments; critical performance indicators and rubrics; and a process for data collection, aggregation, analysis, and reporting.

Curtis and Cheng (Chapter 4) describe a collaborative approach to performance appraisal of ESL teachers within the context of the intensive English for Academic Purposes program at a university in Ontario, Canada. This approach consists of a set of five core competencies in a three-part evaluation system based on self-assessment, peer assessment, and student feedback.

In Chapter 5, Miller and Young report on the introduction of a performance management system for teaching staff at an English Language Center of a major university in Hong Kong. In order to achieve buy-in from all stakeholders, the system developed is both evaluative and developmental.

In Chapter 6, Quirke describes a teacher-driven appraisal tool, referred to as the Performance Enhancement Program (PEP), that was recently developed at his institution in the United Arab Emirates. After providing the theoretical background to the PEP, Quirke outlines how the program was implemented. He then discusses how the PEP is different from other teacher appraisal schemes and makes recommendations on how the PEP might be adapted for use in other teaching contexts.

Stoynoff (Chapter 7) presents an ESOL teacher evaluation system that was used with beginning teachers in a master's in TESOL program in the United States. Although designed for a particular context, Stoynoff stresses that the assessment principles used to design it can be applied to developing credible teacher evaluation systems for both novice and experienced teachers in a wide range of educational contexts.

In Chapter 8, Murphey and Yaode present a rather radical approach to teacher evaluation and appraisal in China. They describe a set of portfolio-based Teacher

Performance Standards. They describe the current forms of teacher evaluation in China, discuss possible implementation problems, and offer suggestions to those wanting to introduce similar types of assessment in their own context.

Part 3, Research in Teacher Evaluation, presents four studies that investigate various aspects of teacher evaluation.

Bray (Chapter 9) reports on an action research project about five ESL teachers' involvement in a competency-based curriculum delivered to migrant students from Europe and Southeast Asia. The aim of the research is to explore the multiliteracies framework that included four primary aspects of literacy pedagogy: situated practice, overt instruction, critical framing, and transformed practice. Bray argues that teachers need to be valued for more than teaching linguistic skills. In the final stage of her study, she observed the participating teachers and evaluated them using the multiliteracy framework rather than looking for a set of discrete teaching skills. Teacher evaluation and professional development, Bray argues, need to foster critical framing abilities that will help teachers equip learners with cross-cultural and critical-thinking skills.

Using a Likert scale questionnaire and a set of open-ended questions, Burden and Troudi's (Chapter 10) study looks into what students think about how they evaluate their EFL teachers in a Japanese university context. The study is informed by a critical and emancipatory theoretical framework that allows the authors to challenge a number of assumptions and practices associated with students' ratings of teachers. The authors raise the issue of the complexity of defining effective teaching and the danger of appraising teachers against mandated standards and comments from students on readily observable facts like "the class started on time." They argue that while students should continue to contribute to teacher evaluation, there is a strong need to establish a teacher-centered and teacher-led evaluation involving a multifaceted process.

In a two-year case study conducted in Turkey, Eken (Chapter 11) intensively explores teacher effectiveness within a framework of teacher training and development. Using a battery of mainly qualitative instruments, the study, holistic in nature, involves trainers, teachers, and students and focuses mainly on their experiences and perceptions of teaching effectiveness. The findings reveal three main areas of teaching that are often not accounted for in evaluation and difficult to capture through classroom observations. These are the teachers' personal qualities, their personal skills and attitudinal qualities, and affective level techniques (the techniques and skills teachers use as part of their teaching methodology to create a positive learning environment and to affectively involve students in the lessons). Though these criteria are not enough to evaluate teachers, Ekin argues that without them teaching cannot be effective. Ekin's most significant contribution is undoubtedly the reexamination of teacher evaluation tools and the development of a set of holistic and analytical evaluation criteria that took place as a direct result of this study.

Davidson's study (Chapter 12), conducted at a tertiary institution in the United Arab Emirates, looks at teachers' views toward students' evaluation of their teaching, classroom observations carried out by administrators, and teaching portfolios submitted each year by the teachers. Not surprisingly the participants of the study showed little agreement on the most effective way of evaluating teachers. In a context where teachers' voices are often not heard, Davidson manages to report on teachers' concerns about the validity and reliability of the way they are evaluated. He argues that in his context, teacher evaluation is a complex and often a contentious issue that is used to form important decisions such as contract renewal, promotion, or passing probation rather than professional development. Although teachers tend to consider classroom observation as the most valid tool for evaluation, he calls for the adoption of a wider range of evaluative tools to do justice to the complex phenomenon of teaching.

The final section, **Part 4, Tools for Evaluating Teacher Effectiveness,** explores tools that can facilitate teacher evaluation.

In Chapter 13, Caroline Brandt examines the issue of self-evaluation. In her study, pre-service teacher trainees recorded their self-talk that facilitated reflection on their experiences of learning to become teachers. The chapter provides an overview of reflection in teacher education and outlines how self-awareness can be increased through self-talk. Finally, Brandt discusses what would be needed to be considered if this form of self-evaluation was to be used as part of the overall assessment of a teacher trainee's performance.

In Chapter 14, Sherry Taylor and Donna Sobel report on a standards-based evaluation tool that they developed in order to evaluate what they refer to as "diversity-responsive teaching"—that is, teaching students from a diverse range of backgrounds and with different abilities in multilingual and multicultural classrooms. This tool has been piloted and was found to have a high level of reliability. As noted, the innovative teacher evaluation tool that they describe can be used for developmental and mentoring purposes, enabling teachers to better meet the needs of their diverse teaching populations.

Finally, in Chapter 15, Fatma Alwan discusses how teaching portfolios can be used to evaluate faculty in her context. After outlining the context of teacher evaluation in public United Arab Emirates schools, she provides a rationale for using teaching portfolios for teacher evaluation. She then discusses how teaching portfolios were piloted and then gradually introduced into all of the public schools. Based on this experience and by drawing on the relevant literature, Alwan concludes by providing a number of invaluable recommendations on how to most effectively introduce teaching portfolios in other teaching contexts.

This book is a practical introduction and guide for teachers, teacher educators, and administrators who wish to implement a coherent, strategic, multiple-measures approach to evaluating teacher effectiveness. It reflects our own approaches to teacher evaluation and appraisal and draws on our combined experience in North America, Europe, the Middle East, and Far East.

PART 1:

Standards in Teacher Evaluation

Quality learning begins with quality teachers. Part 1 provides a foundation for teacher evaluation in the form of teacher standards. Standards are defined as what accomplished teachers should know and be able to do. Both chapters in this part provide an introduction and give important background information related to the establishment of standards for teacher assessment. It is our intention that these chapters contextualize and set the tone for the rest of the volume.

McCloskey, Thornton, and Touba (Chapter 1) share their experience of developing professional standards for newly qualified teachers of English in the context of Egypt.

Their discussion of several important stages within the standards development process allows educators in other contexts to adapt the process to their own educational settings. The authors conclude by offering implications and recommendations to benefit future standards projects in other locations.

In Chapter 2, Burton makes a case for a broader description of responsibility intended to reduce dependence on curricular resources and increase the possibility of professional fulfillment through practical ways using already existing resources. Burton takes teacher standards one step further and looks at experienced Southeast Asian teachers of English and ways in which they can further their knowledge of teaching and develop new skills. Using the TESOL/NCATE standards as a guide, she focuses much of her article on the core domain of professionalism.

Through these two chapters it is hoped that educators around the world can take standards and performance indicators such as those described in these chapters and apply them to their own teaching.

CHAPTER 1

New Standards for a New Era: Developing Tools to Assess the Qualified Teacher

Mary Lou McCloskey, Barbara Thornton, and Nadia Touba

Introduction

A foundation of teacher assessment is the establishment of standards that define what a qualified teacher must know and be able to do. Over a three-year period, we worked to facilitate the development of professional standards for newly qualified teachers of English by a national group of English language educators in Egypt. We document here the processes and outcome of this project for these reasons: the development and implementation of standards is a recent phenomenon; there is little documentation of the processes used to develop standards; the process in Egypt was highly effective at achieving the desired result: standards that truly represented the highly qualified teacher in Egypt, were Egyptian owned and well accepted, and are gradually being institutionalized and used in the process of making decisions regarding teacher education and teacher assessment. This chapter describes the process of goal setting; standards development; validation, review, and revision of standards; awareness-raising and dissemination of standards; working toward official adoption of standards; putting standards to use in educational policy and processes; and recognizing how standards-setting can lead to the discovery of the need for further policy change. We conclude by offering implications and recommendations to benefit future standards projects in other locations.

Background

To qualify as a teacher in Egypt, a student must complete a course in one of the twelve universities in Egypt. However, until recently, there was no clear, shared understanding of what it meant to be "qualified." A teacher from a Faculty of Education in one part of the country could receive completely different training in content and pedagogic knowledge and still be "qualified." While final exams exist at each university as a gateway into the profession, Egyptian universities are traditionally independent and autonomous in setting their curricula and prescribing courses and materials (El Naggar, 2002).

In an attempt to move away from the "I know when I see it" approach to describing qualified teacher status (Wiliam, 2004), the Center for the Development of English Language (CDELT) applied for funding from the Integrated English Language Program II (IELP-II)[1] to embark on a project to set standards for newly qualified teachers of English. The performance standards for pre-service teachers are the output of two years' work on the setting of standards. They provide concrete examples and explicit definitions of what pre-service teachers would have to know and be able to do to demonstrate that they are proficient in the skills and knowledge they have learned. However, the setting of standards in other parts of the world has shown that if standards are to be used to assess teachers in a valid, meaningful, and reliable way, the standards-setting process is vital. The process itself needs to be seen as fair, transparent, and based in the realities of what constitutes good practice (Cullingford, 1999). Above all, the process and products need to be owned by the end users.

The process used for the CDELT standards development project is notable for the care taken to ensure Egyptian ownership of both process and product, leading to both sustainability and maintainability of the standards developed. This chapter documents the STEPS project from conceptualization through implementation. We examine the steps taken and the lessons learned with recommendations relevant to the process of standards development and implementation in other countries and settings.

Part A: Setting Standards

CDELT's Standards for Teachers of English at Pre-Service (STEPS) Project worked with a national group of Egyptian educators to develop Egyptian standards for pre-service teachers. Standards were developed by the STEPS Task Force, which drafted indicators that further describe the standards and then carried out a broad field review involving stakeholders. The standards development phase of STEPS was completed in 2003.[2] The STEPS standards have since been put to use in Egypt, serving as a framework for the Egyptian National Standards Committee to develop teacher standards in the content areas of English, Arabic, Math, Science, and Social Studies. The STEPS project was based on a carefully thought-out and well-principled approach to standard setting that built on successes and challenges from projects working toward change in other contexts (Bishop, 1986). We first interviewed those who led those projects seeking to

---

[1] IELP-II was funded by the United States Agency for International Development (USAID) and managed by the Academy for Educational Development (AED) and AMIDEAST.

[2] STEPS Standards are available at *www.mindspring.com/~mlmcc/Final_STEPS.pdf.*

find out why those projects had failed to be implemented and used in Egypt. Reasons given were: (1) Expatriates led the project—Egyptians were not involved in writing the standards and were only peripherally involved in reviewing them; (2) Plans were not made for dissemination and use of the standards; and (3) Many of the Egyptian individuals involved were quite senior and retired shortly after the conclusion of the project. We took these reasons into account in the design of the project in the following ways.

Egyptian Ownership

For the STEPS project to succeed, its work needed to be widely owned by its Egyptian stakeholders rather than being perceived as the work of expatriates. Therefore, the leadership team included members from Egypt, as well as international consultants from the United States and the United Kingdom. Stakeholders were involved at every stage of the process from conception of the need for standards through outlining and writing standards, to final publication, dissemination, and application.

The STEPS project placed emphasis on Egyptian ownership of standards at a national level using the following means.

Wide Representation

Representatives from twelve Faculties of Education and the Ministry of Education served as members of the STEPS Task Force.

Process to Promote Consensus

Because achieving consensus and decision making in a large group were challenging tasks, activities to learn and practice these skills were a key feature of task force meetings.

Volunteer Participants

STEPS Task Force members were only reimbursed for the expenses they incurred in attending the workshops; they volunteered their time at workshops and for all their work between workshops. The voluntary nature of this work ensured that those who participated in the STEPS Task Force were genuinely committed and made possible the continuance of the work after IELP-II, the USAID-sponsored organization that worked with CDELT, withdrew.

Egyptian Leadership and Authorship

Every effort was made to build the capacity for Egyptian leadership of the project. We counted heavily on the leadership of Zeinab El Naggar, director of

CDELT and co-consultant in facilitating the task force workshops. Participants were given leadership opportunities to help task force members feel and take responsibility for the group. Egyptians played leadership roles in each day of the workshop and led the work teams of the project. During the early stages, consultants acted as facilitators, providing resources, training in various tools and methods for researching and developing standards, and structures for coming to consensus on standards. In the later stages of the standards development process, consultants would raise queries and offer suggestions as to wording. Consultants also played roles at various times as informants and editors. But they did not write the standards, which was the responsibility of task force members. This ensured that the standards genuinely would be the product of Egyptian expertise. A key to the smooth progression of the writing was the preliminary groundwork done to promote shared ownership and the giving and receiving of constructive feedback.

Focus on Dissemination and Use of Standards

We were concerned from the outset that the standards developed by the CDELT Task Force should go beyond being just a document on paper and actually be put into use. We were consistently concerned with sustainability in that standards produced should actually be used to improve education in Egypt. We also focused on maintainability—that standards would continue to be reviewed, expanded, and upgraded by Egyptians and that supporting materials would be developed and revised. Initially, we expected that CDELT would be the national center to assume responsibilities for providing leadership in disseminating and periodically reviewing standards, though since the completion of the STEPS standards, the continuation work has actually been done through the Egyptian National Standards Committee, which included a number of STEPS Task Force members. We also expected that the task force members would be prepared to put the standards to use in their own educational roles, to teach others about the standards, and to plan a schedule for periodic renewal at the conclusion of the project. Activities working toward sustainability included:

- *Focusing on uses of standards right from the outset.* We discussed how the standards we were producing might be used and also considered obstacles to their use.
- *Thorough testing for validity of the standards was key.*
- *Assuring that the task force included both senior staff to provide leadership and status to the product and junior faculty to provide energy and continuity.*

Challenges and Ways They Were Overcome

One of the challenges to the project was the level of written English required for developing standards. We addressed this by providing models and giving clear and specific feedback on the many draft documents. We also edited the standards for consistency and accuracy, subject to the approval of the task force.

A second challenge was developing a group with the ability to develop and write standards as a team. Task force members varied in writing expertise and were used to, and concerned with, taking individual credit for their work. We worked to teach the group members to give and receive constructive criticism and to share ownership of the final product.

A third challenge was that of working without remuneration. Most of the participants expected to be paid to work on an AID project. Project administrators felt that Egyptians would be more likely to own this work if they chose to do it for professional reasons. So, a third challenge was eliciting the motivation in participants to do this work—which involved significant effort in writing and meetings between the workshops—for the good of education in Egypt. A few participants felt that they could not commit their own time to the project and chose to drop out. Those who stayed with the task force communicated to us that their work was valuable and justified.

Building a Professional Community

In order to build a task force willing and able to work together to achieve tangible outcomes, we designed activities that would develop a cohesive task force with good skills for working in groups.

Community-building techniques were essential throughout the standard-setting process, but particularly at its onset. They helped to shape the task force into a group capable of working cooperatively together.[3]

We worked to model sharing leadership for the group, demonstrating the types of interactions and exchanges they would need to participate in as task force members. These included offering and accepting suggestions and improvements in front of the group, politely disagreeing, confirming one another's statements,

---

Table 1.1: Task Force Ground Rules

1. We will work toward consensus about definitions and tasks.
2. We will be practical, not only theoretical, and work toward realistic ways to use standards.
3. We will prepare carefully each day.
4. We will listen carefully to one another and have patience; we won't interrupt.
5. We will complete tasks carefully and on time. We will do our share.
6. We will have team spirit and work cooperatively.
7. We will be honest about our strengths and weaknesses.
8. We will ask questions when we don't understand: the only silly question is the one we didn't ask.
9. Everyone will participate and contribute.
10. We will stay on task and be focused.
11. We will take a break now and then and have fun.

---

[3]   See *http://home.comcast.net/%7Emariluwho/Handouts05/steps_standards.pdf* for examples of activities.

providing additional information, asking for input from someone who had been quiet in a discussion, and negotiating a compromise. These types of exchanges were important in ensuring that the voices of all were heard, particularly in view of the mixed nature of the group, which was composed of junior faculty as well as senior professors.

We also incorporated the exchange of teaching and teacher-training activities as part of task force workshops. Research on group cohesiveness shows that such activities help to facilitate group formation and efficient group working (van Knippenberg, 2000). Short activities at the beginning of each day integrated the goals of the workshop with process goals. Each day had both content goals and a "process" theme—e.g., idioms using a deck of cards in interactive tasks, storytelling, or songs and poetry. We incorporated brief tasks to help participants get to know one another, to review assignments from the evening before, to integrate concepts learned into a song or rhyme, to review or preview material by matching questions and answers or solving a puzzle, etc. The workshops were conducted in ways that followed key principles for cooperative learning outlined by Johnson, Johnson, and Holubec (1994): positive interdependence, attention to group process, opportunities to learn necessary skills for collaboration, both individual and group responsibility, heterogeneous grouping, and shared leadership.

Techniques Used to Facilitate Active Participation

Group tasks and consensus-building activities were used daily during the workshops to elicit engagement and active participation by all task force members. Many of these activities were unfamiliar to task force members, who were accustomed to top-down hierarchical structures in university and ministry meetings. Junior faculty members were surprised and pleased to be invited to participate since their roles in department meetings require them to be silent. Senior faculty members had many opportunities to mentor junior colleagues and were sometimes surprised by the quality of input their junior colleagues provided. We developed the task force's use of consensus-building activities with low-stakes outcome choices. For example, we might take a vote on what time to start our session the following morning. As a result, we later found the task force willing to use the same strategies to determine the contents of the standards document. We also discovered that providing short-time limits for limited decisions often facilitated compromise and consensus-building.

Process in STEPS Standards Development

Developing performance standards is a relatively recent process in EFL contexts. The process used to develop the STEPS Standards may be as valuable as the standards themselves because it served as a rich professional development tool and resulted in standards that were authentically owned by their creators. Thus, we want to outline the process used.

The STEPS Standards were developed during a thirteen-month period from January 2002–February 2003. The number of working members of the task force varied over the time period with a maximum size of about 25 and 16–20 members who participated throughout the project. These included senior and junior faculty members from eleven faculties throughout Egypt along with several representatives from the Ministry of Education. During this time period, the group met four times for workshops of about five days in length. Between these sessions, participants carried out the tasks of developing and revising standards, raising awareness, and conducting the field testing and field review. Task force members sometimes met in small groups and twice met with the Egyptian leaders for follow-on meetings.

1. Reviewing Existing Standards

At Workshop I, consultants collected a wide range of standards documents for task force members to review. These included books and articles about standards and many standards documents. A jigsaw technique was used, with small groups selecting documents to review and presenting their work to the full group. Finding the terminology of standards to be confusing and variable, we began our own standards glossary in which we defined the terms in the ways we would use them in our project. Everyone agreed that this process helped the task force understand what other groups had already done and helped them define the task of developing standards. The group then proceeded to develop a set of "Standards for Standards" that defined what effective standards would look like and provided criteria for evaluating the standards as they were being developed. These are included in Appendix A on page 24.

2. Determining Domains and Developing Domain Teams to Draft Standards

Once we were familiar with approaches to standards and standards development, we clarified our focus—developing pre-service standards for English language teachers—and defined the main domains under which we would develop standards. These differed from domains in other projects because the Faculties of Education/Faculties of English were often responsible for all aspects of teacher development for their students: development of teacher's language proficiency, language knowledge, background knowledge of child development and teaching methodology, specific methodology for language teaching, assessment skills, and development of professional attitudes and practices.

We used consensus-building techniques to help the task force decide on five key domains under which standards would be organized. Then the task force was split into five groups to work on standards in these areas. We based group assignment on individuals' preferences as well as on balancing experience and language skills. Between the first and second workshops, the domain groups produced a first draft of their standards which were further refined during the second workshop.

3. Awareness-Raising

We felt it was important to offer ongoing awareness-raising to get support for the standards and to lay the groundwork for implementation of the standards we were developing. The project worked to build support for the STEPS standards throughout Egypt simultaneously using both top-down and bottom-up approaches to awareness-raising. Throughout the project, task force members presented at conferences, conducted workshops, instructed their students, and talked to other faculty and ministry professionals about standards. Activities included:

- A series of meetings by senior members of the task force held with Faculty Deans, the Ministry of Education, and the Supreme Council of the Universities to gather support and inform officials of the project.
- Seeking views of key stakeholders, including the Ministry, before the start of the official project, through a national meeting, CDELT planning, and various informal contacts.
- An action plan in which task force members raised awareness regarding standards in development. This was undertaken by all task force members between the second and third workshops. Task force members reported reaching 1,140 individuals between April and September of 2002.

4. Reviewing and Revising Standards

During the second workshop, as domain groups worked on the standards, we felt that some groups felt they "owned" the standards in their domain rather than owning the standards overall. This, coupled with the fact that some individuals were too easily satisfied with early drafts, led us to turn to activities that promoted greater involvement of the whole group in writing standards under all domains. Once the task force was ready to embark on the process of writing indicators, groups were reformed to include one member from each domain group and tasks were circulated to assure that everyone would feel ownership of all of the standards.

Standards were revised and draft indicators developed by the new teams, which evaluated the STEPS Draft Standards against the Standards for Standards criteria and made recommendations for revisions. We then carried out an internal validity check before embarking on the field review process.

Performing Validity Checks

A review of the literature revealed little about a methodology for standards validation. The usual approach for standards review was to circulate standards and/or post them on a website and invite comments in the form of responses to questionnaire surveys. We felt that this approach to standard-setting was lacking in both depth and breadth of analysis. We also noted the drawbacks of research by survey alone that have been identified by researchers (e.g., Oppenheim, 1992; Cohen & Manion, 1994). We therefore felt it was important to go beyond these methods in the process of setting our own standards. Furthermore, our experience from other contexts in which standards are already in use has made us very aware of the importance of having standards that are reliable, appropriate, and relevant. As a first step in ensuring this was the case, we had already set out the criteria against which our own standards should be evaluated—our Standards for Standards (Appendix A). We then proceeded to conduct a series of validity checks, outlined here.

Domain Check

Did each standard fit clearly within the domain in which it was placed? We checked this by cutting up the standards and having our 26 participants arrange the strips according to domain. They were then asked to check their domain lists against our draft standards document. In this way, we identified and reconciled several instances where there was a lack of clarity in domain placement.

Construct Validity Check

To check for construct validity, we looked back at what we were trying to measure: what a newly qualified teacher should know and be able to do. We asked participants to think of an ideal teacher and brainstorm that teacher's qualities. We then checked the lists of qualities against our standards.

Concurrent Validity Check

To check for concurrent validity, we asked participants to list what was currently taught in faculties of education. We then used this as a checklist to see whether everything that was taught was covered somewhere within our standards. While this is obviously not a foolproof way of checking for concurrent validity, it gave the task force useful information about the relevance of the standards to what is currently taught in Faculties of Education.

Clarity Check

To check whether our standards would be clear and understandable to the preservice teachers, faculty, and supervisors who would use them, we asked participants to read the standards to one another in pairs, with one partner reading the standards as if he or she were a student teacher. The task was to highlight any words or terms that were unclear to them in this reading. This activity provided a great deal of useful information, and it was decided that the STEPS standards should include an accompanying glossary to be understood by all stakeholders.

Content and Face Validity Check

These activities also checked for content and face validity. Additionally, we required participants to draw a spidergram (a web graphic organizer) of what student teachers learn while they are engaged in teaching practice and had them compare the contents of that diagram to the contents of the standards to see if the standards were complete.

5. Field Testing and Field Review

A field review of the draft standards was designed to collect the opinions of a full range of stakeholders regarding the clarity, comprehensibility, relevance to Egyptian context, coverage, applicability, and usefulness of the standards. The goals were to ensure that the data collected reflect the views of our stakeholder audience by comparing the audience of the field review with our audience of stakeholders; triangulate data to maximize reliability and ensure that we could be confident that any action taken was not based solely on the views of a few individuals. We also put checks in place to prevent multiple responses from a single person.

The task force collected field review data on the standards using three instruments.

Online Survey

We chose an Internet resource tool called SurveyMonkey (see *www. surveymonkey.com*) to enable the task force to gather feedback from a large number of individuals from many segments of education in Egypt. Once the survey questions were determined, this tool facilitated the construction of the survey and collected and summarized responses from anyone who took the survey on the Internet. Each task force member was given ten letters inviting individuals to participate in the online survey and providing them with access information. Again this provided an opportunity for indirect learning: A number of task force members discovered that they could use on-line tools to help with the collection and analysis of data for their own research purposes.

Paper Survey

The task force also provided the Internet survey in paper format for stakeholders who did not have easy access to the Internet. Task force members each took ten copies of the paper survey to distribute to and collect from individuals in identified groups seen as stakeholders (e.g., faculty, deans, teachers, student teachers, parents, and community members). Data from the paper surveys was coded and entered on the online survey for ease of analysis.

Interview Questionnaire

To obtain more detailed qualitative data, each task force member conducted five interviews asking more in-depth questions about the standards and possible uses interviewees may make of the standards. In preparation for this activity, the task force watched and critiqued two interviews—a "good" one and a "bad" one—and discussed ways to conduct an interview effectively, including creating a non-threatening atmosphere, active listening, asking probing follow-up questions, and careful note-taking.

Results of the Field Review

The online survey was collated, and descriptive statistics were developed using both the data analysis tool within SurveyMonkey and Excel. Data from 75 interviews were coded and analyzed using categories developed by a small team of task force members. Our 340 field reviewers showed strong support for the draft standards with 85 percent of the standards receiving an approval rating of 90 percent or more.

All standards that received comments of any type were carefully reviewed. Attention was particularly paid to comments on those standards that attracted less than 80 percent approval. Consultants discussed these standards and came up with changes that addressed the issues identified in the field review. These changes were then presented in a final document for task force review, final revision, and approval. The final standards document was completed at Workshop IV in February 2003.

Part B: The Adoption of Standards in Egypt

The Ministry of Education (MoE) recognized that within Egypt there are numerous organizations and donors providing services to improve education in a number of areas and in different geographic locations. The STEPS project was only one of these. The MoE decided that it would work toward a systematic process for reform and provide centralized guidance to all organizations working toward this reform. On October 3, 2002, the Egyptian National Standards Committee (NSC) was established by Ministerial Decree number 189. The task of the NSC was to develop sets of standards for teachers, curriculum, accreditation and licensing, administration, the effective school, and society involvement (see Figure 1.1).

The STEPS process and document served as model and framework for the generic teacher performance standards and the subject content standards that were developed by the Egyptian NSC. The standards documents were released and published by the MoE at the end of 2003, except for the standards for accreditation and licensing, which have still not yet been finalized.

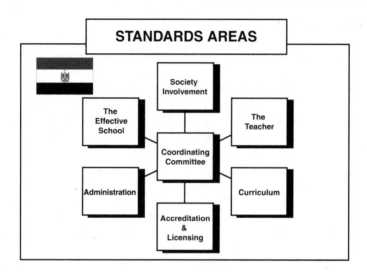

Figure 1.1:   Areas for Standards Development by the National Standards Committee

In 2004, a number of projects were set up to spread the standards-based reform efforts to Faculties of Education (FoEs) to ensure that teachers joining the profession would be competent. FoEs will eventually ensure that all graduates meet all basic standards of knowledge and practical skills needed for effective teaching. The focus is to be placed on the academic and practical preparation that will help graduates provide quality teaching and promote active learning.

On examining the STEPS standards, it is evident that courses taught within the FoEs will need serious review and reassessment in light of the standards. For example, courses taught to students do not include testing or assessment as a distinct field of study so these will need to be developed to meet the standards from Domain 4: Assessment.[4]

Taking Steps to Ensure Smooth Adoption of Standards

With the implementation of a standards-based education system comes the responsibility of ensuring that the context is prepared to support the system. The concept of accountability becomes prominent, and the system must support professionals to meet what is expected from them, rather than using standards-based assessment as a punitive tool. This is not an easy task and takes time to develop.

Developing Rubrics and Exemplars

The standards document cannot itself be used to assess teachers: "Rubrics make the bridge between the standards and the assessments" (Mitchell &

---

[4] See *http://home.comcast.net/%7emariluwho/Handouts05/steps_standards.pdf* for STEPS standards.

Crawford, 1995, p. 79). Rubrics are specific descriptions of expected performance and make explicit the behaviors a teacher will need to exhibit. They provide clear criteria against which a student teacher can assess himself or herself and teachers can assess students. Table 1.2 is a sample rubric under Professionalism that describes four levels regarding seeking professional development opportunities.

The process of developing rubrics has started and is moving quickly. A next step will be to look at exemplars. Exemplars are used alongside rubrics to provide specific examples of what can be expected of teachers who meet standards.

During both formal and non-formal presentations and discussions related to standards, stakeholders have requested that they be provided with exemplars to help them understand and plan for what is expected from them. They argue that exemplars will provide a clear picture of targets and define levels of performance in concrete and meaningful ways. They ask for exemplars that include annotations (examples) that point out specific characteristics of performance at a specific level. The plan is that in the coming years, rubrics and related tools will therefore be used as a means of evaluating teachers against agreed standards.

How Standards Implementation Can Reveal Further Needs for Change

At the present time, in Egypt, there are a number of organizations involved in the lengthy process of developing rubrics and tools that will facilitate the course of action in working with standards in the field. These include the World Bank, USAID, the European Union, and Egyptian partners.

As the work on rubrics progresses, it is understood that many legislative systems have to change. An example of this is creating a promotion system for teachers that moves away from promotion by seniority to one based on competence in actual teaching. The idea is to encourage good, experienced teachers to continue

---

Table 1.2: Sample Rubric
Rubric on Professional Development Opportunities
by Raga Hanna and Mahmoud Mohamed Mohasseb (2006)

STEPS Domain: Professionalism
Standard: 5.2 Improving teaching
Indicator: The newly qualified teacher (NQT) seeks professional development opportunities.

Level 4: The NQT frequently seeks print and on-line resources, regularly attends local seminars, workshops & conferences; gives workshops to colleagues to share ideas; tries new techniques in class and pursues higher studies.

Level 3: The NQT attends one or two professional/academic activities per year; reads on his/her own to grow. Although the NQT does not transfer what is learned to colleagues, the NQT sometimes uses new techniques in the classroom.

Level 2: The NQT seeks an opportunity to grow, i.e., asks about seminars, workshops, etc., but does not take the initiative to attend. The NQT does some reading for self-improvement of teaching.

Level 1: The NQT does not seek opportunities to upgrade or update knowledge.

as practicing teachers in the field and not be promoted into administrative or management positions. To encourage this, the system being piloted is based on a five-level promotion system that ranges from Novice, Developing, Skilled and Proficient, Competent, and Expert teacher based on standard descriptors. The incentive will be academic and financial advancement.

Adoption of national standards will require that the present examination-geared system will need radical change, requiring change and reform efforts in a number of areas in the system. It also necessitates the training of large numbers of in-service teachers who may be resistant to change.

The identification of gaps and needs serves to shape the reform processes, the fact remains that so many entities have to be involved because the management of change is a formidable challenge in any context.

Part C: Implications

Principles for Standards Development

Ensuring Stakeholder Awareness and Buy-In

Our review of earlier projects made it clear that national awareness and owner-ship of a project like this one cannot be assumed. Rather, developing awareness, understanding, and ownership must be part of the planning and process of a project such as this. Strategies include selection of participants, awareness-building and training activities, the field review, application training, and dissemination.

Selection of Participants

Participants should be selected according to their knowledge and leadership ability and should represent both highly experienced members and younger members with high potential, national distribution, and wide representation of a large number of stakeholders. Attention should be paid to developing ownership and commitment to the project through careful community building.

Building Awareness

Participants can all be actively involved in building understanding and awareness of standards through conference presentations, workplace presentations, class sessions with teachers in training, meetings, and informal discussions. Interest-ingly, the implementation of a field review is both a way to collect responses to the standards in development and a way to build awareness.

Field Review

Conducting a field review to reach a wide constituency of educators not only pro-vided valuable feedback for improving the standards, but was also an awareness-building activity in itself. Through the STEPS field review, 340 individuals—English educators from all positions and all parts of the country—were made aware of the new standards and had an opportunity to read and reflect on them. Task force members were requested to personally contact important persons in their home institutions—deans, fellow faculty members, etc.—to request an interview, because we wanted to assure that they became aware of the standards project.

Promoting Top-Down and Bottom-Up Leadership

Our experience in the Egyptian culture confirmed the value of working in both a top-down (developing standards with the authority of educational leaders to-ward practitioners) and bottom-up (developing standards by making use of the wisdom and experience of practitioners) process. Before the project begins, we recommend holding focus group meetings of educational leaders from around the region/country to discuss what standards mean and the history of previous related projects in the local country and to develop an understanding of the needs and goals for standards in the location in which you work.

Ensuring Wide Participation among Stakeholders

Our approach to standards, that is, involving a wide range of stakeholders in the standards development process and promoting even wider ownership of the standards through an extensive field review, has helped to lead—more quickly than we ever expected—to the incorporation of those standards (and a number of those who created them) into the work of the National Standards Committee, and probably also into future efforts to develop certification and accreditation in Egypt. We feel that our approach was validated by this outcome and recom-mend it for similar projects.

Packaging and Disseminating Standards Effectively

As we worked on the standards project, we understood that we were working in an area new to many in the country, and that making the standards docu-ments easily accessible and attractive would increase the possibility that they would be read, understood, and eventually used. From our experience and the responses to our standards, we offer these recommendations for packaging and disseminating standards:

- Write the document in language as clear and widely accessible as possible, and then edit and check it for clarity as part of the validation process.
- Provide a clear layout with adequate white space and large print.
- Make documents widely available in print and online. Disseminate them in many formats and levels: in department meetings, seminars, conferences, workshops, informal discussions, student classes, listservs, websites, etc.

- Develop and include with standards an agreed-upon glossary of standards terminology. Standards development is a fairly new area, and current terminology used is inconsistent. Work to use commonly understood terminology whenever possible, but when there is no agreement, define terms clearly for your purposes and use them consistently. Equal care should be taken with the translations of the standards documents, understanding that new technical terminology may need to be developed if you are working in a language in which standards development is fairly new.

Conclusions

We believe that in large part due to the care with which the standards-setting process was managed, standards in Egypt are gradually being accepted and applied in the area of teacher assessment without the serious concerns and sometimes hostility by educators that have been encountered in other settings. We hope that educators in other contexts will find the tools and techniques we have developed useful in their own processes toward development and implementation of effective standards for teacher education and assessment.

Discussion Questions

1. What were the steps taken to assure sustainability, usability, and maintainability of standards for teachers of English at pre-service in Egypt?

2. Which aspects of this project were designed for the Egyptian setting in particular and which are more broadly relevant and applicable?

3. How did this project work to promote Egyptian ownership of the standards developed? What evidence shows that this was successful?

4. What were the steps taken to assure validity and reliability of the standards as developed? What other steps would be desirable?

5. What is the status of the standards development process, according to evidence in this article? What are future research questions to be addressed regarding standards development?

REFERENCES

Bishop, G. (1986). *Innovation in education.* Basingstoke: Macmillan.

Cohen, L., & Manion, L. (1994). *Research methods in education.* London: Routledge and Kegan Paul.

Cullingford, C. (1999). *An inspector calls.* London: Kogan Page.

El Naggar, Z. (2002). Project document: Standards for teachers of English at pre-service level. Document submitted to IELP-II, April 2002.

Hanna, R., & Mohasseb, M. M. (2006). Sample participant task standards workshop conducted by Mary Lou McCloskey. Alexandria, Egypt.

Johnson, D. W., Johnson, R. T., & Holubec, E. J. (1994). *Cooperative learning in the classroom.* Alexandria, VA: Association for Supervision and Curriculum Development.

Mitchell, R., & Crawford, M. (1995). *Learning in overdrive: Designing curriculum, instruction and assessment from standards.* Golden, CO: Fulcrum Publishing.

Oppenheim, A. N. (1992). *Questionnaire design and attitude measurement.* London: Pinter Publications.

van Knippenberg, D. (2000). Work motivation and performance: A social identity perspective. *Applied Psychology, 49*(3), 357.

Wiliam, D. (2004). Assessing instructional and assessment practice. Paper given at CRESST Conference, UCLA, September 2004.

Appendix A: Standards for Standards

STEPS Standards for Standards Assessment Form					
Domain Assessed: _____					
Content	1	2	3	4	5
Is each standard important and inclusive in scope?					
Does each standard clearly fit in the domain in which it is placed?					
Is each standard appropriate for preservice teachers in Egypt? Does each fit within what newly qualified (beginning) teachers in Egypt actually should know and be able to do?					
Do the standards cover the breadth of the content needed by teachers in this area?					
Do the standards include everything that our teachers need to know in that domain?					
Clarity	1	2	3	4	5
Can student teachers, teachers, administrators, teacher educators all understand what each standard means?					
Are standards consistent across domains?					
Correctness	1	2	3	4	5
Are the standards grammatically correct?					
Are the standards parallel in structure and appropriate in structure?					
Have we avoided sexist language?					

CHAPTER 2

Seeking the Standard:
Using Existing Resources to Support
EFL Teachers in Evaluation Processes

Jill Burton

Introduction

This chapter derives from working with teacher-learners in EFL settings over a number of years as a teacher educator of coursework master's and research students who teach English as a foreign language (EFL) throughout Southeast Asia. These students are already experienced teachers in their own settings when they travel to Australia to investigate ways of furthering their teaching knowledge and skills. Their interests have in common three concerns: how to (1) develop curriculum, (2) design language learning materials, and (3) meet their language learning students' needs more effectively. Evaluation processes are essential to these three concerns.

Sometimes, my students arrive with an already expressed focus on evaluation. Other times, their interest is fired by the potential power of reflective practitioner inquiry and action research that some perceive as ways of separating themselves, even if only temporarily, from institutional reporting requirements. From whichever perspective my students begin, my goal is for them all to make positive connections between institutional reporting imperatives and personal professional goals by, first, understanding the evaluation processes they are part of as language teachers; second, recognizing their own central positions in the development of the teaching profession; and, third, taking responsibility for their own professional actions. It is my experience, however, that many EFL teachers see themselves—and are seen by policymakers and program administrators—merely as implementers. In this chapter, I will make a case for a broader description of responsibility that reduces teacher dependence on prescriptive curriculum resources and increases the possibility of professional fulfillment in practical ways.

Description
Rungporn is a composite portrait of many TESOL professionals I have worked with in Thailand, which I will take as the EFL setting for this chapter.

Rungporn, #1
Rungporn was trained as a primary teacher and works in a rural area in central Thailand. Two years ago, her school began introducing EFL, and as someone with an English major from her tertiary studies, she was put in charge of implementing an English curriculum. She was well aware that with the introduction of the 1999 National Education Act, learner-centred teaching, teacher-conducted research, mentor teaching, and quality assurance would be, in differing ways, key components of her work. Her immediate concern, however, was how to motivate primary school children to learn EFL.

In 2003 and 2004, she attended the usual range of one-off, short in-service activities. She was lucky, however, in being supported to attend two national Thai ELT conferences.

As a first step in implementing an EFL primary-school curriculum, how might Rungporn tap into the national professional EFL resources that these conferences and their publications provided?

Rungporn, #2
During her conference attendance, Rungporn learned about new professional developments and policies, and being away from school provided valuable thinking time; and she looked at publications such as the ThaiTESOL Bulletin.

If Rungporn were to read the first issue of *The PAC Journal* (edited by Farrell, 2001), she could also have discovered the value of keeping a teaching journal, how rewarding collaborative action research can be, and the satisfaction of learning through or while teaching.

But teachers such as Rungporn don't have much time for reading or research. Most teachers, in fact, see research and evaluation as demanding skills that are beyond them and have purposes that conflict with their own teaching; and teachers regularly experience problems with research and evaluations conducted by non-teachers. A study in Australia of the general impact of educational research on teaching (DETYA, 2000) critiqued in a special issue of the *Australian Educational Researcher* (2003) revealed that a number of factors tend to affect teachers' compliance with research outcomes:

- *Publication:* If outcomes are presented in ways and contexts that teachers are not comfortable with, the likelihood of uptake is reduced.

- *Uptake:* Uptake of evaluative research outcomes depends on the relationships and trust among researchers, decision-makers, and teachers.
- *Transience:* The meaning and impact of research and evaluations change, sometimes by the time research recommendations reach teachers.
- *Influences:* Teachers are influenced as much by vernacular theories and their own experiences as by formal evaluations.
- *Knowledge:* Commissioned, formal research and evaluations are only two sources of information about teaching, and teachers are not always included in these processes anyway.
- *Evidence:* All educational stakeholders are influenced by evidence, yet teachers frequently need to be able to explain outcomes and reward individual achievements that fall outside the expected or desired range.

Factors such as these make a strong case for teachers being more closely involved in the design and management of research and evaluation processes on teaching. They also underline the complexity and subtlety of teaching and its evaluation. Action research, inquiry-based learning, and reflective practice are all practical, effective ways in which teachers' central roles in professional decision-making can be acknowledged and supported. Yet many of these points appear to work against teachers being involved in evaluative research processes:

- *Time:* Teachers have little time to follow their professional curiosity.
- *Mentor support:* It's hard for teachers to know what directions to follow without mentors (Stanulis, Campbell, & Hicks, 2002).
- *Identity and voice:* Publication processes and collaboration can mean individual teachers' concerns are lost.
- *The demands of complexity:* Accountability processes often deny the transience and complexity of education (Elliott, 2002), which requires different processes than accountability to prespecified outcomes.

However, teachers' involvement in research and evaluation is also widely recommended:

- *Training:* Teachers who are trained in action research procedures and inquiry-based teaching find such teaching manageable and rewarding (Burns, 1999).
- *Connectivity:* Everything we do is connected, and the particular and the now are significant (Winter, 2003).
- *Reflectivity:* Close observation of small changes can reveal information that can have future, major importance (Sumara, 2002).
- *Narrative:* Writing down what happens supports later reflection *on* action and thus reduces anxiety during future reflection *in* action (cf. Schön, 1987).
- *Questioning:* Effective inquiry processes stimulate curiosity and learning (Luce-Kapler, Sumara, & Davis, 2002).

What might be Rungporn's initial, immediate response to recognizing her own professional dilemmas?

Rungporn, #3

Rungporn felt professionally unsatisfied. Her professional time was totally sidetracked into fulfilling work obligations that she was, rightly, uncertain of. She felt energy-depleted and unmotivated to risk investigating her teaching concerns, which she feared might turn out counter to those of her employer, and therefore jeopardize her hopes of moving up the professional ladder.

But there could be hope for Rungporn outside her immediate professional support system—for example, in innovative adaptation of current evaluative tools used for assessing teacher performance.

Teacher Standards Documents as Frameworks for Professional Support and Renewal

Since promulgating its National Education Act of 1999, Thailand has embraced quality-standard processes. One of the Act's aims is to ensure that educational principles (such as learner-centered development) enshrined in the Act are implemented along with mechanisms and processes for teacher support and evaluation of outcomes. Intended to achieve this, quality standard processes and implementation of curriculum have been largely devolved to school- and community-level management, with a market-driven educational economy to keep teachers accountable.

Meanwhile, the Ministry of Education (MoE) has been developing a set of standards for the teaching profession.[1] In sum, the discussions for these standards have assumed the following expectations that teachers should be:

1. active community members and professionals
2. classroom researchers
3. resources, examples, and mentors for colleagues, the community, and their students
4. effective teachers, setting and implementing realistic goals
5. systematic evaluators of their teaching and able to report learning outcomes.

Working through KHURUSAPHA, the Teachers Council of Thailand is not empowered to enforce the standards. Their enforcement is, as with other MoE policies now, largely up to school communities, with whatever assistance

---

[1] See *www.moe.go.th/web/Nation_Act/index.htm.*

professional bodies (e.g., ThaiTESOL) and teacher education institutions can provide.

Rungporn, # 4

These documents endorsed Rungporn's own professional values but high-lighted that she could be falling short professionally. They reminded her that teaching effectively was important—and that teaching effectively involves planning, implementing, and assessing learning and evaluating teaching. They didn't say anything about subject expertise or teaching resources or how to evaluate teaching in principled, realistic ways. As Rungporn was a dedicated, responsible teacher, she was frustrated.

If Rungporn had logged on to international TESOL's website (www.tesol. org), she would find a link to a standards document (TESOL/NCATE, 2002) designed by a professional body that has consulted with national and international organizations in order to provide leadership from within the profession on teacher education programs. The teacher education standards in this resource are intended to support the preparation of ESL teachers in the school system and complement the standards resources developed for classroom use, such as the *ESL Standards* (TESOL, 1997). The people who designed the document came from a range of professional settings, including universities and primary schools. This U.S. resource has since been used as a base for developing other standards resources, such as EFL teacher standards resources for the People's Republic of China.[2] The TESOL/NCATE resource is therefore a useful base document, potentially adaptable and capable of further development in other settings and related uses. Thailand, like many other EFL settings, does not have a comparable resource (though standards resources were in development at the time of writing as indicated). The explicitness and consistency of the TESOL/NCATE resource mean that it can be adapted and revalidated in a range of settings. As most teachers routinely adapt materials and processes designed for circumstances and purposes different from their own, using this resource as a way of demonstrating how teachers such as Rungporn could fulfill evaluation requirements and personal professional goals is not unreasonable if the initial resource is seen to have relevance to the site of its adaptation. It is how teachers work.

This is not the place to explain the TESOL/NCATE resource itself. Other resources can be found on TESOL's website following the links to standards resources and publications. I will work from the diagram that shows how the standards in the source document are organized around five domains; these make up an ESOL teacher's professional competence (see Figure 2.1).

---

[2] These materials were published in 2006 as the *Integrating EFL Standards into Chinese Classroom Settings* series (edited by Barbara Agor in 4 vols.) by McGraw-Hill.

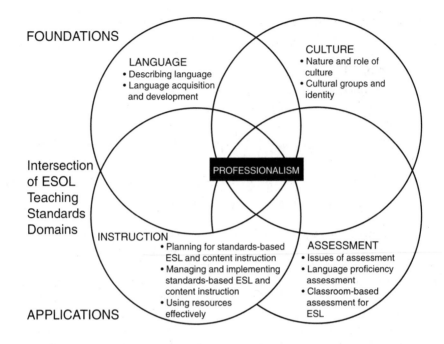

FOUNDATIONS

LANGUAGE
• Describing language
• Language acquisition
  and development

CULTURE
• Nature and role of
  culture
• Cultural groups and
  identity

Intersection
of ESOL
Teaching
Standards
Domains

PROFESSIONALISM

INSTRUCTION
• Planning for standards-based
  ESL and content instruction
• Managing and implementing
  standards-based ESL and
  content instruction
• Using resources
  effectively

ASSESSMENT
• Issues of assessment
• Language proficiency
  assessment
• Classroom-based
  assessment for
  ESL

APPLICATIONS

Source: TESOL, Alexandria, VA.

Figure 2.1:　TESOL Standards for P–12 ESL Teacher Education Programs

The five domains are *language, culture, instruction, assessment,* and *professionalism.* Language and culture are seen as foundational knowledge domains in which teachers must be competent. Teaching competence is applied in the instruction and assessment domains. The four outer domains thus form the content and skill areas of TESOL. How they intersect in each teacher's performance represents that teacher's professionalism.

Each of the five domains is developed and structured in the same way. In this chapter, I will focus on the core domain, professionalism. The overarching standard for professionalism is expressed in the following statement, which I have adapted to address Rungporn's circumstances:

> Teachers demonstrate knowledge of the history of ELT. Teachers keep current with new instructional techniques, research results, advances in the field, and public policy issues. Teachers use such information to reflect upon and improve their instructional practices. Teachers provide support and advocate for ESOL students and their families and work collaboratively to improve the learning environment. (cf. TESOL, 2002; p. 61, for the original text).

This statement captures all the requirements of the Thai MoE developments summarized above.

The TESOL/NCATE professionalism statement is then recast as three inter-connected standards for professionalism: one on ESL research and history, a second on partnerships and advocacy, and a third on professional development and collaboration. I will use the third:

Professional Development and Collaboration

Teachers collaborate with and are prepared to serve as a resource to all staff, including paraprofessionals, to improve learning for all ESOL students. (cf. TESOL, 2002, p. 61, for the original text)

This standard has a supporting explanation and rubric that requires that "teachers take advantage of professional growth opportunities...[and] accept and embrace the role of ESOL advocate and resource person in their schools and districts...[and] are active, contributing members of their professional association(s)" (cf. TESOL, 2002; p. 66, for the original text). Teachers are also required to "collaborate with staff in the school in order to provide a wide range of educational opportunities for ESOL students at all proficiencies of English and with diverse special learning needs...[and] serve as a resource to promote a school environment that values diverse student populations and to advocate for equitable access to resources for ESOL students" (ibid). They are also expected to be "strong models of English language proficiency, although they may not necessarily possess native-like proficiency. Linguistic competence in a language other than English is part of teachers' professional preparation" (ibid). These statements coherently articulate what all ESOL teachers do at differing levels of experience and competence—hence the rubric (see Table 2.1, adapted from TESOL, 2002, p. 67) that acknowledges that teachers are learners throughout their careers. Thus, teachers can be evaluated or evaluate themselves as *approaching* a standard, *meeting* it, or *exceeding* it.

It is my contention that ESOL teachers in any setting could take standards and performance indicators such as these and apply them as a means of self-evaluation and as a contribution to external accountability processes. How could Rungporn have used the standard and rubric?

Rungporn, #5

Rungporn first looked at the left-hand column of the rubric for Standard 5c. Did she have any professional goals? She set plans based on her perceived needs and knew, but had not contacted, her nearest TESOL association and university, which offered postgraduate programs in teacher education. So she judged herself as approaching the standard according to the first performance indicator. As departmental head for the implementation of EFL in the early school years, she worked constantly with school colleagues on this goal. Furthermore, as her colleagues had neither taught nor studied EFL

Table 2.1: Rubric for Standard 5c
Professional Development and Collaboration

These rubrics are additive. *Meets Standard* assumes that the teacher* has also met the criteria under *Approaches Standard*. *Exceeds Standard* assumes that the teacher has also met the criteria under Approaches Standard and Meets Standard.

Performance Indicator	Approaches Standard	Meets Standard	Exceeds Standard
5.c.1. Establish professional goals and pursue opportunities to grow in the field of EFL.*	• Teachers formulate professional development plans based on their interests. • Teachers are aware of their professional associations.	• Teachers implement a personal professional development plan based on interests and reflection, taking advantage of opportunities in professional associations and other academic organizations.	• Teachers engage in a continuous cycle of EFL professional development that is informed by their instructional reflections and analysis. • Teachers take active roles in their professional association(s).
5.c.2. Work with other teachers and staff to provide comprehensive, challenging opportunities for ESOL students in the school.	• Teachers understand the importance of establishing collaborative relationships among EFL staff members and all departments and resource personnel in the school.	• Teachers collaborate with general and specialist school staff (e.g., multidisciplinary faculty teams) to establish an instructional program appropriate for ESOL students at a variety of English proficiency levels.	• Teachers provide leadership to staff in scheduling appropriate classes and instructional opportunities for ESOL students.
5.c.3 Engage in collaborative teaching in general education and content-area classrooms.	• Teachers study and practice a variety of collaborative teaching models (e.g., parallel teaching, station teaching, alternative teaching, team teaching).	**	• Teachers continue to learn about other content areas so they may share greater responsibility for effective instruction and student success in those classes.
5.c.4 Model academic proficiency in the English language.	• Teachers are proficient in the English language.	• Teachers model effective use of the English language for academic purposes.	**

© 2002 by Teachers of English to Speakers of Other Languages, Inc. (TESOL)

* Indicates first occasion of a word changed to reflect Rungporn's situation.

** Cells left empty as content in original is not applicable to Rungporn's situation.

*as a major at university level, she was constantly modeling how to teach
EFL. On performance indicator 2, she found she exceeded the standard. She
estimated that she met performance indicator 3, but was uneasy because
although she constantly worked with teachers who taught the same students,
she never taught alongside them in class. On performance indicator 4, she
was clearly the most proficient EFL speaker in the school, but how proficient
was she?*

*Thus, Rungporn quickly established her strong and weak areas. She de-
cided to start with what she could do for herself.*

*Her immediate plan was to team-teach with a working colleague with
the aim of developing more specific teaching goals for her team. Thus, she
immediately took her inquiry outside her own classroom so that her
decisions could be shared and draw on another's experience and understanding.*

*She and her colleague, Songtida, decided to teach a Big Books project
in which the children developed a book about their families in Thai but
used and learned English words and phrases for some everyday activities.
Through the project students might thus consider how families functioned in
different settings and begin to question cultural stereotypes.*

*Rungporn realized she had begun to think about cultural practices, so
she and Songtida turned to the cultural domain in the TESOL/NCATE
document.*

The supporting explanation for Standard 2.a, Nature and the Role of Culture,
begins: "To enhance the learning of their students, teachers draw on their
knowledge of the nature, role, and content of culture. The nature and role of
culture encompasses such topics as cultural relativism...." (cf. TESOL, 2002, p.
34, for the original text).

Again, Rungporn, and now Songtida, were meeting professional goals. It was
likely that with this unit of work, and taking into account their setting and learner
group, they would exceed performance indicator 2.a.1, could meet performance
indicator 2.a.2, would approach performance indicator 2.a.3, and might meet
or exceed performance indicator 2.a.4 (TESOL, 2002, p. 35–36). These projections would give them yardsticks against which to evaluate their unit of work.
They would be able to draw up similar projections in the language domain also
(TESOL, 2002, p. 18–30), finding here that they might only approach performance indicators because they were less sure of their language skills. Their next
task would be to decide how to keep data on language learning in their project
so that they could report outcomes and account for their teaching. I envisage
the following:

Rungporn, #6

Rungporn and Songtida turned to the Assessment domain in the TESOL/ NCATE document for guidance. The three standards there spoke of assessment, language proficiency measures, and classroom-based assessment. Rungporn and Songtida knew little about assessment or proficiency measures. They were not confident about classroom-based assessment either, but felt more comfortable to start with it, leaving proficiency measures and validity concerns to trained teachers and experts. Perhaps one of their team could attend a course later? Songtida had done a three-day regional workshop on action research and suggested they could consider their teaching innovation an action research project.

Having planned their teaching, what data could they actually collect? Rungporn and Songtida would have their lesson plans, teaching materials, and students' work—these were all part of their normal routine. Additional, observational data might help explain any difference in outcome from expectation. They discussed practicalities. Having two teachers in the classroom for one lesson a week meant that at times one could observe the other, and because they would be in class together they would share teaching experiences and could reflect together.

They decided to use the 2nd teacher as the observer noting specific activities, alternating teaching and observing to note differences in their teaching. Concentrating on groupwork tasks would mean they could both observe and they could start by noting what interested them or "caught their eye." They would use the school video occasionally, when it could be booked and when it could be integrated in the learning activity. Having lunch together immediately after their team-teaching proved unreliable. After two weeks they agreed to keep and exchange daily journal entries on team-taught lessons. They also set aside a half day in the next school break to reflect and write up their experience for the rest of their teaching team.

Their early data and reflection in this project demonstrated that they had more information about what happened in the classroom than would normally be the case, giving them more confidence in course decision-making. But they now had more questions. They therefore wanted to widen the collaboration to include the rest of the School EFL team, and if practicable, their students.

Distinctive Features

Creative Use of Existing Resources

Rungporn and Songtida's first action research experience, then, would begin to raise further questions and widen their potential for collaborative learning. Rungporn's initial worries would evaporate as she was able to describe her situation, her achievements, and her needs more effectively. Creative use of a teacher education resource would lead to team teaching, which would stimulate reflection and discussion of common concerns; all these steps would have been aided by classroom observation and collaborative journaling integrated as part of routine teaching practice.

> **Rungporn, #7**
>
> *Each time Rungporn referred to her journal entries, she saw something more in them. With time, they had become more structured with recurring themes and connections. She found herself adding comments, based on more recent teaching experience, and discovering ideas and information which now fed into her future teaching. She saw now that there were central assumptions and practices involved in and linking every class she taught. Moreover, Songporn's interpretations helped her maintain a sense of proportion.*
>
> *Overall, Rungporn's reflections, based on collaborative, inquiry-based teaching enabled her to work more effectively, and ultimately take more responsibility for her teaching.*

In this chapter, I've demonstrated creative measures that ESOL and EFL teachers can adopt in externally determined standards-based TEFL settings. I've shown that these processes demand very little new of teachers, but nothing that should not be expected (cf. Burton, 2000). I've illustrated how one resource (TESOL/NCATE, 2002) is potentially capable of offering individual teachers some professional independence at their level of expertise or need. I do not suggest that this resource is *the* one to use or that any such resource *has* to be used. I have attempted to portray how teachers operate, how they stumble on resources that for some reason (such as external demands) offer a way forward, and how *such moments can be integrated successfully in professional practice*. The processes I've recounted offer teachers such as Rungporn access to professional development and pathways enabling them to contribute to research and evaluation processes.

Teachers' involvement in Evaluation Processes as a Means of Professional Renewal

A recent Australian study (Butcher, Howard, McMeniman, & Thom, 2003) asserts (p. 43) that benchmarks (e.g., performance indicators in the TESOL/ NCATE resource described) encapsulate trends, and used wisely can stimulate continuous, self-improvement activities that allow analysis and comparison as a means to professional growth and knowledge. The study further argues that for educational research and evaluation to be constructive, all participants in educational processes must be engaged, most particularly, teachers. In my view, *engagement* is qualitatively different from involvement. It implies active, critical participation and taking appropriate responsibility for all actions, as opposed to, for example, mere compliance with externally set procedures. It is this engagement that I have tried to capture with the composite case analysis presented in this chapter.

Used critically, Butcher et al. (2003) continue, benchmarks can support course evaluation and learning assessment and teacher renewal. For example, they enable teachers to *learn* about evaluation and assessment. Portraying this learning was another goal of the case analysis in this chapter.

Caveats

Best Practice

Implicit in the actions of planning, implementing, and evaluating ESOL courses, curricula, and programs is the notion of best practice. The notion raises two pertinent questions:

1. *What is evaluated:* best practice, what's there, what happens, or what outcomes have immediate community impact?
2. *What is the purpose of evaluation:* to determine best practice, what is manageable to teach, or what is easily measurable?

Both questions distinguish between expediency and the ideal. In my experience, teachers are more often concerned with what is desirable or ideal, whereas program managers more often are motivated by expediency. A crude view, nonetheless it may indicate why teachers' participation in design, implementation, and evaluation is necessary—a necessity confirmed in the literature on the status and importance of teacher knowledge and experience (e.g., Freeman & Johnson, 1998; Grossman, 1990; Richards & Lockhart, 1994). In the case described in this chapter, Rungporn and Songtida adopted a responsible, creative, *and* practical approach to evaluation and accountability. Thus, I have presented best practice as the best teaching that teachers can provide *in the knowledge of* what is ideal and possible in their specific circumstances.

Knowing How and Where to Begin

One of the important factors in Rungporn's case was that she and her colleague, Songtida, began at their own levels of professional competence and built on what they already knew and could do. Rungporn invited a teacher she knew she could work with to team-teach a specific course unit, and observe, note, and reflect on their teaching. With one small step, she set up *a project that had good prospects of success*. She and Songtida then had the options of widening and strengthening their circle of collaboration.

In addition, Rungporn was portrayed as *resourceful*. I hypothesized that she found and adapted a document available on the Internet. This kind of strategy might be described as a desperate or extreme measure. Yet such strategies can be very productive if used critically. Teachers who seek resources knowing that none exist that are developed precisely for their circumstances are alert to the purpose and function of the resources they end up finding and adapting. In effect, such teachers adopt a critical or evaluative stance that is very different from that of teachers who are involved only in implementation of externally designed resources.

Conclusion

In this chapter, I have interpreted teacher performance evaluation as part of teachers' professional responsibility. I have argued that EFL teachers should engage in the three main phases of curriculum activity: planning, implementing, and evaluating. I have also argued that their engagement necessarily involves responsibility for decisions in these three curriculum phases. I have hypothesized through a case study of a teacher composed of features and attributes of many teachers I have known in the Thai TEFL context that it is practical for teachers to support their own professional renewal through critical adaptation and use of existing curriculum and performance evaluation resources.

Further, I have suggested that action research can be utilized as a means of inquiry-based teaching that aims to improve evaluation of teaching and its development. As many other teacher educators have argued, development of the teaching profession and individual professional renewal is enhanced by the asking of good questions (cf. Freeman, 1998). This is, indeed, what I mean by *Seeking the Standard.*

Discussion Questions

1. *Consider the nature of inquiry-based teaching:* What are its key features as portrayed in this chapter? To what extent does this account reflect your views on how teachers should manage their own evaluation and professional support processes?

2. *Consider your view of curriculum and the role of evaluation and learning assessment within it:* At what point(s) in implementing the curriculum do you, or someone else, plan evaluation processes? What do they cover? Who do they involve? How are they managed? What data are involved?

3. *Consider the external curriculum resources (i.e., those developed by some-one other than yourself) you use regularly in your classroom:* To what extent do they fit your view of how planning, teaching, and evaluating language curriculum should be conducted? What practical steps could you take to make them work more effectively in your view in your classroom?

4. *Consider a teaching project or activity you will be involved with in the immediate future:* How could you plan the teaching to better reflect your view of how curriculum should be managed? What does this orientation involve ideally? practically? To what extent could this adjustment in your practice cause you to teach differently?

REFERENCES

Australian Educational Researcher, 30(2). (2003, August). Issue mainly devoted to a critique of *The impact of educational research* [cf. DETYA, 2000].

Burns, A. (1999). *Collaborative action research for English language teachers.* Cambridge: Cambridge University Press.

Burton, J. I. (2000, December). Learning from teaching practice: A case study approach. *Prospect, 15*(3), 5–22.

Butcher, J., Howard, P., McMeniman, M., & Thom, G. (2003). *Engaging community—Service or learning?* Canberra: DEST [Department of Education, Science and Training], Evaluations and Investigations Program (Research, Analysis and Evaluation Group).

DETYA [Department of Education, Training and Youth Affairs]. (2000). *The impact of educational research.* Canberra: DETYA Higher Education Division Research Evaluation Program. Retrieved December 11, 2004, from http://www.dest.gov.au/default.htm

Elliott, J. (2002). The impact of intensive 'value for money' performance auditing in educational systems. *Educational Action Research, 10*(3), 499–505.

Farrell, T. C. (2001). Exploring teaching in *The PAC Journal*. *The PAC Journal, 1*(1), 1–5.

Freeman, D. (1998). *Doing teacher research: From inquiry to understanding.* Pacific Grove, CA: Heinle & Heinle.

Freeman, D., & Johnson, K. E. (1998). Reconceptualizing the knowledge-base of language teacher education. *TESOL Quarterly, 32*(3), 397–417.

Grossman, P. (1990). *The making of a teacher: Teacher knowledge and teacher education.* New York: Teachers College Press.

Luce-Kapler, R., Sumara, D., & Davis, B. (2002). Rhythms of knowing: Toward an ecological theory of learning in action research. *Educational Action Research, 10*(2), 353–372.

Richards, J. C., & Lockhart, C. (1994). *Reflective teaching in second language classrooms.* New York: Cambridge University Press.

Schön, D. A. (1987). *Educating the reflective practitioner.* San Francisco: Jossey-Bass.

Stanulis, R. N., Campbell, P. E., & Hicks, J. (2002). Finding her way: A beginning teacher's story of learning to honour her own voice in teaching. *Educational Action Research, 10*(1), 45–65.

Sumara, D. (2002). Notes on writing subjects of action research. *Educational Action Research, 10*(2), 309–317.

TESOL. (1997). *ESL standards for pre-K–12 students.* Alexandria, VA.

TESOL/NCATE. (2002). TESOL/NCATE standards for the accreditation of initial programs in P–12 ESL teacher education. Retrieved December 11, 2004, from http://www.tesol.org/s_tesol/seccss.asp?CFD=219&DID=1689

Winter, R. (2003). Buddhism and action research: Towards an appropriate model of inquiry for the caring professions. *Educational Action Research, 11*(1), 141–155.

PART 2:

Case Studies in Evaluating Teacher Effectiveness

Six innovative and state-of-the-art case studies of successful teacher evaluation and appraisal programs in five different countries make up Part 2. The papers were selected because they represent what we feel are examples of best practice in the field of teacher evaluation.

From the North American ESL context, Kaufman (Chapter 3), Curtis and Cheng (Chapter 4), and Stoynoff (Chapter 7) describe teacher evaluation and appraisal systems that have worked for them in their educational and institutional contexts. More specifically, Kaufman describes the design and implementation of a comprehensive assessment system for teachers that occurred in conjunction with NCATE accreditation at a North American university. Curtis and Cheng share their collaborative approach to performance appraisal of ESL teachers within the context of the intensive English for Academic Purposes program at a Canadian university in Ontario. Stoynoff presents an ESOL teacher evaluation system that his institution used with beginning teachers in an M.A. TESOL program in the United States. Although the teacher evaluation programs described in this part were designed for a particular context, the authors stress that the assessment principles used to design them can be applied to developing teacher evaluation systems for both novice and experienced teachers in a wide range of educational contexts.

An EFL perspective is well documented with contributions from such diverse locales as Hong Kong, China, and the United Arab Emirates. In Chapter 5, Miller and Young report on the introduction of a performance management system for teachers at an English Language Center of a major university in Hong Kong. Quirke (Chapter 6) describes a teacher-driven appraisal tool that was recently developed at his institution in the United Arab Emirates. The final chapter illustrates a new approach to teacher evaluation and appraisal in China. Murphey and Yaode (Chapter 8) describe a set of portfolio-based Teacher Performance Standards that were recently developed for use in the Chinese context.

Authors not only present their teacher evaluation programs and what makes them innovative, but they also discuss possible implementation problems and offer suggestions and recommendations to those wanting to introduce similar types of teacher assessment in their own contexts.

CHAPTER 3

A Multidisciplinary Approach to Assessment in Teacher Education

Dorit Kaufman

Introduction

The need to prepare effective teachers who possess the knowledge, skills, and dispositions to impact positively on learners has motivated inquiry into the links between teaching practices and student learning and has driven the development of standards-based programs and assessment systems. Development of standards across disciplines for improving the professional development of teachers has involved collaborative partnerships among governmental agencies, state education departments, and professional associations (e.g., ACTFL, 2002; NCTM, 2000; TESOL, 2002). Professional standards have been formulated for teacher candidates (INTASC, 1992), for practicing teachers (NBPTS, 2001), and for units of teacher education and educational leadership in colleges and universities (NCATE, 2002). Standards for teacher education programs define the body of knowledge, skills, and dispositions that qualified educators should acquire as part of their professional preparation and the organizational and governance structures of units of teacher education, curricular content, and assessment systems (Darling-Hammond & Bransford, 2005; Williams, Mitchell, & Leibbrand, 2003). Standards for TESOL teacher education programs provide guidelines for the development, review, and accreditation of programs. The review process includes partnership with the National Council for Accreditation of Teacher Education (NCATE), the accrediting organization for units of education at universities.

Institutions of Higher Education in the United States and across the globe are preparing for national accreditation and review of their teacher education programs across disciplines. This process includes alignment of practices with state, national, and professional standards; greater involvement of community stakeholders; enhanced use of technology; collaborative practices across disciplines; and emphasis on assessment and accountability. This focus has led to design of outcome-based measures to assess teacher candidate progress and performance and to monitor their impact on student learning during their clinical practice in schools, as a measure of overall program quality. This chapter explores the design and implementation of a comprehensive assessment system that occurred in conjunction with the NCATE accreditation of the Professional Education Program (PEP) at Stony Brook University (SBU). The assessment system was jointly developed and shared by six teacher education programs that included English, Foreign Languages, Mathematics, Science, Social Studies, and TESOL.

Stony Brook University (SBU) is a Research I university within the State University of New York (SUNY) System in the United States. The University was established in 1957 as the State University College on Long Island for the preparation of secondary school teachers of mathematics and science and has since become one of the nation's leading public research institutions. PEP was created in 1999 as the coordinating unit for all teacher education programs at the undergraduate and graduate levels and the educational leadership programs at the post-graduate level. The University's distributed paradigm for education programs places each of the six teacher education programs in their respective academic departments in the College of Arts and Sciences. This departmentally based model ensures academic rigor in the discipline with integration of pedagogical theory and practice, greater research opportunities for undergraduate and graduate students, and a fertile environment for discipline-based scholarship within and across departments. The teacher education programs combine rich academic coursework in the content discipline with diverse field experiences and clinical practice opportunities in a broad range of educational settings. All programs include a three-semester sequence of discipline-specific pedagogy courses, 100 hours of field experience, and 75 days of clinical practice in schools. A Conceptual Framework that articulates the shared vision and goals for all programs was collaboratively written and approved in 2002. The document includes the major themes that inform curriculum and instruction in SBU's teacher education programs and expectations for candidate proficiencies. It also provides the foundation for a joint commitment to research-based curriculum design, a unified plan for fieldwork and clinical practice, and the development of the unit-wide assessment system for candidates across disciplines.

Description

Recent developments in epistemology, shifting pedagogical approaches in language education, standards-based practices, and educational reform across disciplines have increased interdisciplinary collaborative practices in curriculum planning and assessment (AAAS, 2001). The growing emphasis on language instruction across the curriculum coupled with increased use of English in academic and social contexts have increased the visibility of language educators in educational contexts. The emergence of the content-based instruction (CBI) paradigm further enhanced collaboration across disciplines and increased understanding of the use of diverse academic genres for developing students' critical academic literacy and acquisition of disciplinary concepts (Schleppegrell, 2004). Increased interdisciplinary collaborative partnerships have also generated linked and co-taught courses among content and language educators and integrated language and content assessment (Crandall, 1993; Crandall & Kaufman, 2002; Kaufman & Crandall, 2005; Mohan, 1986; Mohan, Leung, & Davison, 2001; Short, 1993; Snow & Brinton, 1997; Stoller, 2004).

In recent decades, a broad range of instructional paradigms that promote the centrality and diversity of learners, active engagement in authentic and meaningful activities, and cooperative learning have been integrated into classroom pedagogy. Increased emphasis on the centrality of sociocultural theory and processes in preparing professionals has also affected curriculum and assessment design in teacher education (Edge, 2002; Johnson, 2000; Freeman & Johnson, 1998; Hall, 2002; Lantolf, 2000; Prabhu, 1996). Best practices in pedagogy have included fostering learners' autonomy and active engagement, action research, opportunities for experiential learning, construction of knowledge through inquiry and reflective practice, self and peer observation and evaluation, and inclusive approaches (Benson, 2001; Brown, 2004; Burns, 1999; Freeman & Richards, 1996; Gebhard & Oprandy, 1999; Goodlad, 1990; Graves, 1996; Henniger, 2004; Johnson, 1999; Kaufman, 2000, 2004; Nunan & Lamb, 1996; Zamel & Spack, 2002).

The evolution in pedagogy and epistemology paralleled developments in language assessment that underscored increased understanding of the complexity of the learning process and learner assessment. The viewpoint that tests are powerful and provide exact measure of knowledge and performance has given way to a more tentative perspective that recognizes the complexity of the learning process and its assessment. Effective test design, validity and reliability of language assessment paradigms, and ethical issues have been at the forefront of research and debate among linguists and language educators (Alderson, Clapham, & Wall, 1995; Bachman, 1990; Bachman & Cohen, 1998; Bachman & Palmer, 1996; Clapham, 1998; Coombe & Hubley, 2003; Genesee & Upshur, 1996; Rea-Dickins & Germaine, 1998; Shohamy, 2001). Assessment has become more formative and has been integrated into curriculum design and the learning process, attesting to increased awareness of the reciprocal, contextualized, subjective, and dynamic nature of assessment (Fulcher, 2003; Harp, 2000; Spolsky, 1995). Assessment approaches that include authentic assessments, journals, portfolios, self-assessment, and peer assessment have replaced binary assessment paradigms that were prevalent in earlier decades (Brown, 2004; O'Malley & Valdez Pierce, 1996; Purves, Jordan, & Peltz, 1997). Assessment has also become more ethically driven, taking into consideration variability in learner performance (McNamara, 1996, 2000). It has also become more specialized and standards-based and has incorporated advanced computer technology requiring practitioners to familiarize themselves with the theory, practice, principles, and vocabulary of assessment when selecting tests and evaluating their appropriateness for different contexts (Stoynoff & Chapelle, 2005).

The design of SBU's comprehensive assessment system has evolved over a period of several years and incorporated the research-based perspectives discussed as well as input from faculty, teacher candidates, school educators, and administrators. The system was collaboratively developed and implemented by teacher educators from all six programs who brought to the process their own unique disciplinary perspective and insights. It was developed to assess the performance of teacher candidates, faculty, cooperating teachers, and alumni and to evaluate overall program quality and effectiveness. The system is standards-driven and aligned with the PEP *Conceptual Framework*, New York State standards, NCATE standards (2002), the national standards for teacher candidates formulated by the Interstate New Teacher Assessment and Support Consortium (INTASC, 1992), and the standards of the respective specialized professional associations (SPA) across disciplines (e.g., TESOL and NCTM). The focus of discussion in this chapter is on the assessment of teacher candidates. Instruments were developed to monitor the longitudinal development of teacher candidates as they progress through the program and to make authentic, formative, and summative evaluations of their progress at appropriate points in the academic and experiential fieldwork components of the program. Data aggregation and analysis are used to analyze and review candidate performance, monitor and guide their professional development, identify curriculum gaps, and make decisions for improving teaching and learning and program quality. The system has served as a tool for change and improvement to enhance learning and professional growth and promote accountability. Table 3.1 provides an overview of the candidate performance assessment instruments and context of assessment.

Distinctive Features

The challenge for universities preparing new teachers has been the design and implementation of best practices in teaching, learning, and assessment that strengthen the links between instruction and learning at the university and the

Table 3.1: Candidate Performance Assessment Instruments

What Is Assessed	Type and Context of Assessment	Assessment Instrument
Candidates' knowledge, performance, and dispositions throughout the program	Longitudinal assessment of candidates developing professional proficiencies during each of the three pedagogy courses from admission to exit	1. Admission Essay 2. Teacher Candidate Professional Development Form (TCPDF) 3. Dispositions Essay Assignment 4. Portfolio 5. Reflective Journals
Effective lesson design and implementation Candidates' impact on students, in schools	Lesson observation during the Clinical Practice semester and action research	1. Lesson Evaluation Form (LEF) 2. Teacher Candidate Work Sample (TCWS)

effect of teacher candidates on students' learning in schools. The distributed, discipline-based paradigm of teacher education at SBU emphasizes theoretical and practical pedagogical content knowledge and alignment with state, national, and professional standards. SBU's assessment system is distinctive in its interdisciplinary collaborative underpinnings and standards-based approach. In alignment with the national standards for teacher candidates (INTASC, 1992), ten teacher candidate proficiencies were identified to provide a set of performance outcomes for candidates of all six programs (see Table 3.2). These have become an integral part of the unit-wide conceptual framework and assessment system and have provided a focal point around which the assessments instruments are designed to evaluate candidates' development of knowledge, skills, and dispositions.

Table 3.2: PEP Candidate Proficiencies:
Assessing Knowledge, Performance, and Dispositions

1	Understand the central concepts, tools of inquiry, and structures of the discipline	*Knowledge*
2	Understand and apply knowledge of human development and research in pedagogy to design diverse learning experiences that promote intellectual, social, and personal development	*Knowledge and Performance*
3	Understand and appreciate how students differ in their approaches to learning, are sensitive to diversity, and can adapt learning experiences to diverse learners	*Disposition*
4	Apply a variety of instructional strategies grounded in pedagogical content knowledge to creatively develop critical thinking, cognitive and performance skills, and intellectual curiosity for *all* learners	*Performance*
5	Understand and apply knowledge of individual and group motivation and behavior to create a learning environment that encourages positive social interaction, active engagement in learning, and self-motivation	*Knowledge and Performance*
6	Understand and apply knowledge of effective verbal, nonverbal, and media communication strategies to foster active inquiry, collaboration, and supportive interaction in the classroom	*Knowledge and Performance*
7	Plan and adjust learning experiences based on knowledge of the discipline and its pedagogy, curriculum goals, the individual student, and community	*Performance*
8	Understand and apply formal and informal modes of assessment to evaluate learners, monitor learner progress, and inform and improve instruction	*Knowledge and Performance*
9	Actively seek opportunities to grow professionally, including engagement in reflective practice; continually evaluate the effects of their actions on others and are flexible in their responses; open to constructive criticism; and intellectually curious	*Disposition*
10	Foster collegial and communal partnerships to support student learning and well-being, both inside and outside the classroom	*Disposition*

Source: http://stonybrook.edu/pep/guide/candidate.shtml

The multiple instruments that compose the assessment system have proven to be rich and authentic. As formative, they have become an integral part of the learning process and as summative, they assess candidates' development longitudinally as they complete key milestones of the program (see Table 3.3). The journal, portfolio, and dispositions essay are authentic measures that incorporate reflective self-evaluation and feedback from peers and faculty and are developed longitudinally by candidates.

The assessment system is multidimensional and is composed of several assessment instruments that are used in diverse contexts by university faculty and by cooperating teachers in schools. Several of the instruments are used longitudinally throughout the program to assess candidates' growth and to guide their professional development in pedagogical content knowledge and its application in the clinical practice settings. For example, the Teacher Candidate Professional Development Form (TCPDF) assesses candidates' professional growth and their progress toward meeting the ten standards-based proficiencies. The Lesson Evaluation Form (LEF) assesses candidates on the overall ability to create meaningful learning experiences for students of diverse backgrounds and abilities. This includes quality of design and implementation of the lesson, the ability to focus lessons on key disciplinary concepts and essential questions, effective classroom management, promotion of higher level–thinking skills, effective use of multiple learning strategies, effective use of assessment to promote learning, and responsiveness to individual student needs in inclusive settings. Rubrics were developed for each of the assessment instruments to guide the evaluation of candidates' progress, scaffold their development, and enhance their learning.

Table 3.3: Assessment Gates for Teacher Candidates
See *www.stonybrook.edu/pep/assessment.shtml*
for assessment instruments.

Admission to Program 1st Pedagogy Course and Fieldwork	Admission to 2nd Pedagogy Course and Fieldwork	Admission to 3rd Pedagogy Course and Clinical Practice	Program Exit Graduation and Certification
Undergraduate	TCPDF*	TCPDF	TCPDF
2.75 GPA	SPA standards	SPA standards	SPA standards
(3.0 Major)	Dispositions	Dispositions	Dispositions
	Portfolio	Portfolio	Portfolio
Graduate	Fieldwork	Fieldwork	Fieldwork
BA content area	Course Grade	Course Grade	Course Grade
3.0 GPA		NYS LAST Test	LEF**
		2.75 GPA	TCWS***
		(3.0 major GPA)	

*TCPDF – Teacher Candidate Professional Development Form
**LEF – Lesson Evaluation Form
***TCWS – Teacher Candidate Work Sample

Assessment of dispositions is an area that has been challenging for teacher education programs around the globe and has been the focus of much discussion in recent years. Dispositions are defined by NCATE as: "the values, commitments, & professional ethics that influence behavior toward students, families, & communities & that affect student learning, motivation, & development as well as the educator's own professional growth. Dispositions are guided by beliefs & attitudes related to values such as caring, fairness, honesty, responsibility, & social justice" (NCATE 2002, p. 53). In alignment with INTASC standards and New York State Code of Ethics, our disposition assessment consists of formative and summative assessment of candidates' dispositions and attitudes toward teaching as a profession. Our key instrument, the Dispositions Essay Assignment, assesses performance longitudinally over a three-semester period and incrementally increases candidates' awareness and implementation of professional dispositions as articulated in state and national standards. This assignment is intended to raise awareness of dispositions and knowledge of the standards and codes of ethics. Candidates write essays in each of three semesters in which they examine and reflect on their own dispositions and their approach to classroom scenarios. During the first semester, candidates respond to scenarios taken from the published literature, and during the second semester, they respond to general prompts and create their own vignettes. In the third semester, they create their own scenarios based on their experience in the clinical practice setting. Candidates use the INTASC Dispositions, New York State Code of Ethics for Educators, and standards of the Specialized Professional Associations to reflect on and to guide their responses in class discussions and in writing. Candidates' increasingly sophisticated understanding of the personal and professional qualities and dispositions required of committed educators are attested through discussions, reflective journals, and documentation of the school-based scenarios in their portfolios.

Table 3.4 provides an overview of the assessment instruments for monitoring teacher candidates' progress and professional development. These provide quantitative and qualitative data, and they target and reflect the developmental trajectory of candidates as they progress toward professional proficiency and excellence. The features that are assessed are varied, as are the context and the assessors. Assessment by university faculty and cooperating teachers brings together the academic and clinical practice perspectives and provides a measure of inter-rater reliability.

An important element of the Stony Brook University teacher candidate assessment system is the Teacher Candidate Work Sample (TCWS). This instrument was adapted from the Teacher Work Sample developed by the Renaissance Partnership for Improving Teacher Quality (*http://fp.uni.edu/itq/ProjectOverview/Index.htm;* Girod, 2002) and was developed to operationalize the transition from teaching to learning, to producing student learning, and performance accountability (Pankratz, 2004). The TCWS (see Table 3.5) assesses the candidates'

Table 3.4: Monitoring Candidates' Professional Development from Admission to Exit

Assessment Instrument	Features Assessed and Context	Assessor
Teacher Candidate Professional Development Form (TCPDF)	Track candidate knowledge, performance, and dispositions at each of three-course professional education sequence	University faculty School cooperating teacher
Dispositions Essay	Developed through three-course professional education sequence to raise awareness, develop, and assess candidate dispositions as described by INTASC, New York State Code of Ethics, and SPAs (where available)	University faculty
Portfolio	Assess candidate proficiencies, alignment with *Conceptual Framework* themes and pathways and SPA standards	University faculty School cooperating teacher (Review and input to candidate)
Lesson Evaluation Form	Assess candidate performance in clinical practice—five observations per candidate	University faculty School cooperating teacher
Teacher Candidate Work Sample (TCWS)	Assess candidate ability to plan and deliver instruction; assess, and analyze data to improve learning and impact on student learning	University faculty School cooperating teacher (Review and input to candidate)

pedagogical content knowledge and their ability to synthesize the knowledge, skills, and dispositions acquired in the university and apply them in authentic classroom settings. It assesses the candidate's ability to understand the contextual factors and setting for learning; define, plan, and implement learning goals; design and implement an assessment plan; aggregate and analyze data to improve student learning; and engage in reflection and self-evaluation. The TCWS provides a holistic, dynamic assessment of the entire spectrum of knowledge, skills, and abilities and is incorporated as the hallmark of the candidate's professional portfolio.

Development of the assessment system and instruments has stimulated inquiry and partnership among all stakeholders and facilitated monitoring and documentation of teacher candidates' progress in all programs. Assessment data were aggregated and analyzed to evaluate and improve the quality of field experience and clinical practice, academic curriculum, course content and sequencing of elements such as literacy and technology, candidates' performance and their impact on students, and overall program quality.

Table 3.5: Teacher Candidate Work Sample (TCWS)

Contextual Factors— the Setting for Learning	Analyze the learning context—students, school, and community and understand its impact on the formulation of standards-based learning goals, assessment plan, design for instruction, and student learning.
Learning Goals	Design learning goals that are aligned with state, professional, and national standards and grounded in research in the discipline and its pedagogy to formulate a plan to engage all students in meaningful learning using verbal, non-verbal, and media communications strategies to foster active inquiry, collaboration, and supportive interaction.
Assessment Plan	Apply multiple formal and informal modes of assessment that are aligned with learning goals to assess students before, during, and after instruction to monitor learner progress, and inform, modify, and improve instruction in accordance with individual students' needs.
Design for Instruction	Apply multiple instructional strategies that are aligned with the learning goals to creatively develop critical thinking, cognitive and performance skills, and intellectual curiosity for all learners.
Analysis of Student Learning	Use assessment data to analyze the impact of instruction on student learning and formulate plans for adjusting learning goals, assessment, and instruction.
Reflection and Self-Evaluation	Engage in reflective practice to continually evaluate the impact of teaching on student learning and implications for professional development and improved instruction.

Caveats

Preparation of effective teachers involves the design and implementation of a multidimensional assessment system that is performance based and formative in focus to enhance learning and teaching. The development and implementation of an interdisciplinary comprehensive assessment system is a complex endeavor that requires the collaboration and commitment of administrators and faculty across disciplines and departments at the university and educators in the partnering schools in the community. Design and implementation of an effective assessment system includes the development of assessment instruments; critical performance indicators and rubrics; and a process for data collection, aggregation, analysis, and reporting to improve candidates' performance and their impact on all students (see Table 3.6). A web-based user interface and an electronic database management system greatly enhance data collection, aggregation, and analysis. Regular dissemination of results contributes to continued improvement in candidates' performance, curriculum design, and program quality. Commitment to a timeline for ongoing review and revision of the assessment system is critical for ensuring that the process and the system remain dynamic and current.

Table 3.6: Design and Implementation of a
Multidisciplinary Assessment System

Foster unit-wide commitment and support of colleagues across disciplines to ensure interdisciplinary partnership in the development of the system

Secure support of university administrators and enhance participation of community partners

Develop an assessment system in alignment with state, national, and professional standards and the unit's conceptual framework

Develop diverse assessment instruments that are multi-dimensional

Identify assessment coordinator(s) and form an assessment committee

Develop a web-based user interface and an electronic database management system

Develop an ongoing process for data aggregation, analysis, and reporting

Use aggregated data results for candidate and program improvement

Design a timeline and commit to the review and revision of assessment system and instruments

---

Conclusion

A robust assessment system and its implementation for program improvement are at the core of teacher education and the accreditation process. The multidisciplinary approach to assessment design has introduced collaborative initiatives, diverse perspectives, and cross-disciplinary synergy and discourse that have contributed to teaching and learning in all the teacher education programs. The assessment system has provided a holistic, dynamic assessment of the entire spectrum of candidate knowledge, skills, and dispositions, and other aspects of the program and the unit. The standards-based assessment instruments have engaged teacher candidates across disciplines in reflective practice, self- and peer assessment, journal and portfolio writing, and action research. Implementation of the assessment system has captured the relationship among assessment, learning, and scaffolding instruction. Assessment in its formative and summative roles has become an integral part of the learning process, contributing to changes in the curriculum and pedagogical approaches and facilitating learning and improved performance. The process has been both retrospective and prospective and has been powerful in determining candidates' performance and in guiding the developmental trajectory of candidates' professional growth as effective teachers.

Discussion Questions

1. Imagine yourself as a member of the multidisciplinary team on assessment representing the field of TESOL. Outline for your colleagues the knowledge, skills, and dispositions required of teacher candidates if they are to teach English language learners in their content-area classes.

2. Review the TESOL standards for teacher education programs and summarize for your colleagues the major tenets of the standards.

3. Alignment with standards is critical in the preparation of effective teachers. Look up the standards in your state or country. Design a curricular module that aligns with these standards.

4. From your own experience, provide an example of how assessment has helped you to improve instruction.

5. What is content-based instruction? In what way has this paradigm enhanced collaboration of educators from the field of language teaching and other disciplines? What impact has this had on the education of English language learners?

6. As a teacher candidate in a teacher education program, imagine you are assessed on the extent to which you have met the proficiencies listed in the TESOL (2002) Standards for Teacher Education. For each standard, discuss what evidence you will produce to demonstrate that you have met this standard.

   a. Standard 3.c. Using Resources Effectively in ESL and Content Instruction. Candidates are familiar with a wide range of standards-based materials, resources, and technologies, and choose, adapt, and use them in effective ESL and content teaching.

   b. Standard 4.c. Classroom-Based Assessment for ESL. Candidates know and use a variety of performance-based assessment tools and techniques to inform instruction.

   c. Standard 5.c. Professional Development and Collaboration. Candidates collaborate with and are prepared to serve as a resource to all staff, including paraprofessionals, to improve learning for all ESOL students.

Acknowledgement

My thanks to the Professional Education Program faculty and staff whose commitment to teacher education and collaborative spirit have made the development and implementation of the multidisciplinary assessment system possible.

REFERENCES

Alderson, J. C., Clapham, C., & Wall, D. (1995). *Language test construction and evaluation.* Cambridge: Cambridge University Press.

American Association for the Advancement of Science (AAAS). (2001). *Designs for science literacy: Project 2061.* Washington, DC: Author.

American Council for the Teaching of Foreign Langauges (ACTFL). (2002). Program standards for the preparation of foreign language teachers. ACTFL Yonkers, N.Y. Available at http://www.actfl.org/i4a/pages/index.cfm?pageid=3384

Bachman, L. F. (1990). *Fundamental considerations in language testing.* Oxford: Oxford University Press.

Bachman, L. F., & Cohen, A. D. (Eds.). (1998). *Interfaces between second language acquisition and language testing research.* Cambridge: Cambridge University Press.

Bachman, L. F., & Palmer, A. S. (1996). *Language testing in practice.* Oxford: Oxford University Press.

Benson, P. (2001). *Autonomy in language learning.* London: Pearson.

Brown, H. D. (2004). *Language assessment: Principles and classroom practices.* White Plains, NY: Pearson.

Burns, A. (1999). *Collaborative action research for English language teachers.* Cambridge: Cambridge University Press.

Clapham, C. M. (1998). The effect of language proficiency and background knowledge on EAP students' reading comprehension. In A. J. Kunnan (Ed.), *Validation in language assessment.* Mahwah, NJ: Lawrence Erlbaum Associates.

Coombe, C. A., & Hubley, N. J. (Eds.). (2003). *Assessment practices.* Alexandria, VA: TESOL Publications.

Crandall, J. (1993). Content-centered learning in the United States. *Annual Review of Applied Linguistics, 13,* 111–126.

Crandall, J., & Kaufman, D. (2002). *Case studies in content-based instruction in higher education.* Alexandria, VA: TESOL.

Darling-Hammond, L., & Bransford, J. (Eds.). (2005). *Preparing teachers for a changing world.* San Francisco: Jossey-Bass.

Edge, J. (2002). *Continuing cooperative development: A discourse framework for individuals as colleagues.* Ann Arbor: The University of Michigan Press.

Freeman, D., & Johnson, K. E. (1998). Research and practice in English language teacher education (special-topic issue). *TESOL Quarterly, 32,* 3.

Freeman, D., & Richards, J. C. (1996). *Teacher learning in language teaching.* New York: Cambridge University Press.

Fulcher, G. (2003). *Testing second language speaking.* New York. Pearson Longman.

Gebhard, G., & Oprandy, R. (1999). *Language teaching awareness: A guide to exploring beliefs and practices.* New York: Cambridge University Press.

Genesee, F., & Upshur, J. A. (1996). *Classroom-based evaluation in second language education.* Cambridge: Cambridge University Press

Girod, G. R. (Ed.). (2002). *Connecting teaching and learning: A handbook for teacher educators on teacher work sample methodology.* Washington, DC: AACTE.

Goodlad, J. (1990). *Teachers for our nation's schools.* San Francisco: Jossey Bass.

Graves, K. (Ed.). (1996). *Teachers as course developers.* New York: Cambridge University Press.

Hall, J. K. (2002). *Teaching and researching language and culture.* London: Pearson.

Harp, B. (2000). *The handbook of literacy assessment and evaluation* (2nd ed). Norwood, MA: Christopher Gordon.

Henniger, M. L. (2004). *The teaching experience: An Introduction to Reflective Practice.* Upper Saddle River, NJ: Pearson Education.

Interstate New Teacher Assessment and Support Consortium (INTASC). (1992). *Model standards in science for beginning teacher licensing and development: A resource for state dialogue.* Washington, DC: Author.

Johnson, K. (1999). *Understanding language teaching: Reason in action.* Boston: Heinle & Heinle.

Johnson, K. E. (Ed.). (2000). Innovations in teacher education: A quiet revolution. In K. E. Johnson (Ed.), *Case studies in teacher education* (pp. 1–7). Alexandria, VA: TESOL.

Kaufman, D. (2000). Developing professionals: Interwoven visions and partnerships. In K. E. Johnson (Ed.), *Case studies in teacher education* (pp. 51–69). Alexandria, VA: TESOL.

———. (2004). Issues in constructivist pedagogy for L2 learning and teaching. *Annual Review of Applied Linguistics, 24,* 303–319.

Kaufman, D., & Crandall, J. (2005). *Case studies in content-based instruction in primary and secondary school settings.* Alexandria, VA: TESOL.

Lantolf, J. P. (Ed.). (2000). *Sociocultural theory and second language learning.* Oxford: Oxford University Press.

McNamara, T. (1996). *Measuring second language performance.* New York: Addison Wesley Longman.

———. (2000). *Language testing.* Oxford: Oxford University Press.

Mohan, B. A. (1986). *Language and content.* Reading, MA: Addison Wesley.

Mohan, B., Leung, C., & Davison, C. (2001). *English as a second language in the mainstream.* Essex, UK: Pearson.

National Board for Professional Teaching Standards (NBPTS). (2001). *Toward high and rigorous standards for the teaching profession* (3rd ed.). Washington, DC: Author.

National Council for Accreditation of Teacher Education (NCATE). (2002). *Professional standards for the accreditation of schools, colleges, and departments of education.* Washington, DC: Author.

National Council of Teachers of Mathematics (NCTM). (2000). *Principles and standards for school mathematics.* Reston, VA: Author.

Nunan, D., & Lamb, C. (1996). *The self-directed teacher: Managing the learning process.* Cambridge: Cambridge University Press.

O'Malley, J. M., & Valdez Pierce, L. (1996). *Authentic assessment for English language learners: Practical approaches for teachers.* New York: Addison Wesley Longman.

Pankratz, R. (2004). The power of partnerships in becoming accountable for the impact of teacher candidates on P–12 learning. (pdf available at http://fp.uni.edu/itq/Paper_Publication/index.htm)

Prabhu, N. S. (1996). Concept and conduct in language pedagogy. In G. Cook & B. Seidlhofer (Eds.), *Principle and practice in applied linguistics: Studies in honor of H. G. Widdowson* (pp. 57–71). Oxford: Oxford University Press.

Purves, A. C., Jordan, S. L., & Peltz, J. H. (Eds.). (1997). *Using portfolios in the English classroom.* Norwood, MA: Christopher Gordon.

Rea-Dickins, P., & Germaine, K. P. (Eds). (1998). *Managing evaluation and innovation in language teaching: Building bridges.* New York: Longman.

Renaissance Partnership for Improving Teacher Quality. Available at http://fp.uni.edu/itq/ProjectOverview/Index.htm.

Schleppegrell, M. (2004). *The language of schooling: A functional linguistics perspective.* Mahwah, NJ: Lawrence Erlbaum Associates.

Shohamy, E. (2001). *The power of tests: A critical perspective on the uses of language tests.* Essex, UK: Pearson.

Short, D. (1993). Assessing integrated language and content instruction. *TESOL Quarterly, 27,* 627–656.

Snow, M. A., & Brinton, D. M. (Eds.). (1997). *The content-based classroom: Perspectives on integrating language and content.* White Plains, NY: Longman.

Spolsky, B. (1995). *Measured words: The development of objective language testing.* Oxford: Oxford University Press.

Stoller, F. (2004). Content-based instruction: Perspectives on curriculum planning. *Annual Review of Applied Linguistics, 24,* 261–283.

Stoynoff, S., & Chapelle, C. (Eds.). (2005). *ESOL tests and testing.* Alexandria, VA: TESOL Publications.

TESOL (2002). *TESOL/NCATE Standards for accreditation of initial programs in P-12 ESL education.* Alexandria, VA: TESOL.

Williams, B., Mitchell, A., & Leibbrand, J. (Eds.). (2003). *Navigating change: Preparing for a performance-based accreditation review.* Washington, DC. National Council for Accreditation of Teacher Education.

Zamel, V., & Spack, R. (Eds.). (2002). *Enriching ESOL pedagogy: Readings and activities for engagement, reflection, and inquiry.* Mahwah, NJ: Lawrence Erlbaum Associates.

CHAPTER 4

TAPping into Teaching Effectiveness: A Collaborative Approach to Performance Appraisal of ESL Teachers in a Canadian Context

Andy Curtis and Liying Cheng

Introduction

Central to the ESL teaching and learning process is teaching effectiveness. Although one of the most commonly accepted criteria for measuring effective teaching is the amount of student learning that occurs (Theall & Franklin, 2001), what a student learns is not always within a teacher's control—for example, students' attitudes to learning, background knowledge of the course content, study skills, time students will spend on their learning, and their emotional and intellectual readiness to learn. In order to connect theory and practice in teaching effectiveness and apply the findings of previous research studies to our current context, we will present a case study that used a collaborative approach to performance appraisal of ESL teachers within the context of the intensive English for Academic Purposes program (IEP/EAP) at a university in Ontario, Canada. We will describe the existing system of appraisal used by the university and explain why this system is not suitable for the teachers in this particular IEP/EAP program. We will then describe the collaborative approach developed and adopted by the IEP/EAP program called the Teacher Appraisal Program (TAP). The TAP consists of a set of five core competencies in a three-part evaluation system based on self-assessment, peer-assessment, and student feedback. Evaluation of the first year's implementation of the TAP will be discussed, together with recommendations from the teaching and administrative staff for changes to the TAP in its second cycle.

The Background

In 2003, as a result of the appointment of a new director, the School of English at Queen's University (QSoE) in Ontario, Canada, started to explore the

University's annual appraisal program for administrative/support staff.[1] To our surprise, although the University "strongly recommends" appraisals be carried out annually and that continued employment and increase in position and pay are in theory connected to a satisfactory annual appraisal, most QSoE teachers had never had such an appraisal, which meant that some teachers had been at the School for up to fifteen years without ever once being even once formally appraised. The senior administrative team—the school's Director, Program Supervisor, and the two Teacher Supervisors—started to work on creating a collaborative, cooperative Teacher Appraisal Program (TAP) that would complement our new Professional Development Program (PDP), which is described elsewhere (Curtis, 2006). The purpose of this combination of TAP and PDP was to provide a positive and supportive annual appraisal process and procedure, thus enhancing professional development of the teachers involved.

A Diverse and Challenging Context

The School of English at Queen's University was established in 1942, making it one of the longest-established and best-known schools of its kind in Canada. Over 60 years, the program has grown from three staff and one group of international students on short summer programs, to a twelve-month, year-round program employing up to 50 full- and part-time teachers, administrative support staff, and undergraduate student assistants, working with up to 1,000 international students a year coming from more than 30 countries. Although the school is unbalanced in terms of gender, with more than 90 percent of all staff female, it is very diverse in terms of generation, with staff in their teens, 20s, 30s, 40s, 50s, and 60s working side-by-side.

The instructional program is defined as an Intensive English Program (IEP) and as an English for Academic Purposes (EAP) program, with students in classes for a total of 22½ hours per week, with independent study evenings and weekends, for twelve weeks. The average class size is currently fifteen, although this may increase in the near future. According to entry and exit student surveys, approximately half of the students are applying or planning to apply for places in English-medium tertiary institutions, mostly targeting Canadian and American universities, or English-medium institutions in their own countries. However, a growing number of students are enrolling with a view to working for international companies and corporations.

Like most Canadian university schools of English, QSoE is in the difficult and delicate position of being a zero base–funded, cost-recovery, and income-generating unit. The euphemism used by Canadian universities to refer to schools such as ours is "business unit." This means that we receive no funding of any kind from the University, but that we are required to "pay" the university for use of its facilities, such as classrooms and office space, via a percentage of tuition funds received, sometimes referred to as "tuition top slicing." If we are able to cover all of our operating costs, pay the University, and then still generate a surplus,

---

[1]   Teachers at the School of English fall into the category of administrative/support staff at Queen's University. The Teacher Appraisal Program (TAP) we discuss is for ESL teachers teaching at QSoE.

this counts as a revenue stream and goes toward a fund jointly managed by the school and the faculty to which the school belongs (in our case, the Faculty of Arts and Science). This 100 percent "soft money" approach reflects the low priority given to English language schools at Canadian universities within this province and perhaps within the country.

As a result of this model, all employment at the school, for all positions including the head of the school, is by limited-term contract, with a maximum of one year at a time. Even teachers who have been at the school for 20 years have been on 20 consecutive, one-year contracts. Attempting to establish any kind of professional development program or system of appraisal, or a combination of the two within such an environment, is a considerable challenge. We (the management team of the school) have, however, persisted in our attempts as it is perhaps within such uncertain and insecure employment environments that such programs and systems may be most needed in order to achieve teaching effectiveness.

A Profile of the Teacher Population at QSoE

All core teachers at the school, that is, teachers on one-year, full-time contracts, are required to be registered with and certified by TESL Ontario, the provincial governing body for the TESOL profession in this part of Canada. All core teachers have a teaching degree (BEd), teaching experience, and most have international experience (have taught outside of Canada). All of the twelve core teachers at the school are female, and half have been teaching there between two and five years, with the remainder either in their first year at the school or long-standing senior teachers between 15 and 20 years. For most of the last 25 years, the school has used a separate skills model, with the four modalities taught by different teachers, so teachers were hired on the basis of their expertise in one particular modality or skill areas. Over the last two years, the school has been developing and piloting a more integrated skills model, so teachers are now required to have experience in all four modalities and different skill areas. Although the school has moved from a pair-teaching model, with each core class taught by two core teachers, to a model in which each core class has one main teacher, there is still a great deal of sharing of ideas, resources, and materials within a positive, professional, and collegial environment.

Description

The definition of and criterion for evaluating teaching effectiveness is much debated due to the multidimensional nature of teaching, the interaction between teachers and students, as well as the increasingly high-stakes nature of teacher evaluation. Guskey (1998) highlights the issue of accountability in teacher evaluation through professional development and calls for a rethinking of the nature of teacher evaluation. Dunkin (1997) conceptualized the evaluation of teachers' effectiveness through the discussion of its purposes, the category of teachers to be assessed, conceptions of teachers' work, dimensions of teacher quality, and approaches to establishing validity of evaluation. Dunkin also summarized the traditional methods of evaluating teaching effectiveness, such as paper-and-pencil tests and performance measures, and emerging methods, including on-the-job evaluation and portfolio and interviews, and called for the development of more holistic systems for evaluating teachers' effectiveness.

Darling-Hammond (1996) emphasized that teacher evaluation should reflect the knowledge and skills teachers are expected to master as a minimum requirement for responsible practice and should be constructed to encourage the acquisition of the required professional knowledge, skills, and disposition. In discussing the benchmarks for language teachers in Hong Kong, Conium & Falvey (1999) pointed out that the core competencies of an EFL/ESL teacher should consist of language ability, subject content knowledge (language awareness), and pedagogical content knowledge (teaching ability). Accordingly, much of the evaluation work should be improvement oriented (Patton, 1997) and context based (Lynch, 1996), with some elements of the evaluation being more summative in nature (Scriven, 1972). More research has pointed out a combination of both formative (improvement-based and context-based) and summative evaluation. Such a combination can serve the ultimate function of teacher professional development through the appraisal process.

Dunkin (1997) cites Stiggins and Duke's (1990) three types of evaluation systems, with the first being for novice teachers, the second a "system for experienced teachers in need of remediation to correct deficiencies in performance so that they may avoid dismissal" (p. 2), and the third "a professional development system for competent experienced teachers pursuing excellence in particular areas of teaching" (ibid). According to Dunkin, this system would be based on three sets of components: teachers' involvement with setting goals; supervision; and feedback from peers, students, and self-generated feedback, which would enable the teachers to "recheck their performance standards periodically" (ibid). As we are a school with teachers at various stages of their teaching careers, this evaluation system was employed as the basis for our own appraisal system with an emphasis on professional development.

The Teacher Appraisal Program (TAP)

The TAP was developed within this evaluation system consisting of three sets of components—that is, setting goals; supervision; and feedback from peers, students, and self-generated feedback.

Setting Goals

In terms of teachers' involvement in goal setting, QSoE teachers were first asked to generate a list of what we referred to as Core Competencies (CCs), which reflected the knowledge, skills, and abilities they believe an ESL teacher in a program like ours should have. This approach was influenced by the work of Darling-Hammond and colleagues (1995), though the focus of their study was on the licensing of teachers, which Darling-Hammond et al. concluded should "reflect the minimum knowledge and skills all professionals are expected to master as a minimum requirement for responsible practice" (p. 89).

Interestingly, our first attempts at generating this list of competencies were not successful, and in fact led to some tension and anxiety on the part of the some of the teachers, as they felt they were being asked to create something that should have been created by the senior administration. Some teachers felt that this was not their job. This was an unexpected reaction, in fact, the opposite of what we were expecting, as this is much more in line with Darling-Hammond's (1986) notion of the "bureaucratic conception of teaching," in which "administrators plan" and "teachers implement" (p. 532), than the "professional conception of teaching" (ibid). This also proved to be a good example of the difference between the theory and practice of change implementation, as most theories state that when change is imposed on teachers from above, it is unsuccessful because the people most directly affected by the change were not consulted (Curtis & Cheng, 2001; Curtis, 1999, 2000).

Our response to this reaction was to generate a list of competencies that we—the school's Director, Program Supervisor, and the two Teacher Supervisors—believed represented some of the core competencies, but no attempt was made to create a list of *all* teaching competencies, as this may not be possible due to the complexity of teaching and learning, especially in multilingual, multicultural ESL classrooms. The teachers were then asked to review the list; ask us about any of the items on the list; and meet, discuss, and agree upon five Core Competencies (CCs). Here are the competencies originally proposed:

Departmental Knowledge   Change Management
Communication   TESL Knowledge
Classroom Management

Through a group-based, consultative, collaborative, cooperative approach—though, importantly, *not* a consensus-based approach, agreement was reached on the five Core Competencies, which were accepted as presented, expanded upon, and defined. This process served the function of negotiating and understanding the key constructs of the appraisal system, which enhanced the validity of the evaluation.

1. *Departmental Knowledge:* Demonstrates thorough and up-to-date knowledge of the school in all areas, including administrative structures, policies and procedures, curricula, the classroom, contracts, and additional courses. (Additional courses refer to courses taught in addition to the core EAP classes, such as the Introduction to Teaching English as a Second Language course.)

2. *Change Management:* Responds positively and supportively to changes and challenges at the School; demonstrates flexibility and the ability to adapt to new developments; is willing to learn new skills, procedures, and processes.
3. *Communication:* Communicates effectively and professionally with students, teachers, and administrative staff; collects and disseminates information (between different groups at the school); accepts feedback positively from others.
4. *TESL Knowledge:* Demonstrates knowledge of language skills, methodologies, practices, and current developments in TESL; shows an understanding of the importance of student-centeredness and reflective practice.
5. *Classroom Management:* Responds to issues surrounding classroom management promptly, professionally, and effectively.

In addition to the five CCs, a list of Additional Competencies (ACs) was also created that made a list of 23 competencies—five Core, eleven Facilitator of Learning, three Collaboration, and four General (see Appendix 1). In having a core set of competencies, plus three additional competencies selected by the teacher from a negotiated and agreed upon set of nineteen possibilities, we were able to create a program that is both standardized *and* individualized, thereby avoiding the usual either-or dichotomy and dilemma. The process also involved the teachers so they took responsibilities in their own evaluation and development. Each of these CCs and ACs was assessed and evaluated by three different parties: first the individual teacher with self-assessment, the Teacher Supervisor, then the School's Director.

There are three ratings, referred to as Factor Rating Codes in the Queen's system:

- *Exceeded Job Requirements:* High-quality performance that consistently exceeds the requirements of the position
- *Achieved Job Requirements:* Quality performance that meets and occasionally exceeds the requirements of the position
- *Needs Improvement:* Performance that does not consistently meet the requirements of the position

We used these ratings, since our aim was that the appraisal program be compatible with the University's, though we did find these ratings to be problematic, as Needs Improvement, from a developmental point of view, could apply to all areas unless the individual has reached some kind of "perfection" in which no further development can occur. Also, as "quality" is not defined by the University, the difference between "high-quality" and "quality" are difficult to assess, and as with all professional positions, "the requirements of the position" are different at different times of the semester and at different times of the year and can to some extent depend on what is being taught and to whom. In addition, such a rating was based on a norm-referenced evaluation philosophy where teachers are appraised against each other. However, for the first year of our TAP program, we wanted to use the existing rating scales before making any changes.

Feedback from Peers, Students, and Self-generated Feedback

The third of Dunkin's (1997) factors was "feedback from peers, students, and self-generated feedback," parts of which were required as part of the TAP program and parts of which were optional, as we were aiming for a degree of standardization as well as the possibility of individualizing the TAP program to encourage professional development. The two parts of the system required are feedback from students and self-assessment, with peer assessment being an option.

For the student feedback, there were two major changes that needed to be made. First, in previous years, all student feedback had been in the form of open-ended comments. Not only was this difficult for students at the lower levels of English language proficiency, but it also made it extremely difficult to process the feedback, as it was all entirely qualitative. Another limitation of this approach was the fact that written feedback from students was the main or even sole source of documented feedback; an approach not supported by the research findings of Doyle (2004) and others (e.g., Centra, 1993; Doyle, 1983; James, 1997; Seldin, 1999). After stating that "the use of students' rating for evaluating teacher effectiveness is the single most researched issue in all of higher education" (p. 1)—more than 2,000 articles in 70 years, Doyle concludes that "student rating should be only one of several forms of evaluation used to shed light on teaching effectiveness" (p. 9). He goes on to recommend that, in addition to the use of students' ratings, peer-review, self-evaluation, teaching portfolios, and student achievement should also be employed (ibid).

Therefore, before the new TAP was introduced in the winter of 2004, the student feedback process was changed to one based on a mixture of quantitative and qualitative responses and was piloted first with smaller groups of teachers (four) on a shorter course (five weeks). The new student feedback form consisted of a series of statements with a Likert-type scale of numerical responses as well as space for open-ended comments. The first of the statements asked the student to reflect on their overall performance on the course: *I participated in this class regularly and completed all course work.* However, the remaining eight statements focused on the course:

- The lessons were clear and well organized.
- I knew what I was expected to do during class and on assignments.
- The materials and activities were fun and/or interesting.
- The skills, strategies, and structures taught were important.
- The teacher responded positively to students in class.
- His/Her evaluation of assignments was helpful and fair.
- My English language skills improved as a result of this class.
- I would recommend this class to other students.

The Likert-scale was from 1 to 5, with 1 = Strong Disagree and 5 = Strongly Agree. The school then employed a student assistant (a university undergraduate who works for the school, not one of the school's ESL students) to tabulate all the numerical results and provide a summary of the results, including frequency counts, averages, and standard deviations. The benefits of small-scale piloting first were shown by the number of teachers who responded positively to the new system, but who did not understand the notion of "standard deviation." Consequently, the summary forms now include a brief definition of *SD*, as well as a brief definition of which kind of average was being shown (mean), in response to questions from our teachers.

A key part of the TAP program was the Letter of Self-Assessment (LSA), in which each teacher described her roles and responsibilities, accomplishments and achievements, challenges and areas for development. The letters were, on average, approximately two pages (around 1,000 words) and provided the basis for interpreting all of the other documents in the appraisal package. In addition to the LSA, the self- and other-assessed competencies (CCs and ACs) and quantitative student feedback, classroom observation forms could also be included, based on Teacher Supervisor observations, usually of a 90-minute lesson. The form focuses on four areas: organization of the lesson; instructor presentation; class management; and student response, commented on in two main areas of positive aspects and suggestions/ideas. Based on all of these documents, the Teacher Supervisor wrote a half-page of feedback comments, summarizing the evaluation of the teacher's performance over the previous twelve months.

The collaborative approach to the three sets of components of the TAP discussed—setting goals; supervision; and feedback from peers, students, and self-generated feedback—is the essential key to the performance appraisal of ESL teachers within the context of our intensive English for Academic Purposes program (IEP/EAP).

Distinctive Features: A Brief Look at Canadian University Appraisal Programs

To assess how our teacher evaluation program differed from others, we carried out an online investigation of all 22 Canadian university EAP/IEP language teaching units and programs. Having looked more carefully at the websites of each unit and each program, we narrowed the list down by nearly half to twelve programs that seemed more similar to ours based on factors such as size—both in terms of staff and students—and other aspects of the program such as age (how long the program has been offered, length and size, number of weeks, numbers of in-class hours per day and per week).

None of the English language teaching units at these twelve universities gave details as to how its teachers are appraised, evaluated, or assessed. This may be because such details might be considered sensitive or because of some aspects of confidentiality agreements or other union-related restrictions. However, we did find four universities that did give details of their general staff appraisal processes and procedures: Alberta, Brock, Ottawa, and York.

Comparing Different Approaches to Appraisal within Canada

A number of Canadian universities, such as the University of Alberta and Memorial University in Newfoundland, use the nine factors of the Aiken Plan. According to Johnson, Sawatzky, Greenfield, and Allenby (2002), the Aiken Plan is a "standardized factor rating plan. A common (and quite generic) set of factors are applied to all organizations with a given set of weights" (p. 6). The nine factors are:

Complexity/Judgment	Work Experience
Independence of Action (Initiative)	Consequence of Errors
Contacts	Character and Scope of Supervision
Physical Demands	Working Conditions
Education	

A detailed consideration of each of these factors is not necessary here, but in terms of the most relevant factors, Education is worth considering. According to the Memorial University site, Education is defined as: "the level of formalized knowledge required to satisfactorily fill the position. Such knowledge is most commonly acquired as a result of time spent in schools, colleges and universities. It does not consider the education level of the present incumbent" (p. 1). Of interest for our comparison is the fact that the educational level of the present incumbent is not a factor.

Brock University uses Job Evaluation Factors, under which there are four main headings and fourteen sub-headings:

Skill
Technical Know-How	Management Know-How
Human Relations	

Effort
Problem-Solving	What is the thinking environment?
What is the thinking challenge?	Physical Effort

Responsibility
Freedom to Act	Magnitude
Impact	

Working Conditions
Physical Effort	Physical Environment
Sensory Attention	Mental Stress

Interestingly in this classification, education and experience are combined and listed under Skills, with the question to be addressed: "What are the combined levels of education and experience needed to perform the job at a competent level?" (p. 1)

The University of Ottawa describes its Performance Appraisal Program for staff as being "based on the evaluation of two components at the end of each year: the competencies and levels identified for the position and the key objectives established between each manager and their staff members for the period covered by an appraisal cycle. The program therefore seeks to establish and recognize the activities undertaken in a cycle of one year, as well as have some benchmarks for competencies in positions at the University" (p. 1). The program at Ottawa is impressive—if somewhat cumbersome—with no fewer than sixteen areas for appraisal, each of which comes with a focus question and between four and six sub-points—creating a total of 72 factors (pp. 3–18):

Personal Motivation	Planning and Initiative
Teamwork and Cooperation	Client-Service Orientation
Concern for Order and Quality	Critical Thinking
Developing Others	Expertise (Sharing of)
Flexibility	Impact and Influence
Information Seeking	Innovation
Listening, Understanding, and Responding	Organization Awareness
Self-Assertiveness	Self Control
Team Leadership	

York University has developed what it calls a performance management and review program designed to assist "Confidential, Professional and Managerial employees and their managers with the ongoing development and management of employee performance" (p. 1). The program is based on a one-hour interview, carried out in May of each year, with five goals and objectives:

- "Establish employee performance criteria and objectives that will support and reinforce the achievement of the University's Mission, Values and Objectives
- Provide management and employees with a vehicle for communicating and clarifying employee performance expectations and results
- Identify employee training and development needs to support the achievement of employee performance expectations and results
- Assist in the establishment of employee career development goals and the identification and attainment of specific knowledge, skills, and behaviours needed to realize these goals
- Provide a consistent, fair and objective measurement tool for making sound pay, promotion and transfer decisions" (p. 1)

The Queen's University model goes by the name Performance Review and Development Plan and is also available online. Similar to the University of Ottawa program, the Queen's program also has seventeen factors but no multiple sub-factors. The three main factors are: Results; Personal Contribution, and Supervisory, with most – eleven of the seventeen – being Personal Contribution factors, and three in each of the other two areas:

Results Factors: Accomplishment of Objectives   Quality Self-Management (p. 2)
Personal Contribution Factors (pp. 2–3)

Adaptability	Communication
Creativity	Influence and Negotiation
Initiative	Interpersonal Skills
Job Knowledge	Judgment and Problem Solving
Planning/Organizing	Service Orientation
Teamwork	

Supervisory Factors: Leadership, Staff, and Development Supervision (p. 3)

As with the other Canadian university systems for appraisal, evaluation, and assessment of staff, there are recurring themes within the Queen's model and between the different models we surveyed that are relevant for teachers. Examples include teamwork, communication and interpersonal skills, and creativity and problem-solving.

What did we learn from this brief but enlightening survey of different Canadian appraisal programs and systems? First, creating a valid, reliable, and non-threatening teacher evaluation program that helps teachers improve their performance is a complex and difficult task. Second, there are many similarities and areas of overlap in the qualities, characteristics, knowledge, and skills identified in the different programs, which supports the notion of "core competencies" for our TAP. Third, in the same way that long lists of decontextualized words memorized for vocabulary tests may be of less use than a smaller number of words understood in a broader context, it is possible that fewer but negotiated and agreed upon competencies may be more effective than larger, longer "shopping lists." A fourth point, balancing the previous point, is the importance of context, as each of the five systems considered is clearly a product of the context in which it operates, reflecting the values and principles of that environment (Lynch, 1996). The fifth, and perhaps most important result of the survey was that it enabled us to assess the distinctiveness of our TAP program.

One of the distinctive features of our teacher evaluation program is the fact that it exists at all, as all the teaching staff at QSoE are classified within the category of "administrative/support staff," and appraisal of such staff, though encouraged, is not formally required at our university. Therefore, having any kind of evaluation system in place, when one is not required, is unusual. Second, the programs we surveyed appear to be highly standardized, as this is thought to be a key feature of any systematic evaluation procedure. However, using Core and Additional Competencies, we have been able to create a program that is both standardized and individualized, which gives the teachers some choice and responsibilities in how the appraisal is carried out and what is included in the documentation. Also, in most of the programs we examined, there seems to be such an overlap between developmental and evaluative functions of appraisal that the distinction between the two appears to disappear, though it is important to make and keep such distinctions (Bailey, Curtis, & Nunan, 2001; Patton, 1997). Another potentially distinctive feature of the TAP program is its use of triangulation to build up a more accurate picture, by combining self-assessment, peer assessment, and student feedback. The fact that our TAP program was informed by some of the literature on teacher evaluation and by a survey of other Canadian university appraisal systems may also be a unique feature of the TAP program.

Caveats

Based on what we have learned from the first year of the TAP program, we would like to offer some advice, suggestions, and practical ideas on adapting and applying our program to different educational contexts.

Our first suggestion is to start small. Developing any kind of appraisal system is a large and complex undertaking, so piloting is essential. In our case, we discussed the first draft of the program, both the competencies and the other components of the program, with a small group of teachers who trust us and whom we trust. This leads to another realization, which is the importance of trust. If our teachers did not believe that the system was designed as much to show what they can do as to identify areas for development, the program would probably have failed. Similarly, the senior administration at the school had to trust the teachers to enter the spirit of the program, rather than treating it as just one more "hoop" to jump through.

Related to the size and complexity of the undertaking is time. Such programs cannot be introduced quickly. For us, the new TAP program entailed changes in other aspects of the appraisal system, for example, the student feedback forms, so it was necessary to introduce the changes over a period of time. If we had introduced too many changes at the same time, again, the program might have been much less successful than it has been. However, in all organizations that we know of, there are some staff who are resistant to change (Fullan & Stiegelbauer, 1991), so it is important for those who are putting forward the change to expect and prepare for resistance. For us, we pre-empted most of the resistance, which we take to be a natural and normal reaction to change for some, through an open and continuous dialogue, and through making a distinction between collaborative and cooperative approaches versus requiring consensus. Consequently, our teachers understood that we genuinely wanted their needs and concerns to be met and heard, but they also accepted that the senior management of the school would also have to follow an approach that was believed to be best for the school, rather than decision-making on the basis of meeting the needs of a few, usually more vocal, teachers.

We referred to our approach to developing the program as "The 3 F's: Fair, Flexible, Firm." Although these may sound like buzz words and clichés from the business world and may even sound contradictory, we publicly committed to trying to develop a fair system that was flexible and responsive to different and changing needs, but a system in which some parts were required and which had to be completed and complied with as agreed upon.

Conclusion

Our discussion has highlighted the complex nature of teacher evaluation within the context of an IEP/EAP program at a Canadian university. In order to achieve teaching effectiveness, any teacher appraisal system needs to be multifaceted. In our case, the TAP is composed of a three-component system with setting goals (defining core and additional competencies); teacher supervisions; and feedback from peers, students and self-generated feedback. In addition, it is important to define the goals of such an appraisal system, be it developmental or evaluative. Our goal is teacher professional development. However, the nature of any evaluation determines that such a process and procedure will be the interpretation of results from and about the teachers, that is, assigning value to aspects of teaching. Bearing the high stakes of such an evaluation in our profession in relation to pay and job security, it is essential that such a process is conducted through a collaborative approach in which teachers take part in TAPing into teaching effectiveness.

Discussion Questions

1. This chapter discusses the relationship between teacher appraisal programs and professional development programs. How would you describe some of the key differences between the two?

2. According to this chapter, "Darling-Hammond (1996) emphasized that teacher evaluation should reflect the knowledge and skills teachers are expected to master as a minimum requirement for responsible practice." In your professional opinion, what are the knowledge and skills teachers should be able to demonstrate as a minimum requirement?

3. This chapter refers to the work of Doyle (2004, p. 1), who stated that "the use of students' rating for evaluating teacher effectiveness is the single most researched issue in all of higher education." In your teaching and learning context, how important are students' ratings of teacher effectiveness?

4. What other sources of input are sought in assessing teacher effectiveness, and how important are students' ratings in relation to these other sources of input?

5. In the teaching and learning context, the Queen's University model uses three sets of factors: Results, Personal Contribution and Supervisory. How do these three sets of factors compare to those used to assess performance in your education context?

6. The authors describe the approach to developing their program as "The 3 F's: Fair, Flexible, Firm." Is it possible to aim for these in the same place at the same time? Or are they contradictory? Or even mutually exclusive? Give reasons for your response.

7. The conclusion to the chapter emphasizes the importance of a collaborative approach to appraisal. However, this is only one approach. Discuss the advantages and limitations of such an approach.

REFERENCES

Bailey, K., Curtis, A., & Nunan, D. (2001). *Pursuing professional development: The self as source.* Boston: Heinle & Heinle.

Brock University. Human Resources: Employment Information: Brock University Job Evaluation Factors, pp.1–3 (not dated). Retrieved May 1, 2006, from http://www.brocku.ca/hr/employment/Job%20Evaluation/Job%20Evaluation%20Factors.pdf

Centra, J. A. (1993). Use of the teaching portfolio and student evaluations for summer evaluation. Paper presented at the annual conference of the American Educational Research Association, Atlanta, GA.

Coniam, D., & Falvey, P. (1999). Setting standards for teachers of English in Hong Kong—The teachers' perspective. *Curriculum Forum, 8*(2), 1–27.

Curtis, A. (1999). Changing the management of change in language education: Learning from the past, lessons for the future. *PASSA, Thai TESOL 29,* 92–100.

———. (2000). A problem-solving approach to the management of change in language education. *Korea TESOL Journal, 3,* 1–12.

———. (2006). From judgmental to developmental: Creating community through conference. In T. Murphey and K. Sato. (Eds.) *Professional development in language education: Volume Four: Creating professional communities.* Alexandria, VA: TESOL Association.

Curtis, A., & Cheng, L. (2001). Teachers' self-evaluation of knowledge, skills and personality characteristics needed to manage change. *Asia-Pacific Journal of Teacher Education, 29*(2), 139–152.

Darling-Hammond, L. (1986). Teaching knowledge: How do we test it? *American Educator, 10*(3), 18–21, 46.

———. (1996). What matters most: A competent teacher for every child. *Phi Delta Kappan, 78*(3), 193–200.

Darling-Hammond, L., Wise, A. E., & Klein, S. P. (1995). *A license to teach: Building a profession for 21st-century schools.* Boulder, CO: Westview Press.

Doyle, K. O. (1983). *Evaluating teaching.* San Francisco: New Lexington Press.

Doyle, T. (2004) Evaluating teacher effectiveness: Research summary. Retrieved February 22, 2005, from http://www.ferris.edu/HTMLS/academics/center/Teaching_and_Learning_Tips/Research%20on%20Students'%20Evalution%20of%20Faculty%20Teaching/EvalTeachEffec.htm

Dunkin, M. J. (1997). Assessing teachers' effectiveness. *Issues in Educational Research, 7*(1), 37–51.

Fullan, M. G., & Stiegelbauer, S. (1991). *The new meaning of educational change* (2nd ed.). London: Cassell.

Guskey, T. R. (1998). The age of accountability. *Journal of Staff Development, 19*(4).

James, H. (Ed.). (1997). *Evaluating teaching: A guide to current thinking and best practice.* Thousand Oaks, CA: Corwin Press.

Johnson, P., Sawatzky, D., Greenfield, B., & Allenby, S. (2002). Submission to the pay equity task force. Department of Justice Canada Document retrieved May 1, 2006, from http://www.justice.gc.ca/en/payeqsal/4484.html

Lynch, B. (1996). *Language program evaluation.* Cambridge: Cambridge University Press.

Memorial University of Newfoundland. Human Resources: Job Evaluation. Page dated June 15, 2005. Retrieved May 1, 2006, from http://www.mun.ca/humanres/job_eval/aiken_factors.php

Patton, M. Q. (1997). *Utilization-focused evaluation: The new century text* (3rd ed.). Thousand Oaks, CA: Sage Publications.

Queen's University. Human Resources: Work and Career: New Employee: Performance Review: Record of Interview (pp. 1–5). Document dated, 2004. Retrieved May 1, 2006, from http://www.hr.queensu.ca/workand-career/pr-record.php

Scriven, M. (1972). Pros and cons about goal-free evaluation. *Evaluation Comment, 3*(4), 1–4.

Seldin, P. (Ed.). (1999). *Changing practices in evaluation teaching.* Bolton, MA.: Anker.

Stiggens, R. J., & Duke, D. L. (1990). *The case for commitment to teacher growth: Research on teacher evaluation.* New York: State University of New York Press.

Theall, M., & Franklin, J. (2001). Looking for bias in all the wrong places—A search for truth or a witch hunt in student ratings of instruction? In P. Theall, L. Abrami, & L. Mets (Eds.). *New directions in educational research* (p. 109). San Franscsco: Jossey-Bass.

University of Ottawa. Directory of Competencies. Document 10. Document dated December 10, 1998. Retrieved, May 1, 2006, from http://www.hr.uottawa.ca/docs/pdf/T232_Directory%20of%20Competencies.pdf

York University. Human Resource and Employee Relations: Performance Management. Page dated November 3, 2003. Retrieved May 1, 2006, from http://www.yorku.ca/hr/hrservices/pdr/index.html

Appendix 1 Teachers' Core Competencies (CCS) and Additional Competencies (ACS)

Core Competencies

- Departmental Knowledge
- Change Management
- Communication
- TESL Knowledge
- Classroom Management

Additional Competencies

1. Facilitator of Learning

   - Develops (and shares) professional pedagogical materials
   - Effectively manages text materials
   - Demonstrates an ability to deal with issues related to a heterogeneous classroom
   - Shows an understanding of and ability to adapt to the curriculum
   - Balances EAP and communicative language goals
   - Understanding of and ability to balance students' needs
   - Assesses students fairly, according to the standards at the SOE
   - Demonstrates knowledge of goals of level
   - Gives constructive feedback that is both motivating and helpful; performs linguistic analysis effectively
   - Conveys expectations to students
   - Demonstrates an ability to empower students to be independent learners

2. Collaboration

   - Shows respect for others at QSoE and in the greater Queen's community
   - Demonstrates a willingness to work collaboratively with other teachers and staff
   - Shares knowledge and expertise with others easily and frequently

3. General

   - Demonstrates a knowledge of school policies and procedures
   - Demonstrates a professional and personal care for staff and students
   - Shows a willingness to acquire new skills and contribute to the development of the School; takes ownership of self-development; applies lessons from previous learning experiences to present situation
   - Learns and uses technology to improve the services the school provides

CHAPTER 5

What's in It for Me? A Performance Management System to Please Everyone

Lindsay Miller and Jean Young

Introduction

This chapter reports on the introduction of a performance management system for teaching staff at an English Language Centre (ELC) of a major university in Hong Kong. Such a system needs to take into account the policies, procedures, and requirements of a publicly funded tertiary institute while at the same time cater to the needs and aspirations of the staff. The majority of staff in the ELC work on contracts so the need for a reliable and open performance management system is paramount not only to ensure that there is an ongoing process of quality improvement in the ELC, but also to ensure that the needs of individual staff are considered in order to increase staff retention.

In an attempt to achieve a performance management system that pleases everyone, effort has been made to ensure that the current system in the ELC is both evaluative and developmental. The issue of whether appraisal systems can and should be both evaluative and developmental has generated a great deal of discussion. Some argue that the process of evaluation will inhibit staff from opening up about their personal development needs (Barge, 1989), create a role conflict for the appraiser (Torrington & Hall, 1991), have a negative effect on the appraiser/appraisee relationship, or draw attention away from the development aspect (Boswell & Boudreau, 2002). Carlton & Sloman (1992) point out that even if separation of the two aspects is considered desirable, it is difficult to attain in practice. Although the rhetoric of development is often present when teacher appraisal is discussed, the reality may be different; Ellett and Garland (1987) reported that in a survey of U.S. schools, appraisal was primarily found to be summative, for accountability purposes, while Tucker (1997) found that this type of summative assessment was often perfunctory and that teachers tended to receive outstanding scores.

The University

City University of Hong Kong (CityU) is an English medium university in Hong Kong. The university is relatively young, having just celebrated its 20th anniversary. The university has nearly 2,000 teachers and a student population of 20,000 at sub-degree, undergraduate degree, and post-graduate degree level. Most students who study at the university have spoken Cantonese and written Chinese as their mother language. CityU consists of three Faculties (eighteen Departments), four Schools, one College (five Divisions), a Chinese Civilisation Centre, and an English Language Centre (see *www.cityu.edu.hk/cityu/about/cio-fnf.htm* for more information about the university). The orientation of the university is mostly toward science and engineering, although there is also a large business faculty and a relatively small humanities faculty. As such, the types of students who attend the university are mostly non-language majors.

The English Language Centre

The ELC is a service unit within CityU. The main function of the ELC is to offer *English for Academic Purposes (EAP) language courses* to both bachelor's and associate degree students. The ELC also provides language support and *independent learning opportunities* to all CityU students through a Self-Access Centre (SAC), the language lounge, and the informal activities program.

All staff who work in the ELC are classified as non-academic, meaning that the posts are purely teaching positions with no requirement for staff to participate in research.

The Students and Courses

Each year the ELC teaches close to 5,000 mostly Hong Kong Chinese students. Almost all of these students have Cantonese as their mother tongue, and English is either a foreign or a second language for them. ELC students come from all departments within the university. The majority of students have come directly to the university from secondary school, are around 19–20 years old, and are in their first year of study. Students entering CityU must have achieved the basic academic requirements for admission into the university, which includes having an E, or above, in the Hong Kong Advanced Level English examination. An E is roughly equivalent to a score of around 500 on the paper and pencil TOEFL® test. However, many students still require further language support to enable them to follow their studies. Therefore, students entering with an E are required to take six credit units of specified EAP language courses offered by the ELC. Students must take two core courses: Spoken Language (one credit) and Written Language (two credits). The remaining three credits are selected from a range of elective courses: Current Issues, Grammar in Use, Independent Learning, Writing Academic Essays, Language Skills for Research, Writing Effective Lab

Reports, and Presentation Skills. Students attend classes at times convenient to them, and they are assigned to non-discipline specific groups.

The English Language Tutors in the ELC

Currently, there are 34 full-time English tutors in the ELC. All tutors must have a degree plus a post-graduate diploma in TESL (or the equivalent) and two years of teaching experience. However, most of the staff members surpass this basic employment requirement; all of them have substantially more than the minimum required experience, and the majority of them have enhanced qualifications. Around 30 percent of the staff are Hong Kong Chinese (non-native English speakers), and 70 percent are native English speakers from around the world: U.K., U.S.A., and Australia. Although the staff in the ELC work within an academic institution, there is a deliberate policy of employing tutors with good teaching backgrounds and enthusiasm for language teaching, as opposed to those who have aspirations to be academics.

The management structure in the ELC is relatively flat. Apart from the department head, there are five senior tutors who teach 50 percent of a regular teaching load and have administrative duties the other 50 percent of the time. For an individual staff member working in the ELC, there is no obvious career path within the university; there are relatively few promotion opportunities within the Centre and virtually no opportunity of transferring to an academic department.

We now turn to the issue of how the tutors are appraised within this complex system.

Description

The University Requirements for Appraisal

The university gives departments considerable autonomy in developing internal appraisal systems provided they meet with overall university guidelines. The requirements of the appraisal system are at two distinct levels: an Annual Activity Report (AAR) and a formal appraisal on a two- or three-year cycle.

Each year, all members of staff must prepare an AAR in which they have to comment on and show evidence of their work in the past year. The AAR consists of a Qualitative Reflection written by the staff member and details of achievements under these headings:

- Teaching—a list of courses taught and the student evaluations
- Research—a list of publications
- Professional Activities—a list of conferences attended or talks given
- Campus and Community Citizenship—a list of activities undertaken within the university

This annual activity review is submitted to the department head, who is not required to provide any feedback to the staff member concerned or to record any comment, unless a problem is identified.

All university staff members also go through a formal appraisal procedure. This is done every three years for staff on substantiated terms and when coming up for contract renewal (typically every two years) for staff on contract terms. Staff members must prepare a longer reflective document outlining their achievements and support this with a portfolio of evidence, including the annual activity reports for all years since the last appraisal.

Although individual departments are free to customize the appraisal process to suit themselves, the basic model proposed by the university is largely top down, primarily evaluative, requires staff to put relatively more time and effort into the process than managers, and involves little dialogue between appraisers and appraised except in the case of a problem being identified.

The ELC Performance Management System

The ELC has developed a customized version of the university's appraisal system. There are a number of differences:

- Face-to-face dialogue between appraiser and appraisee
- Developmental aspects given a higher priority than evaluative aspects
- Integration of appraisal into a wider Performance Management System (PMS)

In order to achieve the PMS reported on here, three elements were designed (see Figure 5.1):

1. clearly defined and agreed upon *performance indicators* (PI)
2. regular and honest *appraisal of performance* (A) agreed between appraiser and appraisee
3. ongoing support for *professional development* (PD)

Each of the elements in Figure 5.1 interact in a continuous process that is guided by the aims of the Centre and of the individual staff member. Both sets of aims are of equal importance since the benefits received in return for effort expended must be clear to both parties—tutors and appraisers—to motivate continuation of the system. The aims feed into all aspects of the performance management loop: they help in identifying specific actions to be performed; they provide criteria for appraisal; and they help identify needs for current or future professional development.

The ELC has set expanded requirements for the AAR. Staff write a longer Qualitative Reflection document under four headings: teaching, area of responsibility, professional development, and campus and community citizenship.

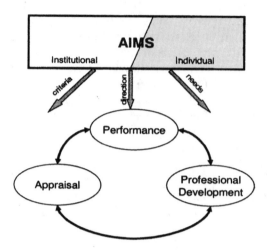

Figure 5.1: Performance Management System

The headings are based on the headings used by the university as a whole, with research having been removed and professional development added. This self-report is supported by a portfolio of evidence, which must include certain specified elements, including the results of student evaluations, an observation report from the appraiser, and peer observation reports written by the staff member after both observing and being observed by another tutor. Staff members meet their appraisers in order to agree to the content of the appraiser's report, which is written and added to the AAR only after this discussion has taken place. The document is signed by the staff member and by the head of department, then placed in the tutor's personal file.

In order to cope with the considerably increased time demands of this customized system, responsibility for appraising teaching staff has been delegated by the head of department to the five senior tutors. Staff members are organized into teams according to their administrative responsibilities, and senior tutors appraise the members of the team they lead, normally between five and seven members of staff. The department head is responsible for appraising the five senior tutors and two senior administrative staff in the Centre. This delegation ensures that the appraisal is done by someone who works closely and on a daily basis with the tutor concerned and so has direct knowledge of performance. It also keeps the number of staff to be appraised by any one person at a level that allows sufficient time be given to the process, and it provides senior staff with an opportunity to develop management skills. Having all annual reports read and signed by the department head maintains a degree of standardization and provides evidence that feeds into the appraisal of the senior tutors.

In addition and in line with university requirements, ELC staff also go through a formal appraisal and contract renewal process every two years. For individual staff members, the process is similar; they prepare a portfolio and have a meeting with their appraisers as usual. The difference is that after completing this process, the AARs and evidence from the previous two years are passed to the Centre Staffing Committee (CSC) for consideration and contract renewal decision. The CSC has seven members: the department head, a senior tutor appointed by the department head, two senior tutors, two tutors elected by and from the staff, and a staff member from an academic department. Members review the portfolios; meet to discuss the individual cases; and assign an overall rating of outstanding, excellent, very good, good, or unsatisfactory. The department head then meets with the individual staff member to report the committee's comments, and after this meeting has taken place, the department head completes a brief written report.

Tutors are encouraged to see the whole performance management system as an ongoing process. They each meet their individual appraiser regularly as part of their administrative duties, and there is a continuous process of feedback on performance. Tutors are encouraged to update their teaching portfolio regularly and are given help in doing this. Appraisers not only provide feedback on teaching and administrative performance, they also provide support for individual staff members in finding ways to achieve their own goals and develop the skills they would like to have, as well as present themselves well through their portfolio. The whole process of performance management begins when a new tutor starts work in the ELC and support for the system is integrated throughout the departmental organization.

How the Performance Management System Works

The PMS is an ongoing process. Tutors need to be aware of how they will be appraised from their first days of service, and they should begin to compile their portfolio as soon as they begin working in the ELC. As it is an ongoing system, it is somewhat difficult to isolate the elements of what happens. However, in considering appraisal a number of questions can be asked:

1. What aspects of performance should be measured? (PI)*
2. How can these performance aspects be measured? (PI)
3. What does the performance aspects measurement mean? (A)**
4. What areas of performance should development focus on? (A)
5. What new skills and knowledge are necessary to bring about this improvement? (PD)***
6. What new skills and knowledge are available for the teacher? (PD)

In answering these questions, we are able to see how the PMS works.

---

*(PI) = performance indicators
**(A) = appraisal of performance
***(PD) = professional development

1. What Aspects of Performance Should Be Measured? (PI)

The aspects that the ELC has identified as important are clearly stated in the job description (Table 5.1 shows the main headings). These include teaching skill and teaching performance; administrative work and areas of responsibility, including, for instance, course coordination, ability to write quality materials, coordinating people, and management skills; professional development; and campus and community citizenship. Separate descriptions have been developed for each specific area of responsibility and are available to staff undertaking these duties.

Becoming familiar with the position requirements is one of the initial tasks of any new staff member, and the first meeting with the appraiser will typically involve examining the job description and related documents and ensuring that there is a common understanding of what is expected. The range of aspects of performance identified sometimes surprises staff, particularly the requirements to maintain the professional image of the ELC, to undertake professional development, and to contribute toward a collegial atmosphere. Discussion of these issues can be very useful in bringing staff to an understanding of the overall purpose and philosophy of the Centre.

The job description and other supporting documents were drawn up in consultation with all the staff of the Centre, and in most cases the initial draft came from the person doing a particular job. The tutor job description was based on one created by one of the authors in a different context. This document was discussed in some detail by all staff meeting in groups of eight to ten staff with the department head, and an ELC tutor job description was drafted based on these discussions. This was then circulated to all staff and underwent some further refinement before being finalized. The statement of teaching philosophy was created in the same way. The process was time consuming; it took more than six months to create the final documents. However, it was important to take this time, as it ensured that all staff understood the criteria fully and were in general agreement about the areas of focus. As research has shown, the involvement of stakeholders in the development of assessment criteria, and allowing time for

---

Table 5.1: Duties of an Instructor

1. To teach classes as timetabled by the ELC
2. To carry out routine student administration and care
3. To carry out student assessment procedures
4. To attend general staff meetings and coordination and evaluation meetings for the courses you are teaching
5. To maintain the professional image of the ELC
6. To be responsible for a particular area of work within the ELC
7. To take part in the professional development system operating within the ELC
8. To contribute to the development of a collegial atmosphere within the ELC and the university
9. Other duties as required by the ELC

system development and implementation have been identified as key factors in effective appraisal systems (Davis, Ellett, & Annunziata, 2002).

2. How Can These Performance Aspects Be Measured? (PI)

Performance is measured via what is included in the teaching portfolio. The key elements of this are the self-reflection in the AAR, the appraiser's report on the staff member over the same period, and the supporting evidence supplied. The evidence must include: for *Teaching*, an evaluative report on a classroom observation done by the appraiser and student evaluations for all classes taught; for *Area of Responsibility*, individual and team work plans; and for *Professional Development*, peer observation reports. Staff members are also encouraged to include any other evidence they consider relevant. Some of this evidence is relatively objective, such as student evaluations. Some are more subjective, like the appraiser's report. This combination of objective and subjective elements in the appraisal system gives a balance to the fact that it is people who are doing the appraising and people who are being appraised.

3. How Can the Evidence of Performance Be Interpreted? (A)

There are two aspects to this question:

How can the process of interpreting the evidence provide useful feedback to support continuing development?
How can consistency and fairness in interpreting the data for judgmental purposes be ensured?

One key feature of the system is that the initial interpretation of evidence is done by the staff member, through the reflective report. The individual tutor has the most intimate knowledge of what has happened and should be the most important source of information about achievements and development needs (Murphy & Cleveland, 1995). Only the tutor is able to provide the essential context to allow items such as student evaluations for any particular class to be interpreted accurately. The process of analyzing and presenting such "objective" data is also seen as useful and developmental in itself since it requires the tutor to reflect on the teaching process, and this reflection is central to professional growth (Davis et al., 2002). Even when considering an external evaluative process such as a class observation by the appraiser, the expectation is that there will be a post-lesson discussion that starts with the tutor's own analysis of what happened in the lesson before any report is written.

By including a balance of objective and subjective appraisal, the system aims to give a more complete picture of overall performance. All staff are valued in the ELC, and it is only by being open and honest about the work they are doing that the tutors' strengths and weaknesses can be seen. This requires a level of trust between appraiser and appraisee that can only be established with time and effort. Piggot-Irvine (2003) identifies a deep problem-solving approach to development issues as one contributing factor to the development of trust, and George (1986) points out that effective appraisal depends more on good interpersonal skills than on policies and systems. If the tutor does have identifiable weaknesses, then both appraiser and appraisee must be willing to acknowledge this, must be clear about the level of seriousness of these weaknesses, and must identify what the Centre can do to assist staff to overcome them: It is a basic tenet that such issues should be raised well in advance of any major decision such as contract renewal so that there is time for remedial action to be taken.

Consistency and fairness are maintained by having all AARs reviewed by the department head, who provides feedback and training to appraisers where necessary. Decisions on appraisal ratings and contract renewal are made by the CSC, which considers a number of cases at any one time and so is able to make informed comparisons. In this way some degree of separation of the evaluative and developmental aspects of the system is maintained: Appraisers are not responsible for making decisions about issues such as contract renewal, although their reports will carry considerable weight with the committee.

4. What Areas of Performance Should Development Focus On? (A)

Tutors who are hired by the ELC are already well-qualified and experienced. In the majority of cases, there are no real performance issues to be dealt with. However, all staff are required to undertake some professional development, and the appraisal system aims to help staff identify areas where improvements can be made. There are several reasons for this requirement: Not only does it contribute to a culture geared toward continual quality improvement, but it helps tutors maintain a greater degree of interest in their work, and this greater interest also contributes to quality teaching. Staff members are judged not only on their teaching and administrative performances, but also on the attempt they have made to move forward with their professional development. If there is evidence that a tutor has made an effort to, say, teach courses that are new or take on new administrative duties, then the tutor is given credit for this.

Staff members are free to identify their own areas for improvement, except where a problem has been identified, but may seek advice from their appraiser. In effect, tutors are encouraged to view their appraisal as a career planning exercise. That is, during the process of discussion with their appraiser, staff members may be able to identify what satisfies them the most in their work, or which areas they would like to be involved with in future. Tutors may choose to develop new skills simply in order to maintain job satisfaction or perhaps to support their long-term career planning. For instance, a tutor may hope to move into textbook writing at a later point in his or her career, and therefore ask to be involved in a materials writing team in the ELC in order to develop useful skills.

Career planning can be considered an essential part of a performance management system (Martin & Kragler, 1999), although it is typically tied to issues of promotion and succession planning. The ELC cannot offer staff much in the way of a career ladder and the nature of the teaching can be repetitive; however, one important thing the department can offer is the opportunity to learn and grow. The way in which administrative duties are assigned supports this; a position does not go to the person who already has the most relevant skills but to someone who wants the opportunity to develop his or her skills. A tutor who has held a position for two years must give it up if someone else requests it in the annual reshuffling of responsibilities. This ultimately benefits ELC since staff who are engaged in their careers are more likely to be happy in their work and to perform well. As Conger (2002) points out, "the degree to which there is a fit between the worker's ability, interest and personality and the work requirements routines, relationships and rewards does increase levels of commitment and productivity" (p. 372).

5. What New Skills and Knowledge Are Necessary to Bring about This Improvement? (PD)

Once a tutor has chosen an area for development, decisions must be made about the focus and support required. This is negotiated by appraiser and appraisee and to some extent relies on the facilities that are available in the ELC. If a tutor has a goal of learning how to facilitate independent learning more effectively, he or she may request teaching assignments involving this, observe and hold discussions with a more experienced teacher, attend in-house seminars, or join the local professional association. However, the goals set have to be realistic. If, for instance, the tutor wants to become a best-selling author, then this is something outside the ELC's resources or requirements.

The appraiser is available to give advice and guidance, but, as with other aspects of the PMS, the onus is on the tutor to identify needs and to actively seek ways of meeting them. It is also important that the appraiser is seen as having enough authority within the department to help staff members achieve their aims (Knibbs & Swailes, 1992).

6. What New Skills and Knowledge Are Available for the Teacher? (PD)

New skills and knowledge can be acquired in a variety of ways: the tutor can learn from teaching a new course or taking on new responsibilities; peers or senior staff may expend time in training the tutor; teacher development sessions can be offered if the need for some new skill or knowledge has a wide audience; and staff are encouraged to attend local or international conferences, or to upgrade their qualifications and are sponsored to do so. The focus for any improvements though are: Are they achievable? Are they interesting or useful for the tutor? Is this change needed in the ELC or at least potentially useful? Are the resources available? If the answer is yes to these, then the tutor is encouraged to pursue the acquisition of new skills and knowledge.

Distinctive Features of the Performance Management System at CityU

The PMS at CityU contains many standard features, including (1) systems of recruitment, (2) staff training and development, and (3) an annual review and appraisal system resulting in a formal report. As with any such system, however, it has developed distinct features that reflect the culture of the Centre. These are (1) the strong focus on joint ownership of the appraisal system, (2) the emphasis on continuing professional development, and (3) the inclusion of career planning, even in a situation where there are few obvious career development opportunities.

Joint Ownership

A feeling of joint ownership was created by involving staff in the design of performance criteria from the earliest stages. The PMS began with a series of staff meeting discussions until all staff were prepared to try out a new appraisal system and felt reasonably confident with the performance indicators. It should be noted that this discussion period was lengthy, taking almost a full academic year and giving all staff the opportunity to present their views. The job description for tutor was written as a group effort; descriptions of the duties for other areas of responsibility were written by the post-holders. It is expected that job descriptions may be renegotiated by staff members on an ongoing basis. This discussion process helps to ensure the strong backing of the staff for the system.

The PMS was not a complete system initially. Feedback was collected during an initial trial, and further discussion and development followed. This trial period took around two years to allow staff to experience a full cycle. This long-term trialing guaranteed that any problems in the system could be attended to and that a shared understanding of the process developed.

Professional Development

The emphasis on professional development was created by requiring evidence of development as one of the performance indicators and by removing some of the evaluative aspects (the need to make decisions about future contract renewal, pay raises, and possible disciplinary action) from the immediate appraiser. This allowed the appraiser to take on more of a mentoring/coaching role to support the appraisee in preparing for the evaluative appraisal by the CSC. The department aims to create a culture of development based on collaborative problem solving, with collaboration between appraisers and appraisees, between teaching staff through the peer observation system, and between members of teams working on various administrative areas. For this to work, staff have to feel that if they are prepared to identify a weakness and then do something about it, that this will be viewed positively by management, and that this approach to their professional development is as important as simply showcasing that they are competent teachers in class.

Identification of weaknesses should result not in criticism but in help and encouragement to improve. This means that there must be development and training opportunities available, but also that a supportive, collegial atmosphere is crucial. Tutors who contribute to such an atmosphere are valued and given credit for this when they are appraised.

Career Planning

Finally, the PMS includes a career planning element, even though there is little in the way of a formal career path available to staff in the ELC. Normally, in addition to helping individual staff members plan their future career and iden- tify the skills they will need to move up, such an element within a performance management system also aims to support well-managed succession planning within an organization, so there is something in it for management as well as for staff. In this context, there is little need for succession planning and few pro- motion opportunities for staff. Career planning therefore has to be interpreted more in terms of developing a broader skill set out of interest, or for possible use elsewhere. As such, the emphasis must be more on what staff members want to learn, rather than on what the department thinks they should learn. As Conger (2002) puts it,

> A career development culture will help people identify and redefine their talents so they can realise the full potential of whatever work situation they find themselves in. Within the context of a career development culture the career planning focus might better be to 'make you and your job everything that you can be together' more than to identify the ideal job. (p. 373)

Caveats

We consider that the PMS described in this chapter is applicable in any language teaching context. However, for the system to work well certain conditions need to be adhered to:

1. *Staffing:* To implement the PMS a language center or department needs to have the individuals to act as appraisers. In the case of the ELC, the five senior tutors took on this responsibility. However, when there are not only lesson observations to conduct, but also ongoing training and career planning discussions, then senior staff need to be prepared to give up time in order to do this.

2. *Training:* All staff members need training, whether they are appraising or being appraised. In our case, a number of workshops and seminars were conducted to help staff get the most out of the system.

3. *Trialing:* When starting any new system of staff appraisal, it is necessary to have a period of finetuning the system in the light of experience and feedback. This PMS was lengthy in its implementation, but the ELC staff were integral in its design.

4. *Cultural Change:* Successful implementation of such a system involves a process of cultural change within the department. The aim here was to move toward a development-focused culture, and this requires an open, trusting atmosphere and a genuine commitment to the process at all levels. As Conger (2002) points out, "The success of a career development culture requires the active support and involvement of three principal actors: top management, supervisors and employees themselves" (p. 371).

Conclusion

The PMS described in this chapter focuses on whole-person development. That is, staff members treat their appraisal not only as an administrative requirement for contract renewal purposes, but also as a way of focusing their professional development.

The PMS operates within a university context, and, as such, must conform to general university guidelines on performance appraisal. However, these guidelines allow the ELC enough freedom to create a system that is unique to staff and that focuses on aspects that teaching staff and management have identified as important. The process of negotiating the details of this system helped to create a development-focused culture.

There is a degree of tension involved in any system that attempts to balance evaluation and development. In the system described in this chapter, the evaluation aspect has been separated to some extent by having decisions made by the CSC. It is also relatively low stakes for most staff, in that non-renewal of contract on performance grounds is rare. The fine grading of appraisal ratings—for example, between very good and excellent—functions mainly as a type of reward, a recognition of good performance. However, the university is considering introducing performance-related pay, and if this goes forward, the evaluation process will become higher stakes for all staff. This is likely to put some strain on the development focus in the current system. We have some reservations about the value of this change; while developing the PMS system at CityU it was apparent that what motivated staff was not small salary increments, but job satisfaction, personal development, and recognition of good performance, which can all be achieved without tying appraisal to pay increments.

In order for a system such as this to operate, a culture of openness must exist and staff must have a willingness to expose their weaknesses in order to develop themselves more. We feel that this has been achieved in the ELC by including all staff in the discussions about the system, by having clearly stated criteria that staff members agreed to, and by not rushing to implement the system too quickly. Through developing such a system, the university benefits by retaining high-performing teachers, and the teachers benefit by being part of the process that treats their appraisal seriously. In fact, the system works by having something in it for everyone.

Discussion Questions

1. In a context you are familiar with, is the appraisal system similar for contract and permanent staff? What are the differences? Why do they exist? Do you think it is reasonable to have more than one appraisal system?

2. The problems of having an appraisal system that is both evaluative and developmental are discussed. Do you agree that these two aspects of appraisal should be combined within one system? What are the arguments for separating them?

3. Describe a teaching context you are familiar with. What constraints does the employment context create for implementing an appraisal system?

4. The context for staff promotion at CityU is described as "flat." Discuss what promotion prospects there are in a teaching context you know, and how this aids or hinders implementing an appraisal system.

5. In the appraisal system described, teachers are required to provide information on four areas: teaching, area of responsibility, professional development, and campus and community citizenship. Would these match your own teaching context (if so why), or would you include other areas for appraisal?

6. Four main issues that are important to consider when implementing an appraisal system are highlighted: staffing; training; trialing; and cultural change. How important are these issues in your teaching context? Are there other important issues you need to take account of?

REFERENCES

Barge, T. (1989). Performance appraisal and personal development...the unholy alliance. *Training Officer, 25*(12), 359–360.

Boswell, W. R., & Boudreau, J. W. (2002). Separating the developmental and evaluative performance appraisal uses. *Journal of Business and Psychology, 16*(3), 391–412.

Carlton, I., & Sloman, M. (1992). Performance appraisal in practice. *Human Resource Management Journal, 2*(3), 80–94.

Conger, S. (2002). Fostering a career development culture: Reflections on the roles of managers, employees and supervisors. *Career Development International, 7*(6), 371–375.

Davis, D. R., Ellett, C. D., & Annunziata, J. (2002). Teacher evaluation, leadership and learning organizations. *Journal of Personnel Evaluation in Education, 16*(4), 287–301.

Ellett, C. D., & Garland, J. (1987). Teacher evaluation practices in our largest school districts: Are they measuring up to "state-of-the-art" systems? *Journal of Personnel Evaluation in Education, 1*(1), 69–92.

George, J. (1986). Appraisal in the public sector: Dispensing with a big stick. *Personnel Management, 18*(5), 32–35.

Knibbs, J., & Swailes, S. (1992). Implementing performance review and career planning: Part two. *Management Decision, 30*(2), 30–34.

Martin, L., & Kragler, S. (1999). Creating a culture for teachers' professional growth. *Journal of School Leadership, 9*(4), 311–320.

Murphy, R. M., & Cleveland, J. N. (1995). *Understanding performance appraisals.* London: Sage Publications.

Piggot-Irvine, E. (2003). Key features of appraisal effectiveness. *International Journal of Educational Management, 17*(4/5), 170–178.

Torrington, D., & Hall, L. (1991). *Personnel management—A new approach.* Hertfordshire, U.K.: Prentice-Hall International.

Tucker, P. D. (1997). Lake Wobegon: Where all teachers are competent (or Have we come to terms with the problem of incompetent teachers?) *Journal of Personnel Evaluation in Education, 11*(1), 103–126.

CHAPTER 6

A Coherent Approach to
Faculty Appraisal

Phil Quirke

Introduction

An appraisal system like the Performance Enhancement Programme (PEP) at the Higher Colleges of Technology (HCT) where I work in the United Arab Emirates (UAE) is one that is standard and coherent and adheres to best practice and principles.

The HCT is a vocational, tertiary series of twelve colleges across the UAE and comes under the Ministry of Higher Education in the country. The colleges hire experienced and qualified faculty from around the world with every department probably having at least five different nationalities among its teachers. The HCT used the experience of its staff to develop the PEP by involving teachers and management from all colleges in an initial PEP Committee resulting in a powerful teacher-driven appraisal tool that focuses on individual goals.

I was part of that initial PEP Committee, and I have been implementing and adapting the original framework for six years. The PEP is supported by teacher-maintained portfolios and focused on teacher development through annual reviews that ensure the process is cyclical and builds on teacher strengths and areas for development year after year.

This chapter gives the theoretical background to the PEP, outlines in detail how the program is practically implemented, argues how it differs from most teacher evaluation programs, and finally suggests how others can implement the program in other teaching contexts.

Description

The PEP is about a coherent approach to faculty appraisal, not evaluation. It is about getting the best from the teaching staff by encouraging reflection and giving teachers choices within a structured program. It is about quality and is therefore qualitative in nature. It does not rely on quantitative data with numbers to be misinterpreted by those removed from the classroom setting. It relies on the qualitative and guided interpretation of all those involved in the teachers' daily working lives.

"Few educational researchers and developers have worked on the evaluation of teachers, who, after all, are the key performers of the curriculum and the classroom....Poor practice in teacher evaluation is quietly accepted, according to teachers, administrators, and researchers" (Peterson, 2000, p. ix). Peterson is not the only researcher who believes that current teacher evaluation practices are in dire need of change, with criticisms being raised more than 30 years ago (Wolf, 1973) and regularly repeated by others (Travers, 1981; Stodolsky, 1984; Wise, Darling-Hammond, McLaughlin, & Berstein, 1984; Scriven, 1987; McLaughlin, 1990; Johnson, 1990) in sometimes very direct language: "Teacher evaluation is a disaster. The practices are shoddy, and the principles are unclear" (Scriven, 1981, p. 244).

These views are hardly surprising when you consider that most current practice is based on a supervisory report that in turn is based on a classroom visit (Bridges, 1992; Peterson & Chenoweth, 1992; Lewis, 1982) or a checklist of what good teaching should involve (Good & Mulryan, 1990). The six major problems with current teacher evaluation practices give us a good framework to build effective appraisal systems by addressing each of them in the design of any new approach.

1. Teachers do not support evaluation schemes.
2. Difficulties are oversimplified.
3. Minimal competency is assessed rather than desired competency.
4. Exceptional teacher cases are not considered.
5. Many systems rely on over-quantification.
6. The general public and parents are not reassured by current practice.

So, a good teacher evaluation scheme must have:

1. Clear purposes to determine good teaching (Scriven, 1973), to acknowledge teacher achievement (Owens, 1991), and to support staffing decisions (Lawrence, Vachon, Leake, & Leake, 1993).
2. Clear criteria for judging teacher quality that accept that teaching is a complex activity dependent on a specific context and delivered to a specific audience.
3. Clear processes for decision-making that accept the inherent subjectivity that occurs in all teacher evaluation.
4. A clear definition of quality teaching that is not based on a minimum competency.
5. Teacher involvement.
6. As many different and varied sources of data as possible (Peterson, Stevens, & Ponzio, 1998).

7. Validity and reliability.
8. Consideration for the multiple roles of teachers.
9. Acknowledgment for exceptional practice built into the system.
10. Transparency of process and protection from political influences (Peterson, 2000, p. 84).

A balanced and effective teacher evaluation scheme should allow teachers to collect data from multiple sources in the form of portfolios or dossiers. There must also be clear guidelines on the form and length of the compilations and, most important, on how they are to be reviewed. The PEP requires a short compilation of four to six pages. How these compilations are then evaluated has been widely discussed with most recommending a teacher evaluation board or review panel using guidelines for review (Peterson, 2000, pp. 257–266). The PEP advocates a guided discussion framework between the teacher and supervisor with the pair summarizing the compilation on a one-page cover sheet.

Seven key stages to the approach are outlined here:

1. Objectives
2. First Meeting
3. Observation
4. Student Evaluations
5. Summative Write Up
6. Teaching Portfolio Extract
7. Final Appraisal Meeting and Record

By going through each of the stages with practical examples, readers will see the tools to implement an appraisal program that merges formative and summative principles into a powerful professional development resource that is driven by teachers.

Stage 1: Setting Objectives

Teachers draw up their objectives based on last year's final appraisal meeting and include objectives on:

1. Classroom teaching—there should not be an innumerable list of unattainable objectives. I often suggest a maximum of one per class, such as "to incorporate more technology in my lessons with at least one class per week focused on softboard delivery" or "to ensure I use more variety in my group work settings."
2. Personal professional development—make sure that these are balanced and not impossible to complete in the year.
3. Action Learning Group—use the objectives as a springboard to action learning.

4. Departmental duty—I would only suggest that a teacher takes this on after his or her first year. Very often teachers see a departmental duty as part of their day-to-day working life and forget to list it.

5. College duty—again I would suggest that a college duty like service on a committee or task force is probably only feasible after the first year, although past experience shows that some teachers quickly move into college life. It is often worth pointing out that the most attainable objective at the start of the year is something like: "To take every opportunity to get involved in college activities." The teacher can then update his or her objectives as these opportunities arise.

6. Duties beyond the college (if applicable)—these are likely to include work on new courses with development and assessment writing or contact with company clients for example.

7. Other—these often come from the previous year's final discussion and tend to involve professional activity that has not been included in the Personal PD objective.

If it is the teacher's first year, I suggest following a format from other teachers. I have included one here that is used by a large number of teachers I have worked with:

Goals	Activities	Person Accountable	Support Group	Planned Completion Date	Output Indicators	Achievement Level

The strength of this tabulated version is that we can easily tie individual objectives into those of the department and the college through the person accountable and support group columns. In other words, department heads draw up their team's goals and objectives using the same format and encourage teachers to participate and enter their names in the support group column. The teacher's table then has this departmental table entry as a major goal giving more details about their participation.

These objectives can be updated during the year. Teachers should realize that the objectives are their own and that they can change them as their duties, responsibilities, and classes change throughout the academic year.

Stage 2: The First Meeting

Many of the doubts about the reasons behind any institutional approach to faculty appraisal can be allayed by managers introducing it in the first meeting in a positive and enthusiastic way. To do this, managers must receive the full support of the institution.

At the first meeting, managers ensure that the teacher is comfortable and confident speaking out and put at ease. This can best be done by active listening (Edge, 1992, 2002), which is basically paraphrasing what the teacher says at key points of the discussion to ensure understanding what is meant rather than imposing one's own interpretation. It is also important to not launch straight into the meeting but instead warm up with a social introduction that demonstrates an interest in the teacher as a person.

Overall, this first meeting needs to cover the following ground:

1. Objectives—ensure that all the objectives are addressed and are obtainable. It is essential to discuss the support the teacher needs to attain his or her goals and that the teacher realizes he or she can adapt his or her objectives at any time during the year.
2. Observations—decide when and how the observation will be conducted.
3. Student evaluations—decide when each class will do its evaluation of the teacher.
4. Support—discuss how the teacher can be supported for each of his or her objectives.

This stage concludes with the teacher sending a final soft copy of his or her objectives to the supervisor by a predetermined date.

Stage 3: Observation

The observation is the most common and most controversial element of any appraisal system. It is the element most feared by teachers who see themselves subjected to a biased view of their lesson by someone who does not know their class or, worse still, has no pedagogic training.

These teacher fears result in an atmosphere that is not conducive to staff development. An additional disadvantage of observations is that "an observer may never be able to observe a natural, undisturbed lesson, because the teacher may well conduct his lessons differently and this in turn will effect how the learners react" (van Lier, 1988, p. 39). A visited class can never be a true representation of the teacher's usual practice because the classroom dynamics and interactions will always be affected by the presence of another person. This observer's paradox is not easily overcome.

One way to start working on these obstacles is to offer the teachers a choice of observation types. There are any number of different observational procedures that can be offered, and each of these can be undertaken by the supervisor, a teaching colleague, or by oneself. Teachers may also suggest using their own observation system, video or audio recordings of lessons (Allwright, 1988; Richards & Nunan, 1990).

It has never ceased to amaze me how few supervisors responsible for teacher appraisals have been trained in observation techniques, and I would suggest that a supervisor should be open to allowing trained observers on their teaching staff to be involved in this stage of the program. Nevertheless, most institutions insist that the supervisor observe their staff, and so I offer a standard approach that I have developed over the last fifteen years. This approach can act as a foundation for all observation types and is based on principles three and four. These are the principles behind all my observations:

Principle 1.   The observer should get to know the class to be observed through a brief discussion with the classroom teacher.

Principle 2.   Every observation must have a pre-observation discussion with the teacher to set out the focus and format of the observation. For example, a teacher might want his or her supervisor to focus attention on certain aspects of classroom practice.

Principle 3.   The observer should record what is happening in the lesson while observing. A teacher-led feedback discussion should be conducted post-observation.

Principle 4.   Every observation must have a feedback hour, which the teacher should lead.

Principle 5.   The observer should provide written comments if the teacher wishes.

Remember that the goal is to provide teachers with insights into their classrooms that will allow them to better develop their teaching.

The Standard Approach

Many teachers are unsure of an exact focus for the observer during the lesson or simply want to see what comes up. This standard approach is based on that scenario, although it can be adapted to any focus required.

The approach can be best explained under the four headings from the observer's record page:

1. **Details** of the lesson to be taught.
2. **Action.** What happens in the lesson?
3. **Comments / Thoughts.** Any thoughts that come to mind based on the lesson.
4. **Summary** of the lesson listing the major strengths and areas to work on.

Details

This section is completed during the pre-observation meeting, and the lesson details that should be noted are:

- Teacher's name, the group to be taught—number of students—the day, date, and time.
- Stages of the lesson, as described by the teacher.
- Focus for the observer, if the teacher determines one.

The result should look something like this:

Chris - E1P - HDYr1 - Room W001 - 16 students	
Monday 23rd Dec, 2003 - 10:15–11:10	
Aim: To improve student reading speed and gist understanding	
1. Warm-up—find the word	5. Discuss writers' views
2. Speed Read	6. Debate
3. Comp Q's	7. Conclusion
4. Combine texts	
Observer focus:	
1. Teacher talk	2. Student participation

It should not be necessary for a teacher to produce a lesson plan. These are the observer's notes taken while the teacher describes his or her lesson at the pre-observation meeting. Most teachers just write brief bullets outlining the lesson and include the materials.

Action

Under the details, I divide the page into two columns. The left-hand column is used to note what is happening in the lesson. The aim is to have enough detail so that the teacher can place, in the lesson, the accompanying comments in the right-hand column. The action is subdivided by the lesson stages and can include: a simple description of what is happening; what the teacher or students say; and movement around the class.

So, the action column for the warm-up stage above would look something like this:

ACTION
Stage 1—Warm-up (10:15)
Teacher at front of class
Students take cards from desk as they arrive. (14 students)
Each card has picture on it.
Students find word on wall matching picture and sit down.
Teacher hands them text based on their word.
Gives them three mins. to read text and turn card back over. (15 students)
Count down begins when last student gets text.

Comments and Thoughts

The right-hand column is used to note any thoughts and comments that the observer has during the lesson. The aim is to phrase the comments and thoughts as questions so that the teacher will lead the feedback session by answering these questions. This ensures that the teacher will reflect on the lesson in some depth.

Try to avoid simple yes/no questions, and remember that *Why* questions will generate more reflection as they require the teacher to discuss the theories behind his or her approach. Teachers must understand that *Why* and *Why not* questions do not imply any form of criticism—they are what I call true *Why* questions. In other words, the observer wants to truly know why the teacher is doing something at a given time. The observer accepts that the teacher knows the class better than anyone and wants to understand the thinking behind the teacher's choices without judgment. So, the page will look something like this:

	ACTION	**COMMENTS**	
10:15	Stage 1—Warm-up		
	Teacher at front of class		
	Students take cards from desk as they arrive. (14 students)	Why not give them the cards at the door?	
	Each card has picture on it.		
	Students find word on wall matching picture and sit down.	Why did you choose these words? What was the problem that Ahmed & Salem had with their cards?	
	Teacher hands them text based on their word.	How did the text refer to the picture?	
15 Ss	Gives them three mins. to read text and turn card back over.	I liked how you allowed Tariq to slip in quietly and move straight into the class.	

Summary

The summary is the observer's subjective view of the lesson and details the strengths he or she has observed as well as the areas he or she would like to see the teacher work on. These areas should not be written as *you MUST do this*, but should be framed as, *What do you think?* questions. So, the summary could look something like this:

SUMMARY	
Strengths:	
Teacher voice and monitoring of students	
Rapport with students	
Staging and flow of lesson—good planning	
Choice of materials—they clearly motivated the students	
Areas to work on:	
Ensuring that all students are on task—e.g., early finishers have something to do while others finish: maybe help the slower students? What do you think? Other ideas?	
Develop the texts and debate—maybe you could look at staging this over two or even three lessons? What do you reckon? The materials are certainly good enough to be worth developing further.	

You can see that the aim is to get teachers to reflect on the lesson and extend and develop the materials used. In order to ensure that the teacher has time to reflect on the observer notes, the feedback session should take place later in the day or the following day. The observer copies the notes and gives them to the teacher so that he or she has time to review them and answer the questions before the feedback session. This approach ensures that the teacher leads the feedback session as he or she recalls the lesson, trying to arrive at a realistic picture of what happened. Often this simple process of description provides the teacher with several insights into attitudes and beliefs of language and learning. As Wallace has noted (1991, p. 53) reflective discussion is a difficult concept and parameters should be set in order to keep the discussion focused. These parameters are, in practice, the points set by the teacher in the pre-course discussion, even though we need to realize that these are flexible. Although this process is time consuming, it is vital because it ensures that the teacher sees that the supervisor has time for his or her development.

Stage 4: Student Evaluations

Student evaluations are, quite correctly, central to most faculty appraisal schemes. It is, however, imperative that these evaluations by our primary clients are conducted and reviewed in a consistent, fair, and transparent manner.

The most important people to involve in the student evaluation of a teaching appraisal form are the respondents (the students), the end users (the supervisors), and those affected by the responses (the teachers). By setting up a working group charged with the development of such a form, you can ensure that the form has validation in the eyes of all parties. The parameters that the group should work by should include a maximum number of questions (I would suggest no more than twelve), the need to include at least one open comments box, and the scale for respondents (I would suggest 1–4, from strongly agree to strongly disagree). For example:

	1 *Strongly* *Agree*	*2* *Agree*	*3* *Strongly* *Disagree*	*4* *Disagree*	*n/a*
The teacher always presents the lesson clearly so that I can understand the main points.					

The group must also be instructed to focus on teaching. It is important that the form does not mix the evaluation of teaching with textbook or course evaluation. If it does, the student evaluations will not reflect an accurate picture of their impressions of the actual teaching.

Once the instrument has been finalized, teachers must be consulted about when it will be administered. At the first meeting, supervisors must find out the best time to give students the form. The student evaluations should preferably not be conducted just before or after a test or so early that the teacher has no time to build up the classroom ambience. I also advise against conducting the student evaluation too late in the course. This is so that a follow-up evaluation can be conducted if required. Once the date has been decided, the supervisor should ensure that the evaluation is conducted as agreed.

I also encourage teachers to regularly get feedback from their students through their own forms or journals. The evaluation should be conducted with the students and a third party or even online.

As with the observation, it is essential that there is a feedback session with the teacher that gives him or her the chance to respond to the feedback summary from each class he or she is teaching. There should be space on the form to record the teacher feedback, and teachers should be given the summary forms for their portfolio. Without this feedback and placing of student feedback in the teacher portfolio, as opposed to some personnel file, the student evaluation becomes a series of abstract numbers that do not reflect on teaching ability.

At the feedback on student evaluation meeting, I find it useful to highlight a main teaching strength and an area that can be worked on. I often begin this meeting with these two points and ask the teacher if he or she considers this a fair interpretation and what two points he or she would extract from the feedback. These should then be included as new teaching goals on the teacher's objectives.

We also need to consider how we approach student evaluations that are mostly negative. It is important that the supervisor put in place a process that is transparent to both students and teachers. The whole aim of the PEP is to ensure professional development through improved teaching, so the process must mirror this aim. I always speak to the teacher openly and start with an observation and discussion with the students. I then bring students and teacher together in an open discussion and 95 percent of the time this helps alleviate any miscommunication and misunderstandings. If that fails, I involve a third party, such as the student counselor, to get to the root of the students' dissatisfaction, and then have the three—students, third party, and teacher—work together to draw up an action plan to address the student grievances. This action plan then becomes part of the teacher's new teaching goals. All students should understand that the supervisor and institution will not indiscriminately change a teacher. It is far more effective to work with all parties and reach a consensus to improve both teaching and learning.

Stage 5: Summative Write-Up

The summative write-up is my personal addition to the PEP, but one that I have found indispensable for most teachers when they are developing professional development teaching portfolios for the first time.

The summative write-up is a subjective personal summary of the teacher's work during the year by the supervisor. It is written by the supervisor to the teacher with a paragraph on each objective that is included in the teaching portfolio extract as the teacher wishes.

I have found this summative write-up, which takes me about half an hour to write and rarely covers more than two sides of A4 paper, is useful for three reasons. First, it allows me to check that I really know the teacher's work over the year—not always as simple as it sounds when you have 102 staff reporting to you. Second, it does wonders for the teacher's morale and motivation when he or she realizes that you do know what each teacher has been doing. Finally, and most important, it gives teachers a true prop for their portfolio extract.

Stage 6: Teaching Portfolio Extract (TPE)

The four to six page teaching portfolio extract (TPE) is the teacher's summary of the portfolio, which is a private record of the year's work and can take any form. The portfolio is not a public document. It is simply where the teacher stores the material he or she refers to in the TPE and which can be accessed quickly. The extract must include a self-evaluation with reflection on teaching, reference to student evaluations, and reference to line supervisor's comments. It must adhere to the honesty principle in that anything stated in the extract can be supported by documentation in the portfolio.

One of the main worries that teachers have is the time they will need to write their portfolio extract. I always provide them with a model from when I was teaching. This is a six-page extract that breaks down as follows:

Page 1:   The teacher's objectives (already written and updated during the year).

Pages 2–3:   The teacher's self-evaluation based on objectives (this needs to be written by the teacher, but by using the objectives as the framework and by following the guide of the supervisor's summative write-ups, this should not take more than a couple of hours at an absolute maximum).

Pages 4–5:   The supervisor's summative report.

Page 6:   The student evaluation summary table.

This is the easiest format as most of the portfolio extract is already written, and it guarantees meeting the TPE requirements of including student evaluations, supervisor comments, and self evaluation.

Having said that I give teachers no set format, I find it interesting how the extracts differ and reflect teachers' personalities. I have had those that follow the outline to those that are a six-page narrative meeting all the requirements by taking quotes from supervisor emails, write-ups, and other documents, and official and informal student feedback. Other extracts I have received fall somewhere between the two using parts of the model with the teacher's own self reflection built around it. Once the teacher has submitted the TPE, the supervisor should review that it is acceptable before calling the final appraisal meeting.

Stage 7: Final Appraisal Meeting and Record

The power of the final appraisal meeting is that it not only looks back and reviews the last year, but also draws on that review to look forward and set goals for the coming year. This ensures a truly cyclical process.

This final meeting should take between 40 minutes to an hour and follow the TPE. The teacher should talk the supervisor through the extract focusing on the coming year with the following points being covered:

1. The objectives for the year.
2. The evidence in the portfolio that meets the requirements of reference to student evaluations, reference to supervisory comments, self-reflection, and the honesty principle. This final point could include the teacher being asked to produce documents from his or her portfolio referred to in the extract.

3. How the objectives and extract match departmental and college goals.
4. Supervisory comments for the year.
5. Teacher comments for the year.
6. Teacher goals and priorities for the coming year. This is the most important part of the meeting as it provides a continuation from one year to
   the next and ensures that the PEP is truly cyclical. The goals should be
   written up by the teacher after the meeting and used as the framework
   for the first meeting of the following year.
7. The support that the teacher will require to meet these future goals
   focusing on the professional development needed. This could be, for
   example, computer training in Excel or WebCT.

A cover sheet should be completed and then signed off by both supervisor
and teacher. This is then attached to the TPE and submitted for final director
signature before filing in the personnel records. This ensures that teachers
know exactly what is going into their personnel files, and the transparency of
the program is assured.

Distinctive Features

The PEP is, I would argue, not an especially innovative program. It is, however,
significantly distinctive in that it is the only program I have encountered in
more than twenty years of teaching that meets all the best practice principles
of teacher appraisal. It is a process that:

- is fair to all
- is based on sound principles
- allows problems to be detected early and therefore acted upon quickly
- assures both consistency in approach and documentation when applied
  correctly
- is driven by teachers

Any appraisal program should have a personnel evaluation strand and a
professional development focus as it is concerned in a fundamental way with
people's personal and professional well-being. This merging of formative and
summative evaluation has often been argued against by experts who suggest
that the two should be separated. I posit that no appraisal scheme can be truly
effective unless it brings the two together as the PEP does.

Providing constructive feedback to enable continual enhancement of professional performance is another key feature of any effective program. The PEP
approach ensures this as it is based on the empowerment of teachers by:

- allowing them to determine their objectives
- ensuring they drive their developmental goals

- giving them the opportunity to build up a teaching portfolio
- ensuring they are involved in the decisions as to what goes in their personnel files

Caveats

The PEP, as described in the preceding sections, can be easily adapted to any educational context. Adhering to the principles stated here, and ensuring that the process is transparent to all parties and is teacher driven from the outset will help ensure success.

Conclusion

This chapter has reviewed one teacher appraisal program that is developed from sound principles. The process is not set in stone and is continually evaluated by those being appraised. Feedback on the program is encouraged, and it is always exciting to see how teachers, students, and managers suggest improvements. The one factor that cannot be changed is the time that the process takes for supervisors. I have little sympathy for those arguments that suggest a comprehensive appraisal program such as the PEP is just too time-consuming. Surely, if we are focused on quality education, our primary concern should be for teaching faculty. The teachers have the most interaction with our primary clients, the students, so if we can assure teacher satisfaction through fair and rigorous appraisal, then we can also ensure we meet student needs and institutional excellence. If we do not have the time for these, then we have our priorities seriously misplaced.

Discussion Questions

1. How can you draw on the experience at your institution to develop, overhaul, or adapt the current teacher appraisal system? Who should be involved? How can agreement be reached on what changes are needed?

2. What are the main problems in your institution's evaluation practices? Based on these problems, what practices need to be included or addressed in a new or revamped appraisal system?

3. Brainstorm all the sources of data that could be used to demonstrate a teacher's work through the year. How can each of these be used in the appraisal scheme?

4. Are observations necessary in teacher appraisals? Why? Why not? What other ways can we use to review and explore teaching practice?

5. How can students be involved in faculty appraisal without formal evaluation forms?

6. Can an extract truly reflect everything a teacher does in a year? What format could be used to provide a better instrument to review the teacher's work?

7. How can you adapt the faculty appraisal approach in this chapter to your institution?

References

Allwright, D. (1988). *Observation in the language classroom*. London: Longman.

Bridges, E. M. (1992). *The incompetent teacher*. Philadelphia: Falmer.

Edge, J. (1992). *Cooperative development: Professional self-development through cooperation with colleagues*. Harlow: Longman.

———. (2002). *Continuing cooperative development: A discourse framework for individuals as colleagues*. Ann Arbor: University of Michigan Press.

Good, T. L., & Mulryan, C. (1990). Teacher ratings: A call for teacher control and self evaluation. In J. Millman & L. Darling-Hammond (Eds.), *The new handbook of teacher evaluation: Assessing elementary and secondary school teachers* (pp. 191–215). Newbury Park, CA: Sage.

Johnson, S. M. (1990). *Teachers at work: Achieving success in our schools*. New York: Basic Books.

Lawrence, C. E., Vachon, M. K., Leake, D. O., & Leake, B. H. (1993). *The marginal teacher*. Newbury Park, CA: Corwin Press.

Lewis, A. C. (1982). *Evaluating educational personnel*. Arlington, VA: American Association of School Administrators.

McLaughlin, M. W. (1990). Embracing contraries: Implementing and sustaining teacher evaluation. In J. Millman & L. Darling-Hammond (Eds.), *The new handbook of teacher evaluation: Assessing elementary and secondary school teachers*. (pp. 403–415). Newbury Park, CA: Sage.

Owens, R. G. (1991). *Organisational behaviour in education*. Englewood Cliffs, NJ.: Prentice Hall.

Peterson, K. D. (2000). *Teacher evaluation: A comprehensive guide to new directions and practices*. Thousand Oaks, CA: Corwin Press.

Peterson, K. D., & Chenoweth, T. (1992). School teachers' control and involvement in their own evaluation. *Journal of Personnel Evaluation in Education, 6*, 177–189.

Peterson, K.D., Stevens, D., & Ponzio, R. C. (1998). Variable data sources in teacher evaluation. *Journal of Research and Development in Education, 31*(3), 123–132.

Richards, J. C., & Nunan, D. (1990). *Second language teacher education.* Cambridge: Cambridge University Press.

Scriven, M. (1973). *Handbook for model training program in qualitative educational evaluation.* Berkeley: University of California Press.

———. (1981). Summative teacher evaluation. In J. Millman & L. Darling-Hammond (Eds.), *The new handbook of teacher evaluation: Assessing elementary and secondary school teachers* (pp. 244–271). Newbury Park, CA: Sage.

———. (1987). Validity in personnel evaluation. *Journal of Personnel Evaluation in Education, 1,* 9–24.

Stodolsky, S. S. (1984). Teacher evaluation: The limits of looking. *Educational Researcher, 13*(9), 11–18.

Travers, R. M. W. (1981). Criteria of good teaching. In J. Millman (Ed.), *Handbook of teacher evaluation* (pp. 14–22). Beverly Hills, CA: Sage.

van Lier, L. (1988). *The classroom and the language learner.* London: Longman.

Wallace, M. J. (1991). *Training foreign language teachers: A reflective approach.* Cambridge: Cambridge University Press.

Wise, A. E., Darling-Hammond, L., McLaughlin, M. W., & Berstein, H. T. (1984). *Teacher evaluation: A study of effective practices.* Santa Monica, CA: RAND.

Wolf, R. (1973). How teachers feel toward evaluation. In E. House (Ed.), *School evaluation: The politics and process* (pp. 156–168). Berkeley, CA: McCutchan.

CHAPTER 7

Building a Context-Specific Teacher Evaluation System for an ESL Program

Stephen Stoynoff

Introduction

Any attempt to assess teacher performance pivots on what constitutes *effective* or *competent* teaching. Based on a review of the learning-to-teach and the effective teaching literature, Reynolds (1992) concludes that competent teachers should be able to perform these basic teaching tasks:

- Plan lessons that enable students to relate new learning to prior understanding and experience
- Develop rapport and personal routines that are fair and appropriate to students
- Establish and maintain rules and routines that are fair and appropriate to the students
- Arrange the physical and social conditions in the classroom in ways that are conducive to learning and that fit the academic task
- Represent and present subject matter in ways that enable students to relate new learning and prior understanding and that help students develop metacognitive strategies
- Assess student learning using a variety of measurement tools and adapt instruction according to the results
- Reflect on their own actions and the students' responses in order to improve their teaching (Reynolds, 1992, p. 26)

These tasks offer teacher supervisors a research-based framework within which to situate their judgments about teacher actions and a conceptual basis on which to build a credible teacher evaluation system.

Good teacher evaluation systems adopt recognized evaluation standards and assessment principles. Determining the purpose and defining the *construct of interest*—the characteristic to be measured—are essential preliminary steps in the development of an assessment. When the construct of interest is defined in terms of a conceptual or theoretical framework, it strengthens the validity argument for using the assessment for its intended purpose. In this volume, teaching effectiveness is the construct of interest, and in this chapter it is operationally defined as the ability to fulfill the seven key tasks reported in Reynolds' synthesis of the research on effective teaching.

This chapter presents an ESOL teacher evaluation system that was used with beginning teachers in a master's in TESOL program in the United States. While this system emerged from a particular context, the assessment principles used to design it can be applied to developing credible teacher evaluation systems for both novice and experienced ESOL teachers in a wide range of contexts.

Description of the Evaluation Context

This evaluation system operated at a large, public university in the United States where it was used with student teachers enrolled in a graduate degree program in TESOL. The student teachers (hereafter referred to as teachers) were employed by the university's intensive ESL program, and they received a graduate assistantship in exchange for their work in the program. Teachers spent one academic year (approximately 30 weeks) performing various duties in the program, including serving as classroom assistants, observers, and ESOL teachers. During the final ten-week term, teachers were assigned fifteen to twenty ESOL students and assumed full responsibility for delivering a course that met four hours a week.

Each teacher was paired with a mentor teacher. Mentor teachers were highly qualified ESOL teachers who possessed a minimum of ten years' experience in the ESL program. Teachers met with their mentors an average of five hours a week and received feedback on every aspect of their performance from advice on classroom management to the use of instructional techniques. Teachers also had regular access to the ESL curriculum coordinator who held weekly meetings in which mentors and teachers jointly planned and exchanged ideas on how to implement the ESL curriculum in their classes. This level of intensive mentoring and extensive collaboration appears to be unusual, at least in terms of the 40 studies of novice teachers Kagan (1992) reviewed.

Principles for Teacher Evaluation Systems

When the term is applied to teachers, *evaluation* refers to a process of acquiring, considering, and judging information related to teaching and learning. Two predominant justifications are made for conducting teacher evaluations: to promote professional development and to hold teachers accountable. Some researchers argue these are divergent and irreconcilable aims. This has led to a distinction in the literature between evaluations that provide teachers information about their performance so they can adjust and improve their practice *(formative)*, and evaluations that provide decision-makers information about teachers' performance so supervisors can make formal determinations related to employment *(summative)*. Outcomes of summative evaluations include decisions to retain, dismiss, reassign, promote, or adjust teachers' salaries (Andrew & Barnes, 1990). Since the consequences of the two evaluations are quite different, teachers and supervisors must be clear about the purpose(s) of an evaluation before undertaking it.

In an introduction to research on teacher evaluation, Good (1996) notes there may not be unanimity with respect to all the practices used to evaluate teachers, but there are some principles advocated by most educational experts. They include establishing the purpose of the evaluation, choosing appropriate evaluation procedures—given the institutional values and aim of the evaluation—and developing context-specific evaluation systems. Other principles gleaned from the assessment literature include planning the evaluation, involving stakeholders in the process, using multiple sources of information, considering the consequences of assessment, and evaluating (validating) the assessment (Moss, 1992).

An authoritative publication—*The Personnel Evaluation Standards* (Joint Committee on Standards for Educational Evaluation, 1988)—developed by a distinguished panel of teachers, scholars, and school administrators codified many of these principles (Stufflebeam & Sanders, 1990). The Joint Committee's standards emphasize the need to define performance expectations; consider the evaluation context; specify the process and procedures; select appropriate procedures based on the evaluation purpose; use systematic data-gathering methods; organize and record data accurately; limit sources of bias; and evaluate the efficacy of the evaluation system. Table 7.1 displays a set of assessment principles that reflect prevailing professional standards of evaluation and questions to guide development of context-specific teacher evaluation systems.

The Evaluation System

Purpose of the Evaluation

The teacher evaluation system described here fulfilled two purposes. It collected information used to conduct formative evaluations of teaching effectiveness and summative evaluations of professional performance during the employment period. Hence, the first evaluation functioned as a professional development tool for the teacher while the second served as an accountability measure for the program.

Using data collected during the formative evaluation, the supervisor (a graduate faculty member) judged certain aspects of the teachers' performance and provided them constructive feedback orally and in writing. Classroom observations were the principal source of data for formative evaluations, and teachers negotiated the focus of the classroom visit and the data-collection procedures

Table 7.1: Principles for Developing Context-Specific Teacher Evaluation Systems

Principles	Questions to Ask
Establish the purpose(s) of the evaluation and ensure stakeholders understand it.	What is (are) the purpose(s) of the evaluation? What decision(s) will be made based on the results of the evaluation? How will the purpose(s) of the evaluation and any decision(s) based on the results be communicated to teachers?
Acknowledge important factors affecting the context of the evaluation and ensure stakeholders understand them.	What are the social, institutional, and political realities affecting the context of the evaluation? How are teachers informed of them?
Plan the evaluation and include stakeholders.	What steps will be followed in conducting the evaluation? Who will participate in the process? What opportunities will participants have to discuss both the process and the results?
Consider the range of possible information sources and procedures for collecting it.	What sources of information on teaching effectiveness are available, and what procedures can be used to collect it? Which sources and procedures are most appropriate and practical given our context and the teacher(s)?
Use multiple sources of information and utilize systematic and uniform data collection procedures.	Which sources of information and procedures will we use? What protocols and documents do we need to facilitate systematic collection of information and uniform organization of results?
Present evidence the evaluation system is suitable for its intended purpose(s).	What evidence is there this evaluation system measures teaching effectiveness?
Justify use of the system by presenting compelling evidence to support it.	How convincing is the evidence this system is a good measure of teaching effectiveness?
Align evaluation decision(s) with the expressed evaluation purpose(s).	Are decisions about teaching effectiveness based on the collected evidence, consistent with the established purpose(s) of the evaluation, and supported by sufficient evidence?
Consider the consequences of the evaluation.	What benefit is there in conducting the evaluation? What harm is there in conducting the evaluation?

with the supervisor during pre-observation meetings. Peers and mentors also engaged in formative assessments of teacher performance, but these assessments usually employed less systematic procedures, although they yielded valuable additional information that teachers used to improve their practice. Teachers learned about the purpose and how the results of the formative evaluation were to be used during an initial group orientation meeting held the first week of the academic year.

A single summative evaluation was conducted at the end of the academic year and several weeks after the teachers' ESL courses concluded. The supervisor analyzed the information contained in a teaching portfolio, which consisted of multiple artifacts related to teacher performance, and, after considering the cumulative body of evidence, decided whether the teacher had performed satisfactorily. It was a holistic assessment based on the answer to two questions: *Did the portfolio demonstrate teacher growth during the period covered by the evaluation? Did the portfolio contain sufficient evidence to render a reasonably reliable judgment about the teacher's ability to perform key professional tasks competently?* Teachers were informed orally and in writing at the beginning of the evaluation period about the purpose of the summative evaluation as well as the assessment criteria that would be used to evaluate portfolios. At the end of the evaluation period, the supervisor met with each teacher individually and discussed the evidence and the supervisor's decision.

Context of the Evaluation

Evaluations cannot be considered apart from the social and political contexts in which they occur because these factors affect the design and suitability of an evaluation system for its designated purpose. Both social and political factors influenced the evaluation system that emerged in our context.

The TESOL and ESL programs were separate administrative units of the university, and each had a distinct academic culture. The administrative autonomy of the two programs was a political reality, and it meant teachers assumed two roles and operated in two academic cultures simultaneously. Their employment-related duties were assigned and directed by ESL faculty while their degree-related activities were supervised and directed by graduate faculty in TESOL. Despite having disparate organizational structures and serving different functions within the institution, personnel from the two units forged close working relationships and built a collaborative evaluation system that reflected a set of shared values (Stoynoff, 1999).

In a study of two graduate TESOL programs in the United States, Ramanathan, Davies, and Schleppegrell (2001) reported how local contexts affected the characteristics of programs, especially in terms of the subtle "pressure to conform to the prevailing ideologies of the departments" where the programs were housed (p. 300). Our program operated in a department in which the ideological underpinnings embraced the reflective practitioner perspective. This philosophy views teachers as self-directed individuals capable of observing, analyzing, understanding, and judging their work by critically considering and reflecting on it (Doyle, 1990). Teachers are assumed to have an intrinsic desire to perform their professional roles competently and to be capable of gaining insights and improving their practice by examining and thinking critically about teaching and learning (Sprinthall, Reiman, & Thies-Sprinthall, 1996).

Organization of the Evaluation System

Although this evaluation system described evolved over a period of several years, the most successful version consisted of five separate meetings. These consisted of an initial group orientation followed by a series of individual meetings that included a planning session, pre- and post-observation meetings, and a portfolio conference. The initial meeting occurred at the beginning of the academic year, and the rest were distributed over a twelve- to fifteen-week period that commenced just before the teachers' ESL teaching began.

Each meeting served a distinct function. In the first session, teachers learned about the general steps in the evaluation process, the purpose of each evaluation, and the participants' responsibilities. Teachers, mentors, ESL program administrators, the TESOL supervisor, and ESOL students were stakeholders and therefore participated in the evaluation system. During an individual planning meeting, teachers and the supervisor considered ways to collect information for the formative and summative evaluations and devised a schedule for obtaining observational data over the ten-week ESL course.

Teachers videotaped two or three of their language lessons in the first few weeks of the ESL course and reviewed the tapes to learn more about themselves. There are numerous published accounts of the prevalence and value of self-observation as a professional development tool (Richards & Farrell, 2005; Bailey, Curtis, & Nunan, 1998). Teachers who participated in our evaluation system confirmed what the research reports had already told us: It is helpful to observe oneself teaching, and it stimulates insights that often improve performance.

In addition to self-observation, the evaluation system utilized peer and mentor observations. These observations were conducted near the middle of the term and after teachers had the opportunity to further develop their teaching skills and confidence. Richards and Lockhart (1991–1992) reported peer observation was an important method of collecting information on teachers' performance, and it can contribute to professional development, especially when it is not used as part of a summative evaluation. Peers and mentors directed their attention to specific aspects of a teacher's performance. Some of the most frequent teacher requests were for feedback on how well they were managing small group activities, pacing lessons, explaining subject matter, and interacting with students. Interestingly, these were many of the same aspects of teaching that Richards and Lockhart (1991–1992) found their experienced teachers targeted for feedback.

While there are clear benefits to conducting observations, they make most teachers anxious. To assuage some of the anxiety associated with being observed, we adopted an observation sequence that began by having teachers observe themselves (on videotape); in subsequent weeks of the term, they were observed by a peer, by a mentor, and finally by a supervisor. Sequencing the observations like this acknowledged the developmental nature of learning to teach and afforded teachers opportunities to improve their performance before the supervisor rendered judgments. Including multiple perspectives and multiple samples of teaching performance in the evaluation system increased the likelihood of capturing convergent or divergent perceptions. It also ensured the system generated sufficient samples of performance upon which to base judgments.

Sources of Information on Teaching Effectiveness

Classroom observation is a widely used source of information on teacher performance, but there are others. In a discussion of approaches to evaluating ESOL faculty, Pennington and Young (1989) identified six sources in addition to observation; these include teacher interviews, standardized teacher assessments such as the National Teacher Examination, student ratings, student performance (both on teacher-developed and standardized measures), peer evaluation, and self-appraisal. The TESOL literature also includes reports of evaluating teachers based on information from teaching journals (Bailey et al., 1998), group journals (Cole, McCarthy, Rogan, Schleicher, 1998), professional conversations (Pennington & Young, 1991), and documents created or completed by the teacher or other stakeholders.

Given the challenge of assessing teaching effectiveness and the significant consequences of summative evaluations, teacher evaluation systems should be designed to collect as much relevant information as is practical and to ensure it is as reliable as possible. Data triangulation is a process used in ethnographic studies to increase the researcher's confidence in the reported data by using multiple sources, theories, researchers, or methods (Carter & Nunan, 2001, p. 227). Integrating multiple data sources, collection methods, and stakeholder perspectives into a teacher evaluation system reduces the risk of bias and increases the reliability of inferences based on the evidence.

Information Sources and Collection Procedures for the Evaluation System

The evaluation scheme relied on six sources of information (teacher, peer, mentor, ESL supervisor, TESOL supervisor, and ESOL students), five data-collection methods (observation, teaching journal, records, questionnaire, and portfolio), and multiple samples of performance and artifacts.

Collection procedures were standardized to make them more systematic and uniform. For example, the supervisor's observations were conducted using the three-stage clinical model of supervision developed by Acheson and Gall

(1987). The three stages consisted of a pre-observation meeting in which the focus of the visit was negotiated, the observation visit, and a post-observation feedback meeting. This is a collegial model characterized by a collaborative spirit in which the teacher and supervisor work cooperatively to promote the professional development of the teacher. During classroom visits, the supervisor "focuses on the teacher's actual classroom performance," and the goal is to collect information that can be used to improve the teacher's effectiveness (1987, p. 6). For several supervisor accounts of using a clinical supervision model with experienced second language teachers in international contexts, consult Gaies and Bowers (1990).

In our case, the supervisor and teacher used the pre-observation planning sessions to determine the aim of the observation and to establish appropriate data-collection procedures. A variety of procedures were used. For example, when teachers wanted feedback on the nature of the oral exchanges in their classrooms, especially in terms of the amount of teacher versus student talk, the supervisor used the Flanders Interaction Analysis System or created a verbal flow chart (Acheson & Gall, 1987). When teachers sought feedback on the pacing of a lesson, the supervisor adopted an ethnographic approach, recording brief field notes of what was occurring during the lesson at five-minute intervals. Other data collection documents were developed or adapted from published protocols in the teacher evaluation literature (e.g., seating charts and instructional clarity rating scales).

Teaching journals were a valuable record of teachers' thoughts, questions, and reactions to their teaching experiences. Although the impetus for a journal entry was often attributable to a particular classroom experience, many teachers were prompted to make an entry as a result of conversations with peers, mentors, or the supervisor. Professional conversations are a largely untapped source of information in teacher evaluation (Pennington & Young, 1991) in part because they are difficult to capture but also because it is difficult to document their impact on teacher development. Entries in the teaching journal provided evidence of teacher reflection and professional growth during the evaluation period, and they revealed the effect of professional dialogues on teacher development. A few basic procedures were established to standardize this data-collection method. Teachers were required to make at least two entries per week, and each had to be at least 200 words in length and dated. The supervisor reviewed entries weekly and would engage the teacher in an oral or written dialogue when it seemed especially important to do so.

Written records represented another major source of information. In addition to producing lesson plans and supplemental instructional materials, teachers produced a number of employment-related documents. These included a current resume that listed professional activities and achievements during the period covered by the evaluation. Other noteworthy written records were (a) mentor and peer feedback on the teacher's lesson plans and selected pedagogical materials; (b) narrative assessments of the teacher's performance completed by the mentor, ESL program administrator, and TESOL supervisor; (c) student ratings; and (d) samples of student writing obtained at the beginning and at the end of the teacher's course.

Numerous documents were developed to make the evaluation process and data-collection procedures explicit to participants. For instance, a time line listed the different stages in the evaluation process and explicated the activities that occurred at each stage; another document described the basic components of the system (i.e., multiple observations, teaching journal, various written records, student ratings, and portfolio). Other documents outlined procedures for developing and evaluating the portfolio, including specifying the number and type of artifacts to be gathered and the assessment criteria to be applied to the portfolio. In a discussion of pre-service ESOL teacher evaluation, Johnson (1996) noted the importance of clarifying the purpose of the portfolio as well as the criteria used to evaluate the contents.

Suitability of the Evaluation System for Its Purpose

Does this system measure teaching effectiveness? There is construct validity evidence that it does. The system is based on research on teaching effectiveness and teacher evaluation as well as evidence of teachers' ability to perform seven tasks linked to professional competence. Additionally, those who designed and used the system (teachers, ESL program staff, and TESOL faculty) believed it faithfully represented the range of professional activities teachers are expected to perform.

Evidence to Justify Use of the Evaluation System

Considerable evidence exists to support using this system. First, teacher performance was conceptually linked to a set of indicators of effective teacher actions drawn from studies of the construct of interest. Second, the system was based on sound assessment principles that included collecting empirical evidence over an extended period of time, triangulating both data-gathering methods and perspectives, adopting systematic collection procedures, and specifying the portfolio contents and evaluation criteria. These characteristics of the system contributed to more consistent judgments about the teachers' performance and thereby improved the reliability of the evaluation system. Finally, evidence exists that the system was carefully planned, included stakeholders, and reflected the institutional values of the context from which it emerged. Therefore, based on the cumulative evidence, we determined the system was suitable for our purposes and that we could justify using it with our teachers.

Alignment of Evidence with Decisions

The teaching portfolio contained a cumulative record of the teacher's performance during the evaluation period, including artifacts collected from the classroom visit and meetings related to the formative evaluation. In the case of the formative evaluation, the supervisor made a single, low-stakes decision based on the evidence: Did the teacher attempt to improve performance relative to this aspect of teaching? A higher-stakes decision was made in the summative evaluation, and therefore it was based on substantially more information than was collected for the formative evaluation. In fact, the supervisor used all the evidence in the teaching portfolio to decide whether the teacher had performed satisfactorily. Both decisions were consistent with the evaluation purposes and supported by direct evidence.

Consequences of the Evaluation

There were several consequences to implementing the evaluation system described here. As teachers engaged in various evaluation activities and collaborated with colleagues, they learned more about themselves and were able to construct a more complete professional profile for the supervisor than would have been possible with a system that relied on fewer sources of information and less systematic procedures. Applying research-based evaluation standards and principles increased the quality of the information used to make decisions about teacher performance, and this benefited teachers, supervisors, and the ESOL students. Finally, the system effectively balanced the need to perform summative evaluations with the desire to contribute to the ongoing professional development of teachers.

Distinctive Features

This teacher evaluation system is consistent with prevailing perspectives on second language teacher education, including these assumptions:

- Teachers benefit from evaluations that focus on performance, use multiple data-collection procedures and sources, and are sensitive to the context and consistent with the purpose of the evaluation.
- Teachers have a stake in evaluating and improving their teaching effectiveness, and they should participate in the design of the evaluation, collection of the information, and consideration of the results.
- Teachers are capable of using self-knowledge and reflection to improve their professional performance.
- Teachers are capable of increasing their professional competence at any stage in their careers.
- Teachers develop professional insights and competence over time.
- Teachers value a collaborative approach to evaluating and improving their teaching effectiveness.

These key features distinguish the system:

- It utilizes multiple methods to collect information from multiple sources over time. Data are gleaned from direct observations, a teaching journal, numerous written records, a student questionnaire, and the examination of a teaching portfolio that contains a cumulative record of the evaluation. Information is obtained and analyzed from multiple perspectives, including those of the teacher, supervisor, colleagues, and students.
- Teachers participate in the design and implementation of the evaluation system, sharing responsibility for collecting, analyzing, and judging information on their performance.
- The system is context specific, yet its primary features are applicable to novice or veteran teachers working in a variety of ESOL situations.
- The system cultivates the reflective capacity of teachers through the integrative use of observations, a teaching journal, multiple written records, student questionnaires, and a portfolio.
- The evaluation occurs over an extended period, and this permits the collection of multiple samples of performance.
- It represents a collaborative approach to faculty evaluation that shares responsibility for improving teaching effectiveness.

Conclusion

More efficient evaluation systems than this one are certainly possible. Yet, given the centrality of effective teaching to the success of student learning in language programs, teachers and administrators ought to be willing to commit the resources required to deploy robust teacher evaluation systems. Collecting unsystematic and limited information on teaching performance produces superficial and ephemeral knowledge about a teacher's competence. Rather than an isolated, periodic event imposed on the teacher by superiors, evaluations of teaching effectiveness ought to be a rich, continuous, collaborative process that contributes to greater understanding of one's teaching and improved practice. This evaluation system provides both a framework and an impetus for this to occur.

Discussion Questions

1. What factors affect the quality of an evaluation system?

2. In what ways are formative evaluations similar to and different from summative evaluations of teachers?

3. What values and practices are likely to contribute to more effective teacher evaluation systems?

4. Reflect on a teacher evaluation system that you are familiar with or would like to implement. How is teacher performance evaluated? What procedures contribute to the effectiveness of the system? What are the consequences of the evaluation? How can the evaluation system be improved?

5. Identify a situation in which a teacher evaluation is needed and (a) predict the factors that will affect the context of the evaluation, (b) identify the sources of information and collection procedures to be used, (c) suggest how the system can be evaluated (validated), and (d) note any consequences of implementing the system.

REFERENCES

Acheson, K., & Gall, M. (1987). *Techniques in the clinical supervision of teachers: Pre-service and in-service applications* (2nd ed.). New York: Longman.

Andrew, T., & Barnes. S. (1990). Assessment of teaching. In W. Houston (Ed.), *Handbook of research on teacher education* (pp. 569–598). New York: Macmillan.

Bailey, K., Curtis, A., & Nunan, D. (1998). Undeniable insights: The collaborative use of three professional development practices. *TESOL Quarterly, 32*(3), 546–556.

Carter, R., & Nunan, D. (2001). *The Cambridge guide to teaching English to speakers of other languages.* Cambridge: Cambridge University Press.

Cole, R., McCarthy, R., Rogan, P., & Schleicher, L. (1998). Interactive group journals: Learning as a dialogue among learners. *TESOL Quarterly, 33*(3), 556–568.

Doyle, W. (1990). Themes in teacher education research. In W. Houston (Ed.), *Handbook of research on teacher education* (pp. 3–24). New York: Macmillan.

Gaies, S., & Bowers, R. (1990). Clinical supervision of language teaching: The supervisor as trainer and educator. In J. Richards & D. Nunan (Eds.), *Second language teacher education* (pp. 167–181). Cambridge: Cambridge University Press.

Good, T. (1996). Teaching effects and teacher evaluation. In J. Sikula (Ed.), *Handbook of research on teacher education* (2nd ed.), (pp. 617–665). New York: Macmillan.

Johnson, K. (1996). Portfolio assessment in second language teacher education. *TESOL Journal, 6*(2), 11–14.

Joint Committee on Standards for Educational Evaluation. (1988). *The personnel evaluation standards: How to assess systems for evaluating educators.* Newbury Park, CA: Sage Publications.

Kagan, D. (1992). Professional growth among preservice and beginning teachers. *Review of Educational Research, 62*(2), 129–169.

Moss, P. (1992). Shifting conceptions of validity in educational measurement: Implications for performance assessment. *Review of Educational Research, 62*(3), 229–258.

Pennington, M., & Young, A. (1989). Approaches to faculty evaluation. *TESOL Quarterly, 23*(4), 619–646.

———. (1991). Procedures and instruments for faculty evaluation in ESL. In M. Pennington (Ed.), *Building better English language programs* (pp. 191–227). Washington, DC: NAFSA.

Ramanathan, V., Davies, C., & Schleppegrell, M. (2001). A naturalistic inquiry into the cultures of two divergent MA-TESOL programs: Implications for TESOL. *TESOL Quarterly, 35*(2), 279–305.

Reynolds, A. (1992). What is competent beginning teaching? A review of the literature. *Review of Educational Research, 62*(1), 1–35.

Richards, J., & Farrell, T. (2005). *Professional development for language teachers.* Cambridge: Cambridge University Press.

Richards, J., & Lockhart, C. (1991–1992). Teacher development through peer observation. *TESOL Journal, 1*(1), 7–10.

Sprinthall, N., Reiman, A., & Thies-Sprinthall, L. (1996). Teacher professional development. In J. Sikula (Ed.), *Handbook of research on teacher education* (2nd ed.) (pp. 666–703). New York: Macmillan.

Stoynoff, S. (1999). The TESOL practicum: An integrated model in the United States. *TESOL Quarterly, 33*(1), 145–151.

Stufflebeam, D., & Sanders, J. (1990). Using the personnel evaluation standards to improve teacher education. In J. Millman & L. Darling-Hammond (Eds.), *The new handbook of teacher evaluation* (pp. 416–428). Newbury Park, CA: Sage Publications.

CHAPTER 8

A China Initiative: Portfolio-Based Teacher Development and Appraisal

Tim Murphey and Qiu Yaode

Introduction

In the spring of 2003, we and many other collaborators began work on the China EFL Standards project, collaboration between the International TESOL organization, McGraw Hill, and NFLTRA (National Foreign Language Teaching and Research Association). China's NFLTRA leaders had become aware of TESOL's extensive involvement in the research, construction, and establishment of several standards and wished to take advantage of their expertise. TESOL, of course, wanted to involve as many knowledgeable Chinese in the task as possible in order to ground and situate the work. The project had five writers (two Chinese and three Americans), one project leader (Barbara Agor), one Teacher Development coordinator (Tim Murphey), and more than 20 Chinese inspectors and collaborators (Qui Yaode, was one of these).

Four volumes were created for the project: one for primary teachers, one for junior high school teachers, one for senior high school teachers (Agor, 2006a, b, & c), and a fourth volume to guide portfolio-based teacher development with teacher performance standards (Murphey, 2006). Each of the first three volumes is a collection of narrative units of real or imagined classes in which a teacher guides students through a unit spanning several days or weeks. The narratives in these volumes illustrate effective teaching, with occasional real problems and with ample reference to the teacher performance standards and a set of learner standards. The units are not meant as direct models to be followed, but rather as illustrative examples of good teacher work that can be modeled and borrowed from, as appropriate for teachers in their local contexts.

The fourth volume, our focus here, is entitled *Portfolio-Based Teacher Development and Appraisal with Teacher Performance Standards* (PBTDA hereafter)—which entails rather radical proposals for teacher evaluation and appraisal in China. A professional development function of Volume Four is also to get teachers interpreting and personalizing the narratives in the first three volumes, using the appropriate volumes to reflect on their own teaching. The proposals in this fourth volume will be our main subject. We begin with a brief overview of the forms of evaluation for teacher performance already in place in China and then describe what the CEFLS project proposes and its distinctive features. Then we will look at plans for application, some possible problems, and conclude with hope.

We also need to acknowledge that, given the supply and demand in China, we are really not talking about a high-stakes situation in which the ideas we propose are used for firing anyone. We see the implementation of our proposals as a way for schools and teacher groups to form learning communities and collaboratively stimulate in-service learning and development. In some cases, this in-service learning will mean teachers learning and improving their English itself as they develop and model this learning for their students (Murphey, 2003). In other cases, teachers will be developing more pedagogically oriented skills, beliefs, and attitudes through the use of the tools we are proposing.

Current Forms of Evaluation of Teacher Performance Already in China

In China, evaluations of teachers' teaching have existed for many years, with English teachers being no exception. However, at present there is no ongoing standard practice directly under the control of the Educational Ministry. Currently, each school or institution has its own teacher evaluation system. There are some differences, of course, between evaluating teachers to hire them and evaluating them in-service. Schools regard recruiting teachers as one of the most important procedures in the whole teacher-evaluation system.

Initial Qualifications

Employment is largely in the hands of the school leaders, but with possible variations. Generally speaking, when the teachers are recruited, their education degrees must match the descriptions of the recruiting schools. For example, kindergarten teachers currently need to have studied for two years in a vocational school that specializes in preschool education and graduate with a certificate. Elementary and secondary school teachers need to have at least a two- to three-year course in a college or university and graduate with a teaching certificate. The percentage of schools requiring more and more education is changing as more people are being educated. In Beijing, all secondary school teachers now must have a B.A. or B.S. degree from a university. Some key schools that are affiliated with universities even request a certain percentage of graduate degrees among their staff. Universities are also the same. In some universities, they recruit only teachers with a Ph.D.

Yearly Teacher Evaluations

Once teachers start their jobs, they are evaluated regularly in the present system. But this evaluation is quite simple. Once a year, usually at the end of the academic year, teachers write a brief summary about their performance that year. The summary includes their attitudes toward the government policy, toward teaching, toward social activities, and toward colleagues. It also might include their workload and their publications, research accomplishments, and public service. After writing the summary, teachers will either talk about them within their own group of colleagues or hand them in to a superior. Every year, three to five percent of the teaching members get a salary raise according to the opinions of their colleagues based on their performance during the academic year. Usually a more serious evaluation of work is done when they are a candidate for this salary raise.

The purpose of raising salary is to praise the good teachers and encourage others to do better in the future. However, many teachers have complained about this evaluation system. They said that it's very difficult to judge whether a teacher is really good or not. Most teachers do the same things every day. Besides, the level of the students can also determine teachers' success and performances. If the students are originally very good and highly motivated, teachers need not work very hard and they still can help students get into the universities. If students are very weak and poorly motivated, no matter how hard the teachers try, their effect seems to be in vain.

Students' Semesterly Evaluations of Teachers

In addition to peer evaluations, students are also invited to evaluate teachers. In fact, teachers are evaluated every semester by their students. From these evaluations, we discover certain teaching problems and who is popular and greatly loved by students. Nevertheless, the evaluation from the students can be only a reference since some teachers do not get high scores because they are strict with students and students don't usually like the strict teachers. Also, in some cases, if teachers give students high marks, students like those teachers and give them high evaluation scores. Because of this, in some schools, the salary-raise "honor" goes to different persons by turns instead of choosing "good" teachers. As Mr. Zhang Xin* said, "We love to be evaluated by students, because it can enhance our work and create a communication channel between teachers and students. But students' evaluations should not be the only determinant to evaluate us."

---

*All cited teachers' names are pseudonyms.

In-Service Training

In many schools, teachers are now requested to attend a weekly training program organized by the teacher-training department of that district. A record of attendance is kept, and all teachers should participate in the training. The training itself has two purposes: One is to provide explanations and keys to students' testing papers on a regular basis, and the other is to invite scholars or experts to talk about educational issues. However, some teachers rightly criticize top-down explanations and just receiving answer keys. Miss Liu said, "We teachers like to receive further education. But we hope that we could have better guest speakers. If they could provide us with the more advanced teaching ideas, we would all enjoy them."

Evaluation Forms and Evaluators

Teachers don't want to be evaluated frequently—once every semester, or maybe even once a year, is ideal. Mr. Zhang Xin worries about the result of the evaluation: "Evaluation is a good thing. What if we find something wrong with a particular teacher? Can we fire him or her? If not, what is the point of evaluation?" Mr. Zhang Xin's concern raises an issue of the function of evaluation. Is it to uplift teachers? To find fault with teachers? To improve teachers' teaching skills? Once this is clear, evaluation will bear its real purpose.

Currently, there is no standard evaluation form from the Ministry of Education, and the evaluation of teachers' teaching by their colleagues, school principal, or headmaster is not required. Even if administrators do have a certain evaluation form, they do not use it often or widely. Each local school and district has its own rules and ways of working. Teacher evaluation is regularly done by students, but not by peers or principals due to lack of staff and time. Schools don't have specialists to evaluate teachers because no one can be an expert in every subject. If there is someone who does it, they do it in addition to their regular job and thus lack time they have to teach and there are too many teachers to evaluate.

Even if peer evaluations are not good, and students dislike teachers, administrators will still keep them because there are not enough teachers. Miss Wang, in charge of academic studies at her school, speaks of the legal system: "We don't have the right to unemploy people. If we dismiss them, they would come to you every day for further explanations or hassle you all the time. In order not to get into any trouble, we dare not fire anyone. The system fails to support us. At present our employment system still needs developing."

While implementing the evaluation system, many teachers think Chinese should have a national standard system—that is, every school should have the same criteria and same procedures for evaluation. There is no standard practice, and the salary raise could be done more systematically and rationally. The new standard of English curriculum was published in 2006 and teachers were apprised of the possibilities for evaluations.

CEFLS Proposals

The two main tools that we were contracted to develop were a set of teaching performance standards and a portfolio process for teacher development. From the outset, Volume Four was described as something that would help Chinese English educators develop a portfolio-based teacher evaluation system through teacher performance standards.

Over the two-year period, we developed a set of Teacher Performance Standards (TPS) with the help of our colleagues in China and feedback from the general public, as well as suggestions from TESOL's Standing Committee on Standards. While both the TPS and portfolios could be used in an evaluation process, from their inception we preferred to see them as generating reflection and teacher development rather than being judgmental sticks to hold over teachers' heads. We chose to see them and present them, and believe they are tools for self- and collaborative appraisal and inspiration rather than intimidating pronouncements of degrees of quality.

There are also several important ways of working with the TPS and portfolios that we propose and see as desirable. First, we hope teachers will use the TPS to confirm some of the wonderful things that they are doing already. This is a process to recognize and validate their own practices. Second, we hope that groups of teachers together will decide for themselves what each degree of goodness means in their own particular situations in the application of the TPS. As we suggest in the volume, teachers will need to discuss examples that fit their situations as to how they are discovering, approaching, meeting, or exceeding any particular standard in their particular situations. We have found time and time again how "top-down, one size fits all," does NOT work in all educational practices. We hope we have provided tools that can be adapted locally and situationally. Third, we hope teachers and inspectors will take advantage of the opportunity to learn from each other collaboratively and, for example, produce newsletters of good practice in their region.

Teacher Performance Standards

From the outset, our description of the TPS stresses that student learning is the ultimate goal and that, according to research, the teacher is the most important factor in learner progress. However, students learn best when teachers, too, are learning:

> Student learning and well-being is the goal of effective teaching. Thus, it is also the goal of TESOL's teacher performance standards. Improved student learning, however, does not happen without teacher learning (Darling-Hammond, 1997; Darling-Hammond & McLaughlin, 1999). According to research and meta-analyses conducted over many years (Hattie, 1992; Marzano 2000, 2003a; Sanders & Horn, 1994; Wright, Horn, & Sanders, 1997), the teacher is probably 'the single most

important factor affecting student achievement' (Marzano, 2003b, p. 1). 'Change efforts have found that the fate of new programs and ideas rests on teachers' and administrators' opportunities to learn, experiment, and adapt ideas to their local context' (Darling-Hammond, 1997, p. 214). Thus, the CEFLS project participants looked seriously at how the Chinese education system can offer opportunities, through these performance standards, for teachers to engage in their own locally situated professional development. (Murphey, 2006)

There are 21 standards within eight essential domains that come from surveying many other existing sets of standards, looking at what recent research is telling us, and also looking at domains that already exist in one set of standards in China (Ministry of Education, 2001). From this last set of standards, one particular aspect we included was the Chinese emphasis on attitudes and effect that we found very appropriate.

The Eight Domains for the China EFL Teacher Performance Standards
Domain 1. Knowing Students
Domain 2. Appreciating Attitudes
Domain 3. Planning, Delivering, and Reflecting on Instruction
Domain 4. Constructing Knowledge of Languages, Language Learning, and Critical Thinking
Domain 5. Exploring and Applying Culture
Domain 6. Assessing Teaching and Learning
Domain 7. Connecting Beyond the Classroom
Domain 8. Expanding Professional Horizons

Portfolios

The primary tool of teacher development that we propose is, in fact, the teachers' own professional lives as reflected in their portfolios. The constructing of portfolios has the potential to greatly affect teacher development as teachers reflect on their practice and collect artifacts that represent good practice and data from their own classes. Constructing one's own portfolio is performing a kind of "appreciative inquiry" on oneself; it can greatly boost one's self-esteem, motivation, and desire to reflect and improve on areas that are weak. No teacher training method could be as individually relevant to teachers' unique needs as identifying their individual strengths and good work and then building on that. This is what portfolios have the possibility to do.

Seldin (2004) describes portfolios as "a collection of materials that document teaching performance," bringing "together in one place information about a [teacher's] most significant teaching accomplishments" (p. 3). Martin-Kniep (1999) refers to portfolios as "collections of purposeful and specialized work, capturing a process that can never be fully appreciated unless one can be inside and outside someone else's mind. They validate current expectations and legitimize future goals . . . . Portfolios are history in the making" (p. 3). Teachers can be very creative as to what they wish to insert in their portfolio and to share with others. Some include student work, their own reflections, observations from other teachers and parents, lesson plans, innovative activities, or even a video of their class. Portfolios are collections of a teacher's processes and products to show someone what they are proud of and how they have developed. They often include a philosophy and vision statement for their work and a resume of their activities and employment history (Murphey, 2006).

However, even the best of tools can be used inappropriately to harm rather than promote healthy development. While researchers agree (Kilbane & Milman, 2003; Martin-Kniep, 1999; Seldin, 2004) about the possible benefits to portfolios, they also admit to their use and misuse at times, for evaluation purposes.

Allow us to present a simple analogy here. Ideally, teachers want all children to work hard and improve the best they can. Nevertheless, standardized tests and some classroom tests would still label some of these children failures and perhaps stigmatize them for life, reducing them to underperform to their abilities. A more open educational approach would motivate children to do the best they could, accept it, and build on it. When we ask teachers to do portfolios, we are also asking them to showcase their good work along with their problems and reflections. Ideally, what they produce will involve three reflective and collaborative processes that will be combined in their portfolios: (1) the affirming of what they are doing well with, (2) the seeding of knowing about what others are doing well that they might be capable of incorporating into their own teaching, and (3) the acknowledgment of quandaries and problems and how they are thinking about them. It is especially the honest attention to this last one that can keep portfolios from being just a boring task of pretending everything is going well for the administrator and make it one of deep learning and development that can improve teachers' lives. We see this as a healthy balance between acknowledging what one is doing well; being open to the innovations and options in our immediate environment that we might model; and honestly acknowledging mistakes, problems, and what we do not know yet. Stories and reflections on failures can provide us with a wealth of developmental stimulus when they are encouraged and accepted, not condemned. This is the genius of professional teacher portfolios when they are done with a minimum of top-down (standardized) evaluation.

One: Appreciative Inquiry

"Because teachers and administrators are important change agents in their own education and the education of their students (Wu, 2004), we need to acknowledge the excellence that is already present in their work and celebrate it (cf. Appreciative Inquiry, Cooperrider & Whitney, 2002)" (Murphey, 2006.) Appreciative inquiry is a twenty-year-old field in business management that has shown remarkable results and only recently has been applied to education (Henry, 2003). The basic idea is that workers (students and teachers) tend to be more motivated when leaders concentrate on what they are doing well and encouraging more of that than on focussing on what is wrong. Research also shows that many of the "problems" that traditionally would have been corrected with great effort often simply disappear when people focus on appreciating what they are already doing well.

At the beginning of Volume Four we assert that appraisals can be done with a variety of "eyes." We propose the teacher's own eyes are the most effective and necessary for productive change and learning to occur. We also admit that while teachers in general can be given more self-confidence through doing self-appraisals, we still want to know what others think. As Martin-Kniep (1999) says, "Teachers learn best from other teachers, provided they can articulate what they think and know in ways that honor their different ways of knowing and thinking" (p. 15).

Finally, "Teachers know that students who take responsibility for their own work learn and grow, and the same is true of teachers. Therefore, we propose a process that does not marginalize the role of supervisor, but places it in a different sequence. This model also enhances the effectiveness of those supervisors who were not trained in English teaching. For them to review portfolios in depth would be difficult and very time consuming. A group of teachers collaboratively appraising each other's portfolios can leave their reports in Chinese in the teacher's portfolio that administrators can then read and more quickly understand" (Murphey, 2006).

Two: Cooperative Dialogue, Calibrating Meanings, and Community

If teachers and administrators attempt to apply the portfolios and TPS individually and without cooperative dialogue (Edge, 2002), the process will very likely flounder and die. It is the socio-professional act of groups of teachers deciding themselves what kinds of portfolios they wish to do and what the TPS mean exactly for them that will generate the professional conversations necessary for professional development. Our greatest hope is that through these conversations they will develop a sense of community, a sense of excitement and support for and by colleagues.

Thus, we have guided measurably and indicated in several places that it is the teachers who need to talk and decide many of the processes of portfolios and the meanings of the standards. Here is an example from the CEFLS V4 (Murphey, 2006).

This is a partial PAATPS grid with a few examples of what may be appropriate behaviors and activities for teachers at the primary school level. Some blanks have intentionally been left for you to fill in what you might think is appropriate from your own professional life. We invite you to put your examples in the boxes marked "Another example."

Domain 4, Standard 2: Teachers guide students and themselves to use effective communication and learning strategies that can also be applied in a range of academic and social contexts.			
Exceeding	Another example	My students and I are creating a class book of our communication and learning strategies.	Another example
Meeting	Another example	I am asking students for help when I need it and modeling using other resources.	Discussions of good learning strategies with students have become common.
Approaching	Playing with the language with students at different times during the day is becoming frequent.	I'm not so afraid of making mistakes in front of my students now.	Another example
Discovering	I am open to the possibility of learning with my students.	Another example	Another example

Three: Collaborative Learning and Communicating beyond the School

Expanding on the concept of community, we also hope with the increase in professional conversations within the schools that teachers will want to know more about what is happening in other schools as well, broadening their awareness and their impact. One way to do this is for inspectors to create regional newsletters for their teachers and encourage them to share their best work with other teachers in the area. These could plausibly be once-a-semester newsletters at first, open to all comers, or rotating from one school to the next to encourage all to share and take part. The volume also addresses principals and inspectors directly in the narratives and activities that are proposed for workshops and in-service training. It even proposes that inspectors and principals could show the way by creating their own portfolio.

Distinctive Features

Five of the distinctive features of the initiative have been adequately described: portfolios, teacher performance standards, local adjustment for relevance, a collaborative self-determined teacher process, and an openness to change of the tools to teachers' contexts and times. Let us look here at the use of narratives.

Within the last 15 years, there has been a social turn in SLA and language teaching research (Block, 2003) with a strong ethnographic element to it (Watson-Gegeo, 1988; Day, 2002) that validates the telling of stories by learners, teachers, and researchers as a way of sharing knowledge in more comprehensible ways. Even in the extremely rationally oriented business world, they are recognizing the value of stories for strengthening knowledge management and communities of practice (Brown, Denning, Groh, & Prusak, 2004).

The four volumes in the CEFLS series are structured around narratives that can help teachers more easily grasp the difficulties and contradictions of our profession while at the same time providing models of success and persistence and everyday genius. We hope the stories will make reading the volumes easier and more attractive to teachers and that they will learn more because of them. We are also encouraging teachers to tell their own stories by doing portfolios and collaborating with other teachers because when they do they reveal their values and learn from one another more readily.

Annette Simmons (2001) says that becoming conscious of our stories can help us become more congruent and live the stories we tell. We need to be conscious of the stories we tell ourselves to reach this congruence, and telling others helps us be more conscious of them. Her personal vision story mirrors many of the things we hope to happen with our CEFLS project:

> *My vision story is something I don't often share. It sounds corny but it keeps me going. I believe that the human race is evolving new collaborative behaviors that will help us transcend the threats we face. If we evolved an opposing thumb to survive, then we can evolve more collaborative behavior to survive the environmental and war threats we currently face. My story keeps my hopes alive, gives me a job to do, and gives me peace even if the results I seek are not realized in my lifetime (p. 239).*

Caveats

Possible problems with implementation and application of the model that we foresee include:

1. Dispersion of the ideas
2. Buy-in by administrators, inspectors, principals, and teachers
3. Getting people to try it out initially
4. Documenting the successes for others

While trainings for teachers and supervisors are planned in 2005 and 2006, with the volumes available in 2006, we foresee a need for a top-down adoption by universities and the Ministry of Education for this project to have an impact. Without support, the things we propose are applicable but may not be widely known and tried out.

Qiu Yaode described our initiative to many teachers and asked for their comments in January 2005. It was clear that teachers already recognize a need for different kinds of evaluation for teachers involved in different types of careers:

- Miss Liu Minghua, a twenty-year veteran high school teacher, said, "Teacher evaluation is a good thing. But there is no standard practice. Each situation must be dealt with differently. For example, leaders cannot judge a teacher only on how many published research papers there are. What if the teacher is assigned to teach lots of periods per week, where can he or she find the time to write? In this case, the leaders should evaluate this teacher's teaching instead of asking him to produce research papers."

Teachers are also concerned about who does the evaluations:

- Mr. Li Jun, who has been teaching in junior high school for only two years, says, "We cannot only let senior teachers evaluate young teachers. What if the senior teachers have traditional ways of teaching, but the young teachers have new approaches? If they don't like our way of our teaching, I'm sure they will under-evaluate us and put us in an unsatisfactory group. We should have people who could represent us all to evaluate us, not only one person."

On the other hand, teachers are worried about the evaluations being superficial social evaluations:

- Miss Fang Hongxin, fifteen-year veteran, says, "It's very hard for teachers to evaluate each other. We don't want to say something bad about that particular teacher. We want everybody happy. So usually we almost say the same thing to each individual person. We don't want to degrade anybody."
- Miss Shen, working at the educational evaluation center, says, "Right now, we really don't have a standard evaluation system. We allow local authorities to do them as they see fit. Situations are quite different from school to school, from district to district. But we do hope that through evaluation we could praise the good ones, and give warnings to the 'undesirable ones.'"
- Mr. Zhao, a high school teacher, brings up the perennial question of time: "Evaluation is a good thing as long as it does not give us a lot of burden. We are afraid of being asked to comment on others again and again. Meanwhile, we also feel nervous when we know that we are evaluated again and again. Our life is already hard enough."

Most of these quotes describe the process as evaluation done by another. Keeping the title in mind, *Portfolio-Based Teacher Development and Appraisal*, we want to stress that our project is first and foremost for teacher development and done by teachers in service of students' learning. When that is done well and teachers are developing, then that should be the most important part of an evaluation. But we realize that conventional ideas about evaluation will not go away easily, and thus our attempt is to wrap it up inside of a larger, more holistic process of professional development and hopefully allow "evaluators" to slowly become appraisers of development over time, rather than judges for a moment.

There is also danger that the teacher performance standards will be misused. National standards to many people, and actually in many places, may be used to the detriment of situated local knowledge and flexibility, as Cochran-Smith and Lytle (1999) describe so well:

> The standards movement—and with it the proliferation of classroom, school, school district, city, state, and national policies—now dominates the agenda regarding instruction, curriculum, assessment, promotion policies, and other aspects of school life....Part of what these developments have in common is a set of underlying assumptions about school change that de-emphasizes differences in local contexts, de-emphasizes the construction of local knowledge in and by school communities, and de-emphasizes the role of the teacher as decision maker and change agent. (p. 22)

By contrast, we see the China TPS as a general framework that describes good teaching as we now understand it to be and yet admits that no set of standards will ever be complete and that adaptation is normal in remaining relevant to our contexts and developing through time. It is our hope that through the tools of portfolios, local teacher-produced newsletters, storytelling, and teacher-directed portfolio appraisal practices that the TPS will be continually revised and adapted to the local and changing contexts: "A healthy amount of humility should be a component of any knowledge stock that we wish to see grow and develop" (Murphey, 1989, p. 315). Or in the words of Voltaire, "Doubt is not a pleasant condition, but certainty is absurd."

We do not yet know of another instance of standards being used so flexibly. As the portfolio practices and TPS begin to be applied, we will need to document successes and describe local applications so that others will have clearer models of how these apparently contradictory forces can indeed work together. Without the dissemination of such stories (Brown et al., 2004; Simmons, 2001), the modeling of these practices may not be as fast as it could be. Sullivan (2004) gives us hope in describing her study of 61 principals and foreign language department chairs in middle schools and high schools who overwhelmingly found portfolios and their own state standards (Rhode Island) useful for evaluating teacher candidates to hire.

Conclusion

The Portfolio-Based Teacher Development and Appraisal volume was introduced in 2006, and the initiative was monitored with a view to understanding the dynamics of applying what was proposed. While it was somewhat daunting to introduce something like this in the largest and fastest-growing country in the world, we pursued our mission. We feel that the initiative is a gem; however, much depends on situated applications, or to paraphrase Michael Jordan, "We can accept failure but we cannot accept not trying." Failure will surely come at different places and times. But when we see it as feedback to be adjusted to, it is welcome information to learn from and improve education more broadly.

Discussion Questions

1. Compare your country's history of teacher assessment measures with China's present system. What parallels do you see? What differences?

2. Compare and contrast how student, peer, and administrative evaluations of teachers are used in China and in your situation. What is similar and what is different? How do you think each should be used?

3. To what extent are teacher portfolios used in the teacher assessment systems you are familiar with and with what success? What aspects of the plans for China might make portfolios a more viable alternative in the systems you know?

4. Portfolios and Teacher Performance Standards put more weight on self-assessment. What are the principle advantages to allowing more self-assessment (some of which are mentioned in the chapter) and what are some of the dangers?

5. Why have the authors put so much emphasis on "local adjustment for relevance," "collaborative self-determined teacher processes," and "an openness to change"?

6. Narrative, telling stories, is singled out as a distinctive feature in this chapter. From your own experience, what importance has telling your own story of development, or hearing others tell theirs, played in your understanding of teaching and learning?

7. This chapter cites as a possible problem with the implementation of portfolios and TPS the "buy-in by administrators, inspectors, and principals and teachers." If you were in the authors' shoes what could you do to allow for more "buy-in" by the end users of your proposals?

REFERENCES

Agor, B. J. (Ed.). (2006a). *Integrating EFL standards into Chinese classroom settings, primary level (grades 3–6).* Singapore: TESOL/McGraw-Hill.

——. (Ed.). (2006b). *Integrating EFL standards into Chinese classroom settings, junior level (grades 7–9).* Singapore: TESOL/McGraw-Hill.

——. (Ed.). (2006c). *Integrating EFL standards into Chinese classroom settings, senior level (grades 10–12).* Singapore: TESOL/McGraw-Hill.

Block, D. (2003). *The social turn in second language acquisition.* Washington, DC: Georgetown University Press.

Brown, J., Denning, S., Groh, K., & Prusak, L. (2004). *Storytelling in organizations: Why storytelling is transforming 21st century organizations and management.* Burlington, MA: Elsevier Butterworth Heinemann.

Cochran-Smith, M., & Lytle, S. (1999). The teacher research movement: A decade later. *Educational Researcher, 28*(7), 5–25.

Cooperrider, D., & Whitney, D. (2002). *Appreciative inquiry: The handbook* (1st ed.). Euclid, OH: Lakeshore Publishers.

Darling-Hammond, L. (1997). *The right to learn: A blueprint for creating schools that work.* San Francisco: Jossey-Bass.

Darling-Hammond, L., & McLaughlin, M. (1999). Investing in teaching as a learning profession. In L. Darling-Hammond & G. Sykes (Eds.), *Teaching as the learning profession: Handbook of policy and practice* (pp. 376–411). San Francisco: Jossey-Bass.

Day, E. M. (2002). *Identity and the young English language learner.* Clevedon, UK: Multilingual Matters.

Edge, J. (2002). *Continuing cooperative development: A discourse framework for individuals as colleagues.* Ann Arbor: University of Michigan Press.

Hattie, J. A. (1992). Measuring the effects of schooling. *Australian Journal of Education, 36*(1), 5–13.

Henry, R. (2003, August). Leadership at every level: Appreciative inquiry in education. *New Horizons for Learning.* Retrieved June 25, 2004, from http://newhorizons.org/trans/henry.htm

Kilbane, C., & Milman, N. (2003). *The digital teaching portfolio handbook.* Boston: Allyn & Bacon.

Martin-Kniep, G.. (1999). *Capturing the wisdom of practice: Professional portfolios for educators.* Alexandria, VA: Association for Supervision and Curriculum Development.

Marzano, R. J. (2000). *A new era of school reform: Going where the research takes us.* Aurora, CO: Mid-Continent Research for Education and Learning.

——. (2003a). *Classroom management that works: Research-based strategies for every teacher.* Alexandria, VA: Association for Supervision and Curriculum Development.

———. (2003b). *What works in schools: Translating research into action.* Alexandria, VA: Association for Supervision and Curriculum Development.

Ministry of Education of the People's Republic of China. (2001). *English curriculum standards* (for general school) *(Draft version).* Beijing: Beijing Normal University Press. Translated 2003.

Murphey, T. (1989). Sociocognitive conflict: Confused? Don't worry, you may be learning! *ETC., 46*(4), 312–315. (Journal published by the International Society for General Semantics.)

———. (2003). NNS primary school teachers learning English with their students. *TESOL Matters, 13*(4) 1, 6. Retrieved November 1, 2004, from http://www.tesol.org/s_tesol/sec_document.asp?TRACKID=&CID=192&DID=1001

Murphey, T. (Ed.). (2006). *Portfolio-based teacher development and appraisal with teacher performance standards* (Companion to integrating EFL standards into Chinese classroom settings series): *CEFLS Volume IV.* New York: McGraw Hill.

Sanders, W. L., & Horn, S. P. (1994). The Tennessee value-added assessment system (TVAAS): Mixed-model methodology in educational assessment. *Journal of Personnel Evaluation in Education, 8,* 299–311.

Seldin, P. (2004). *The teaching portfolio.* Bolton, MA: Anker Publishing.

Simmons, A. (2001). *The story factor: Secrets of influence from the art of storytelling.* New York: Basic Books.

Sullivan, J. (2004). Identifying the best foreign language teachers: Teacher standards and professional portfolios. *The Modern Language Journal, 88*(iii), 390–402.

Watson-Gegeo, K. A., (1988). Ethnography in ESL: Defining the essentials. *TESOL Quarterly, 22*(4), 575–592.

Wright, S. P., Horn, S. P., & Sanders, W. L. (1997). Teacher and classroom context effects on student achievement: Implications for teacher evaluation. *Journal of Personnel Evaluation in Education, 11,* 57–67.

Wu, Y. (2004, May). *Aspiring after continued teacher development: A study of effective university EFL teachers in China.* A presentation at the Fourth International Conference: New Directions in ELT, Beijing, China.

PART 3:

Research in Teacher Evaluation

The chapters in Part 3 investigate issues and practice within teacher evaluation and appraisal. The studies were selected because they represent different research paradigms (qualitative, quantitative, and action research) from a variety of different educational contexts.

Bray (Chapter 9) reports on an action research project about ESL teachers' involvement in a competency-based curriculum delivered to migrant students in Australia. In her study, Bray observed teachers and evaluated them using a multiliteracy framework rather than looking for a set of discrete teaching skills.

Burden and Troudi (Chapter 10) investigate student perceptions of teacher evaluation processes and procedures at a Japanese university. Using both quantitative (Likert scale questionnaire) and qualitative (a set of open-ended questions) measures, they look into what students think about how they evaluate their EFL teachers. Their study challenges a number of assumptions and practices associated with student evaluation of teachers. The authors raise important issues and cautions regarding teacher appraisal by students.

In a longitudinal two-year case study, Ekin (Chapter 11) explores teacher effectiveness within a framework of teacher training and development. Her study, conducted in Turkey, employs predominantly qualitative instruments and actively involves trainers, teachers, and students. The primary focus of this study is on stakeholders' experiences and perceptions of teaching effectiveness.

The final chapter looks at teachers' views on how they are evaluated at a tertiary institution in the United Arab Emirates. More specifically, Davidson (Chapter 12) examines teachers' views towards students' evaluation of their teaching, classroom observations carried out by administrators, and teaching portfolios submitted each year by the teachers. The author also reports on teachers' concerns about the validity and reliability of the way they are evaluated.

The chapters in Part 3 help inform the practice surrounding teacher appraisal and evaluation. Results of these studies provide us with a much bigger picture of how English language teachers are evaluated and identify controversial issues within the area of teacher evaluation.

CHAPTER 9

Insights for Teacher Evaluation from an Action Research Study

Lyn Bray

The Multiliteracies framework was developed by a group of academics from Australia, Britain, and the United States[1] who came together in New London, New Hampshire, in 1994, to discuss the role of language and literacy education in our rapidly changing world. They called themselves the New London Group, and the ideas they generated at that meeting became the basis for a paper entitled "A Pedagogy of Multiliteracies: Designing Social Futures" that appeared in the Spring 1996 edition of the *Harvard Educational Review* (New London Group, 1996). The paper attracted much international interest and became a focus for research and teacher development, especially in Australia and South Africa (Kalantzis & Cope, 1997).

Introduction

A few years ago I had the privilege of working with a team of ESL teachers in Adelaide, South Australia. I was conducting a study into the Multiliteracies curriculum framework (New London Group, 1997) in which I proposed to collaborate with this team to investigate the links between the theory it presented and the practical considerations of day-to-day teaching in their context. I met with five teachers initially to establish whether they were interested in participating; to their credit, they all volunteered their time and attention. So we engaged in a process of reflection, information, action, and further reflection to see what the Multiliteracies were all about and to try to apply some of its principles. By the time the process was complete, I found I had achieved, besides the stated outcomes of the study, a rich understanding of the quality of their teaching.

While some forms of evaluation may be summative in nature, my belief is that the interests of learners and learning institutions are best met by an

---

[1] Courtney Cazden (United States), Bill Cope (Australia), Norman Fairclough (United Kingdom), James Gee (United States), Mary Kalantzis (Australia), Allan Luke (Australia), Carmen Luke (Australia), Sarah Michaels (United States), and Martin Nakata (Australia).

ongoing process of teacher renewal, where evaluation is a part of a cycle of action and reflection, an organic process of change, adaptation, and progress. Teacher evaluation, in this view, is qualitative and sensitive to individual differences. It is embedded in professional development, and teachers thrive when recognized for what they already know. As we see from Cochran-Smith (2003, p. 373),

> [W]hen teaching is rightly regarded as an intellectual activity and when it is acknowledged that teachers are motivated, at least in part, by love of learning, then it becomes clear that what is needed are more opportunities for teachers to work with others in learning communities; raise new questions about students, subject matter, assessments, equity, and access; and generate local knowledge through collaborative analysis and interpretation.

In view of this, teacher evaluation should focus on growth and flexibility rather than the acquisition of specific skills. A set of pedagogical concepts like those in the Multiliteracies framework can provide stimulating input for teachers to reflect on and make use of.

The rationale behind the Multiliteracies is that the advent of computing and information technologies means a great deal more to teachers than a new tool to teach with and a new communication need to consider. It is reshaping our whole society as it becomes more global and interconnected. With this massive social change going on, educators need more than ever to develop ways of preparing learners to design their own "social futures" (New London Group, 1997), futures we can barely anticipate. Teaching literacy is more than ever the most fundamental and powerful imperative of educators in every field. Given the abundance of information available now, and communication that is encoded not only in written script but in voice and body language and in visual presentation, critical literacy skills are more important than ever to make sense of it all. Moreover, critical awareness of learning processes contributes to a learning approach that is effective long after formal schooling ceases. The Multiliteracies framework, then, was designed to address the recent changes in society resulting from the new technologies, and as such represented a step forward in the knowledge and understandings of the participating teachers.

The five participants in the study were ESL teachers in a state-wide program called the Advanced English Migrant Program (AEMP). Their students were adult migrants from a variety of countries in Europe and Southeast Asia whose English language skills were considered to be advanced enough for a course that would prepare them for the workplace or for further study or training. Many of them were university graduates in their original countries. They took the course at the Institute of TAFE (Training and Further Education), where the focus was on vocational training for the South Australian workforce. The competency-based curriculum, called the Certificate III in Advanced English Proficiency, accordingly emphasized skills for vocational preparation.

The team of full-time and part-time teachers shared responsibility for teaching this curriculum to two classes. They were all university graduates with Bachelors' degrees, had specific ESL qualifications such as a certificate or a graduate diploma, and were experienced teachers. Here is a brief introduction for each of the teachers; their names have been changed for reasons of confidentiality.

- Anita taught the group of subjects called the "Core," which was compulsory for all the students. She was particularly interested in critical literacy.
- Barbara took four subjects: Listening Skills Extension, Pronunciation Practice, Oral Presentations, and Australian Language and Studies (ALAS). She often emphasized the idea that the students were "intelligent adults."
- Colin was responsible for teaching computing skills as an elective subject. His professional background was primarily in teaching visual design.
- Deirdre taught two subjects, Advanced Reading and Advanced Writing. Students in these subjects were more advanced in these skills and were expected to produce longer pieces of work and operate at a more academic level.
- Eva had duties as coordinator and also taught the "Core" as well as ALAS. She was the most experienced teacher with this curriculum and had developed many of the resource materials and compiled the student workbooks.

These teachers joined with me in an exploration of the Multiliteracies framework, in particular the associated concepts of the four aspects of literacy pedagogy: Situated Practice, Overt Instruction, Critical Framing, and Transformed Practice. Of these, Critical Framing proved to be the most controversial in that some teachers resisted applying it in the classroom, while others welcomed the opportunity it provided to stimulate the thinking of the students. In this way it powerfully revealed the nature of the teachers' attitudes to their own practice.

Critical framing is defined by the New London Group as: Interpreting the social and cultural context of particular designs of meaning. This involves the students' standing back from what they are studying and viewing it critically in relation to its context. (New London Group, 1997, p. 43)

The term *designs of meaning* is interpreted here as including both texts studied in class (either reading passages or samples of speech for listening comprehension) and learning experiences (individual lessons or units of study) designed by the teachers and participated in by the students. Critical Framing is based on principles of critical literacy; it is the aspect of the Multiliteracies that directly addresses the skills we need to effectively make sense of the profusion of information we are increasingly surrounded by, and to choose a proactive response to it.

While Critical Framing is concerned with issues of reflection and change, it goes further than the reflective process that occurs in many classrooms, where a teacher guides students through a detailed examination of an assessment task in order to formulate ongoing study strategies. The emphasis in the Multiliteracies framework is on real-life uses of language rather than the academic study of language for its own sake. Critical Framing is concerned with seeing how texts function in different social and cultural contexts and how learning can be applied in ways that enhance effective participation in society.

Description

The aim of the study was to develop understandings about the Multiliteracies framework in the context of ESL teaching for adult migrants, with particular attention to the important aspect of Critical Framing.

These questions were explored in the study:

- In what respects were the teachers already practicing Multiliteracies principles?
- What features of the framework did they judge to be of value?
- What new ideas did they pick up on when given the opportunity to put them into practice in their teaching?
- How did they perceive Critical Framing in the context of their classroom practice? (Bray, 2000, p. 23)

The procedures were designed to be sensitive to the perceptions and opinions of the ESL practitioners, to involve consultation with them and careful consideration of their views and understandings. The emphasis was on interviewing the teachers and discussing the issues with them, in the belief that:

> Both research and pedagogy can be guided by a concern for listening carefully and critically to the voices of those embedded within the day-to-day life of the institutions we are concerned with. (Goodson & Mangan, 1996, p. 67)

According to this view, much can be learned from those who are working every day with students toward their learning goals, and their accumulated knowledge is to be valued.

An initial round of interviews was conducted with individual participants to establish features of their teaching practice that might be consistent with the Multiliteracies framework. Each recorded interview explored these questions:

- What do you do to give students real-life practice of the skills they acquire?
- How do you draw on the past experience of your students?
- How do you present new information to the students?
- What are the different ways you look at a text? (Bray, 2000, p. 29)

The participants were given reading materials to study before and after the next step, which was a workshop. The readings were:

- *Multiliteracies: Rethinking What We Mean by Literacy and What We Teach as Literacy [in] the Context of Global Cultural Diversity and New Communications Technologies* by Mary Kalantzis and Bill Cope (1997)
- *A Pedagogy of Multiliteracies: Designing Social Futures* by the New London Group (1997)

The workshop was held to discuss their understandings from the literature, to clarify the concepts involved, and to explore how the framework might be applied in their own settings.

Next, each teacher collaborated with the researcher in choosing and applying some aspect of the framework. A planning session with the researcher was arranged to facilitate interpretations of the Multiliteracies and the translation of theory into practice. The researcher then observed the teacher in the classroom, either in person or by way of audio recording, according to the teacher's preference, and debriefed immediately afterward. Finally, an extended interview was conducted with each teacher in which the teacher was asked to review this teaching and identify which elements were perceived as being derived from the Multiliteracies framework.

In this way the participating teachers were interviewed before and after working with the framework in order to identify any growth or change in their perceptions about their teaching. The recordings were selectively transcribed and analyzed for the way the participants revealed their understandings about their teaching and about the four aspects of the Multiliteracies.

The procedure of working with the participants to help apply the Multiliteracies in the classroom was designed to put the ideas into a more practical perspective, calling on the researcher and practitioners to weigh what the framework had to offer and to debate and develop ideas about using it in practice. By observing the teachers in action, the researcher was able to obtain additional evidence of a more objective nature. At the same time, the study allowed the participants some space to develop their own ideas and try them out. According to Kemmis and McTaggart (as cited in Nunan, 1992), action research should be:

- carried out by practitioners
- collaborative
- aimed at changing things (Nunan, 1992, p. 17)

These features were in evidence in the following ways:

- The participants were given choices as to which part of the framework to focus on and were invited to make up their own minds about it.

- They collaborated with the researcher to establish a plan and carry it out.
- By participating in the study they had an opportunity to try to improve their teaching practice.

The design of the study, then, was aimed at providing the teachers with as much opportunity as possible to engage actively with the process as well as with the information presented.

Three factors in the teachers' practice emerged as the study progressed. First, as teachers they all engaged in Critical Framing as they situated the students' learning in their life worlds and related lessons to their needs. The workshop revealed a team of teachers who were accustomed to a discourse of discussing students' learning in these terms. Second, they encouraged Critical Framing capabilities in the students to differing degrees, according to their beliefs about what they should teach. Third, they exhibited different attitudes toward the new ideas presented by the Multiliteracies framework. In this area, the degree of acceptance or resistance expressed by the teacher was sometimes at odds with the teaching that was observed.

Anita

In the first interview, Anita provided a list of activities she had designed for her class, all of which showed an eye for practicality and transferability to real life. For example, the class would role-play a formal meeting in which the course itself was analyzed and discussed as if in an actual management setting.

She had developed a process of telling anecdotes about her own life and encouraging the students to do the same, in order to illustrate the lessons and to draw out similar experiences that students may have had. In this way both teacher and students would frame their past experiences and their language and culture learning in a critical way.

Anita saw Critical Framing as "an extra tool [for the students] to work with" and as "the thinking bit" of the framework. At the end, she said she enjoyed working with Multiliteracies and expressed a belief that her teaching approach had changed for the better. This was in evidence in the adjustments she had made in designing reading activities to encourage critical awareness, and certain students had responded well to this.

Barbara

While Barbara appeared to want to learn about new ideas, she also expressed resistance to those that did not fit with her existing beliefs. She felt that her pronunciation class had enough work to do developing comprehension skills without having to address Critical Framing as well. Nevertheless, she routinely used authentic texts in all her classes, and in choosing these, she herself was framing her teaching critically.

Barbara welcomed the opportunity to invite the researcher to speak to her Listening class about the Multiliteracies framework, to provide an authentic listening experience. This proved to be a form of Critical Framing in that the presentation served to frame the learning experience in two ways. First of all, it provided a justification to the students as to why the researcher would be observing their lesson. This served to keep the teacher's decision-making transparent to the students. Second, it offered them a broad perspective for the learning they were undertaking, placing it in the global context of educational theory and societal change. In this way, students were given an opportunity to reflect on their own learning and to understand it more deeply. This is surely one of the more important aspects of Critical Framing as "interpreting the social and cultural context of particular Designs of meaning" (New London Group, 1997, p. 43), where the design is the learning experience itself.

Colin

Although he was intellectually interested in learning about Multiliteracies, Colin could not initially see any relevance between it and the teaching he was responsible for:

> My job in computing is to match the students' ability with national standards. The quickest way for me to get there is for the students to replicate existing works, but of course, that denies, that disempowers the student in the designing process (Bray, 2000, p. 55).

However, he agreed to try to add a Critical Framing component by helping the students interpret the quality of the material they found on the Internet.

Two lessons were observed. The first, according to Colin, was simply a technical computing lesson, while the second was "Multiliteracies inspired" (Bray, 2000, p. 56). He was pleased to see that he could improve the quality of the students' learning by inserting suitable questions and taking a more reflective and contextualized approach, without the need for taking more class time.

Deirdre

This young teacher picked up on the idea of communication being visual as well as printed text, and on the strength of this, she decided to present a lesson on the use of graphics to represent statistical information. Her view was that by dealing with this already familiar material students would be able to learn the English vocabulary and expressions associated with the area, such as "pie chart" and "bar graph." In the process of coming to this decision, Deirdre had to stand back and look at the material from the students' perspective, and in so doing exercised Critical Framing.

However, the links that Deirdre made were not effectively transferred to the students, and although she claimed to have enabled them to reframe their existing knowledge, this was limited by the fact that she left it to them to make the connections with real-life situations. She stated in the final interview that learning materials could relate to different spheres of life, but that the integration of ideas was up to the individual student, not something a teacher could "force along" (Bray, 2000, 63). In holding to this opinion, she resisted one of the main ideas from the Multiliteracies framework, which is that critical awareness is an important part of what students must learn.

Eva

Eva's ideas were already in line with Multiliteracies concepts in many ways. She was quick to see the connection between the question about real-life practice and the Work Experience provided in the curriculum and said that her teaching included specific preparation for this. In class, she led discussions about culture: the students' home cultures and their adaptation to Australian culture. Whenever she introduced a new topic, she justified it to the class in terms of both the linguistic features they would learn from it and the application of the language to real life. In this way, the Critical Framing she used in devising the topic was communicated to the students so they could see the reasoning behind the teaching.

However, there were some signs that Eva was set in her ways. One was that her class discussions on culture were rather closed in that she would express her opinion first and then call on the students to support it. The most pronounced indication, though, was that she withdrew from the study before the point where she was to plan and implement a lesson. While it is true that she was busy, the fact remains that she did not place a high enough priority on the study to maintain her participation.

Relevant Literature

It is recognized that a continuous, cyclic process of reflection and action can contribute to the professional growth and renewal of language teachers. Donald Freeman's book, *Doing Teacher Research—From Inquiry to Understanding* (1998), is a well-known contribution to our ideas about inquiry-based teaching. Jill Burton points out that "reflective teaching enables teachers to think more effectively" (Burton, 2003, p. 9). Among the participants in this study, we can see this most clearly in Anita and Colin, who found for themselves that their thinking about Multiliteracies helped them improve the quality of the questions they asked their students.

The need for a reflective approach to professional development is driven by the complex nature of the task of teaching a language. Woods (1996, p. 14) examines the fact that a teacher's perspective of a particular lesson can be greatly at odds with that of a student, according to the criteria he or she brings to bear on the judgment of success. He suggests that each point of view has its own validity. So, too, an observer (an evaluator or, in this study, a researcher) can come away from a lesson with a different idea again of its success. A snapshot approach to evaluating a teacher is limiting and unlikely to reveal underlying patterns of classroom relationships or the intentions of the teacher (Woods, 1996, p. 17). Therefore, an overreliance on observation was avoided by including extended discussion with the participants, both one to one and as a group.

The complexity of the teaching task is partly a result of the interrelated and interactive relationships between the knowledge, values, and ethical dispositions of the teacher. A report by Scarino and Papademetrė draws attention to this aspect of the teaching of language.

> A system of categories, no matter how robust, cannot capture the integrated nature of teachers' work.... [W]hat is important is a notion of purposeful action in complex, contextual, real-life situations which call for initiative, judgment and self-awareness. (Scarino & Papademetre, 2004, p. 4)

Furthermore, the amount of experience a teacher has is not as important as the quality of the attitude that teacher displays toward his or her own practice. What matters most is the self-awareness the teacher brings to teaching, the ability to "take a stance towards ongoing improvement" (Scarino & Papademetre, 2004, p. 5). This stance became increasingly evident as the researcher collaborated with the participants and reflected on their responses. What emerged from this process was a concern that, whatever skills teachers display, whatever understandings or experience they have, the question is whether they take up a stance of examining their practice critically and adjusting it in the interests of the students' learning.

Distinctive Features

The quality of the teaching that emerged prominently from this study was the intensely personal nature of the teaching and learning that went on. When Anita, for example, revealed certain things about her background in order to elicit stories from the students, this led to a certain amount of self-exposure for her and for the students. She said she appreciated the way it could improve their confidence: "I think it makes them feel important, acknowledging what they've got to offer" (Bray, 2000, p. 41). This was her way of affirming her students as adults with experience of the world and capable of reflecting on it, and of using that experience as a resource for her language teaching.

Eva, too, spoke about the need to build trust within the class so that students would willingly engage in discussions, expressing their opinions and justifying them: "As the trust builds the language skills base builds" (Bray, 2000, p. 64). Cultivating an atmosphere of trust among the students and between the students and the teacher was an important foundation for the development of critical-thinking skills and the ability to express an argument effectively and persuasively in English. One topic the class engaged in was the idea of acculturation, in the form of the four stages of settlement identified as: euphoria, irritation and hostility, gradual adjustment, and adjustment. Students were encouraged to reflect on whatever stage they currently found themselves in, which was an "extraordinarily exposing exercise" as they recognized similarities in each other's responses (Bray, 2000, p. 64).

Just as culture is negotiated and contested in a language classroom (Pennycook, 2001, p. 34), so too the teachers debated their professional viewpoint in the workshop. Barbara, with her keen respect for the intelligence and dignity of her students, said in one interview that a critical approach might be appropriate for certain "cynical Europeans," but not necessarily for students from cultural backgrounds that do not encourage it. In the workshop, when the teachers talked about the debates the students had as part of the course, there was general agreement that they had great difficulty with rebutting each other's arguments. Consistent with her earlier comments, Barbara attributed this to the culture of the students, implying that the difficulty was to do with deeply entrenched attitudes and values. But Anita offered a contrasting view: "They just haven't done it before" (Bray, 2000, p. 40).

We can see from this how challenging the study was at a personal level for the teachers involved. As researcher, I was aware of suspending my own judgment of the teachers' practice in order to permit them to reflect for themselves. The quality of their teaching was revealed in the nature of their reflections, their willingness to engage in the process of self-reflection, and their openness to change as needed.

This is not as straightforward as it seems. Deirdre, for instance, expressed interest in Critical Framing but failed to encourage it in her students, as evidenced by the lesson that was observed. What she got confused about was that, in her thinking about her lesson plan, she herself used Critical Framing skills in order to ascertain the needs and perspectives of her students; however, the students were actually never given much opportunity to take on the role of Critical Framer for themselves. Conversely, Barbara underestimated her own ability to teach Critical Framing. As we have seen, she saw as problematic the cultural predisposition of some students to avoid critical approaches to learning, and felt that this constrained her to teach only linguistic skills. However, the talk given by the researcher on the Multiliteracies was a wonderful case of Critical Framing in which learners were encouraged to step back from their learning and look at it in a broader context. Once again, the teacher's evaluation of her own teaching was not to be taken at face value.

The gap between what teachers say they do and what they actually do is good reason for an evaluation process to include some kind of observation as a reality check. The difficulty with such procedures is their intrusiveness, at the very least a problem of "observer's paradox" (Labov, 1972, p. 256) in that the presence of an evaluator (or a microphone or camera) can of itself influence the behavior of the teacher and the students being observed. What helped to reduce this effect was the sense of control they had about the conduct of the study as a whole, since they were consulted on several aspects of the procedures and content. Their focus, as they conducted the observed lessons, was not on their own performance but on the responses of the students and what they seemed to be learning. The results of the observations were further balanced and extended by the discussions and interviews where they could express their views.

By giving the teachers some control over the conduct of the study and keeping their focus on their teaching and how it affected the learners, the researcher was able to build a relationship of trust with the participants. The study was built on an assumption that the teachers were professional people who wanted the best for their students.

Here, then, was a paradox worth striving for: *the focus of the teacher evaluation was never on evaluating the teachers.* Instead, the Multiliteracies framework itself was under scrutiny as much as the teachers and their practice. This was the perspective offered to the teachers right from the beginning, that their experience with their students and with the particular course was as valid as the theory provided by the New London Group. The process was a collaborative one, whereby teachers and researcher worked together toward improved learning for the students.

Caveats

One of the major outcomes of the study was that, although teachers had mixed responses to the idea of teaching Critical Framing skills to the students, they all made use themselves of these skills in designing their lessons. The process involves stepping back from the requirements of the curriculum and the students' preferences to make judgments about what learning experiences will be most effective in supporting their language development toward their life goals. In doing so, teachers will often draw on their own life experiences and preferred ways of learning. For example, Barbara used listening tasks from the educational radio station "Radio National" because this was her own preferred source of listening. On the other hand, Barbara also used the soap opera *Neighbours* as listening material, even though this conflicted with her personal taste in entertainment; the reason for this was that it gave students an example of more everyday conversational language (Bray, 2000, p. 50–51). In either case, the teacher takes up a frame through which to view her own experience in a way that will make it accessible to, and useful for, the students.

If teachers employ Critical Framing as part of the design process when planning lessons and materials, then one way they can pass on these skills to the students is by communicating the design process to them. By making the lessons transparent in this way, the students can themselves pick up on skills of Critical Framing for their own ongoing learning. A teacher whose skills in this area are limited or impoverished cannot provide effective leadership in the development of these skills in the learners.

> [W]hat teachers know and can do is the single most important influence on how and what students learn. (NCTAF, 1996, cited in Cochran-Smith, 2001, p. 8)

What these teachers demonstrated, then, was openness to learning about teaching, a willingness to reflect on their teaching practice and to continually improve. Learners acquire language in many different ways, so a teaching approach that works well with one group may not be appropriate for another. Teachers must develop a repertoire of techniques and be constantly extending it; they must adjust and fine-tune their strategies to suit the needs of their students, and also to respond to changing institutional requirements or even shifts in wider societal or cultural expectations. As the New London Group (1996) points out, we are living in a rapidly changing world that is reshaping itself as it comes to terms with new technologies of information and communication.

Critical Framing is a key feature of the process of ongoing continual improvement for teachers. The understanding they bring to bear in designing appropriate lessons and learning experiences for their students applies equally to their own learning and professional development. Critical Framing is also interrelated with cultural awareness[1] in that communicating across a cultural divide involves taking up a different "frame" or perspective, which usually means developing a kind of empathy for the other person. English language teachers generally do this as a matter of course, which is why they so often develop a close personal bond with their students.

In contrast, it must be noted that language proficiency tests are inclined to assess only the linguistic rather than the socio-cultural competence of language learners (Bray, 2005). The unfortunate "washback" effect of this is that social and cultural communication aspects of learning may be neglected in the classroom (Coombe, 2005, p. 33). However, social and cultural communication skills are crucial for students who are hoping to live in another country and make their way within its educational institutions and social systems. Teachers, therefore, need to be able to develop these cross-cultural skills in their learners, and this is why it is so important for them to be valued for their Critical Framing abilities. Teachers with an ability to apply critical perspectives will be better equipped to develop a learner-centered teaching approach, and they will be more likely to seek to cultivate cross-cultural skills and understandings in their students. By recognizing and encouraging this, we can hope for a kind of "wash forward" effect into language classrooms, where teachers will reject the limitations of a narrow linguistic approach and encourage, in their turn, the Critical Framing abilities of their students.

---

[1] As Angela Scarino notes, this concept is an important one for teacher development and deserves further examination.

Conclusion

This action research study was designed to explore the Multiliteracies curriculum framework in the light of the experiences of a team of teachers in a program for migrants preparing for work or further study. Procedures included interviews and a workshop to find out about the teachers' views about their own practice and about the framework, as well as an opportunity for them to choose an aspect to develop for a lesson, which was then observed by the researcher and evaluated in a final interview. In this way the study was designed to involve the teachers as much as possible and encourage them to engage with the process as well as the content of the research.

As they examined their teaching practice and responded to the ideas presented in the framework, the teachers revealed a lot about the strengths of their teaching and what made it effective. When given the chance to discuss their students and learn about some new ideas, the teachers demonstrated a professional attitude toward ongoing improvement. In particular, Critical Framing was an essential part of the process of designing learning experiences for their classes.

It became clear that the participants were teaching in a very engaged and personal way, which required a relationship of trust to be built up between teacher and students. In a similar way, participating in the study was personal and challenging for the teachers themselves, as they negotiated different perspectives among themselves in the workshop and discovered problems in their own teaching practice. A crucial feature of the study was giving the participants control over some aspects of the procedures and providing a secure environment for them to engage critically with new ideas.

In a rapidly changing world, Critical Framing is necessary for effective evaluation of the mass of information available to us. It is important for language teachers, both in designing learning experiences for their students and in pursuing their own ongoing professional development. It also has a cultural dimension in that communicating between cultures requires a shift of "frame" or perspective, an ability that is crucial for students aiming to study abroad. Teachers need to have highly developed social and cultural communication skills and a critical awareness of the needs of students in order to create a "wash forward" effect into language classrooms.

Conducting professional development for language teachers has a lot in common with teaching language, as it involves building on existing knowledge, creating a supportive environment for people to engage critically with change, and generating a cycle of reflection and action toward continuing improvement. By collaborating with teachers and focusing with them on student learning, evaluators can use their position as outsiders to encourage and promote the teachers' professional growth.

Discussion Questions

1. This study used the Multiliteracies framework as a starting point for professional exploration and debate. Here are some other suggestions: needs analysis, task-based learning, Total Physical Response, Systemic Functional Linguistics, and "top-down" and "bottom-up" approaches to learning language. Can you think of more?

2. Looking at your list, which includes your suggested topics, which of them might be a useful focus for professional development among the teachers in your work context?

3. How would you find agreement among your group of teachers on a suitable starting point?

4. What reading materials and other resources would you seek out to inform your exploration of the issue?

5. What procedures could be implemented in your context? How might you draw on the teachers' experience to develop a sense of collaboration?

6. What practical outcomes could you and the teachers work towards, e.g., a report, teaching materials, improved student feedback, a published article?

7. How would you evaluate the effects of your professional development program on the students?

Acknowledgments

I would like to express my appreciation for Jenny Barnett and Jill Burton for their support and inspiration for the study, and Angela Scarino and Bill Kennedy for their valuable feedback on this paper.

REFERENCES

Bray, L. (2000). *"Multiliteracies" for Adult Learners of English: An investigation of how the Multiliteracies framework may be applied in the Advanced English Migrant Program.* Thesis submitted for the degree of Master of Education in TESOL, University of South Australia, Adelaide.

———.(2005). How a theory of language can shed light on English language assessment. In C. Coombe, P. Davidson, & D. Lloyd (Eds.), *Proceedings of the 7th and 8th current trends in English language testing (CTELT) Conferences, Vol. 4.* UAE: TESOL Arabia.

Burton, J. (2003). *Seeking the standard.* Paper presented at CULIO'S 5th International Conference, Bangkok. Retrieved December 20, 2004, from http://www.bath.ac.uk/~edsajw/values/jbCULIpap.htm

Cochran-Smith, M. (2001). Constructing outcomes in teacher education: Policy, practice and pitfalls. *Education Policy Analysis Archives, 9*(11). Retrieved September 12, 2004, from http://epaa.asu.edu/epaa/v9n11.html

———. (2003). Sometimes it's *not* about the money: Teaching and heart. *Journal of Teacher Education, 54*(5), 371–375.

Coombe, C. (2005). Washback and the impact of high-stakes tests on teaching and learning. In D. Lloyd, P. Davidson, & C. Coombe (Eds.), *The fundamentals of language assessment: A practical guide for teachers in the Gulf.* Dubai: TESOL Arabia.

Department for Employment, Training & Further Education (South Australia) (1997). *Certificate III in advanced English proficiency (second language).* Adelaide.

Freeman, D. (1998). *Doing teacher research—From inquiry to understanding.* Boston: Heinle & Heinle.

Goodson, I. F., & Mangan, D. M. (1996). Computer literacy as ideology. *British Journal of Sociology of Education, 17*(1), 65–79.

Kalantzis, M., & Cope, B. (1997). Occasional paper No. 21: *Multiliteracies: Rethinking what we mean by literacy and what we teach as literacy [in] the context of global cultural diversity and new communications technologies.* Sydney: Centre for Workplace Communication and Culture.

Labov, W. (1972). *Language in the inner city: Studies in the black English vernacular.* Philadelphia: University of Philadelphia Press.

New London Group. (1996). A pedagogy of multiliteracies: Designing social futures. *Harvard Educational Review, 66*(1), 60–92.

———. (1997). Occasional paper no. 1: *A pedagogy of multiliteracies: Designing social futures.* Sydney: Centre for Workplace Communication and Culture.

Nunan, D. (1992). *Research methods in language learning.* Cambridge: Cambridge University Press.

Pennycook, A. (2001). Rethinking the tools and the trade of English language teaching. In Z. Syed & D. Heuring (Eds.), *Tools of the trade: Teaching EFL in the Gulf. 2000 Conference Proceedings, 1st Annual Teacher-to-Teacher Conference.* Abu Dhabi: Military Language Institute.

Scarino, A., & Papademetre, L. (2004). *Considerations in developing standards in teaching,* Background paper No.1 in the development of Standards in Teaching Languages and Cultures. Unpublished report prepared for the Department of Education and Children's Services. Adelaide: Research Centre for Languages and Cultures Education, University of South Australia, Adelaide.

Woods, D. (1996). *Teacher cognition in language teaching: Beliefs, decision-making and classroom practice.* Cambridge: Cambridge University Press.

CHAPTER 10

An Evaluation of Student Ratings of Teaching in a Japanese University Context

Peter Burden and Salah Troudi

Introduction and Theoretical Framework

There is an ongoing concern that university principals in Japan are using end-of-semester summative evaluations by students as the sole criteria for part-time lecturer retention or as a punitive measure to remove tenure in establishments with diminishing student enrollment. This is despite assertions that ratings should only be used to "make crude judgments" (d'Apollania & Abrami, 1997, p. 125), and as they are easy to abuse, should "never be the sole basis for evaluating teaching effectiveness" (Seldin, 1993, p. 40). Yet student evaluations are often invalidated through poor administration procedures, timing, and instructions (see Cashin, 1995, and Seldin, 1993, for a summary), which can lead to negative effects on teachers' careers.

Decisions to introduce teacher evaluation in the 1990s in Japan do not exist in a vacuum, so it is impossible to discuss classroom processes and evaluative decisions without considering the relationship to social and economic structures. As critical research explores and critiques power relationships that are in many instances simply taken for granted, an aim is to analyze these existing power relations and confront status quo assumptions. Research in the critical paradigm seeks to be *emancipatory,* moving away from a causal linear process, with an emphasis on discovery involving both insight and intuition.

This study seeks to identify and challenge underlying assumptions about student evaluation. In particular, the study focuses on *why* giving a closed-item questionnaire to students who have had just one semester in a university is considered to be *inherently suitable* for decisions including teacher retention. There is also a wider political question of who defines and articulates knowledge about teaching and whether teachers should be benign recipients. The study is also an attempt to create opportunities to discuss and debate with others involved in the educational process and help to "establish critical communities of enquirers" (Carr & Kemmis, 1986, p. 40).

Teacher Evaluation

Arguably, learners are not, in fact, "evaluating" but "rating" narrowly defined definitions of classroom practice that are then interpreted or "evaluated" by some source ultimately unknown to the student. Ratings are often used for summative evaluation focusing on judgments about instructor's teaching effectiveness, and less so for formative evaluation, which uses the ratings diagnostically. But are students aware of their usage? Because summative evaluation is increasing in Japan, questions remain as to whether students in their first semester of university are competent to evaluate teachers, especially when college teaching is so different from high school. Does this encourage faculty members to elicit satisfaction from their students by whatever means necessary or for reward by the administration, while faculty who elicit dissatisfaction, no matter the reason, may suffer consequences without the chance to defend themselves? Whether ratings actually assess teaching behavior or reflect characteristics of a course over which the teacher has little control, or of the raters themselves, are crucial questions—especially when ratings are used administratively.

Seldin (1993) notes that the number of institutions using ratings of teachers in the United States had climbed to 86 percent in 1993, and teachers were expected to improve their teaching because of student feedback. Students are seen as participants in the process. Smith and Carney (1990) note that many students have a cynical attitude that teachers themselves may "inadvertently promote through haphazard or scornful administration" (p. 1). As the use of results may be unclear to students, evaluation often becomes a "perfunctory exercise of little impact" (p. 6), which jeopardizes reliability and validity. Abbot, Wulff, Nyquist, Ropp, & Hess (1990) have observed that emphasis by institutions on the use of standardized ratings sometimes requires that students fill out the same form on every instructor at the end of every semester, which may heighten their indifference. Teacher concerns about fairness and usefulness have led to claims that only 23 percent of faculty made changes to their teaching based on student evaluations (Senior, 1999), the majority being fairly superficial changes, such as altering handouts. Infrequent use of student ratings to improve teaching can probably be traced to concerns teachers harbor about fairness and usefulness as serious doubts remain over content validity. There is insufficient evidence to establish the dimensions of effective teaching or whether the dimensions are compromised when rating across a wide range of courses, as teachers are not all using the same methods that are equally applicable to helping students learn.

We can also question to what extent ratings are influenced by variables unrelated to effective teaching such as lenient grading, as suggested by Greenwald and Gillmore (1997). That one or two disgruntled students who do not find the teaching style compatible to their learning styles can produce a significant difference in the final rating is often overlooked in the dangerous pursuit of high mean scores. Cashin and Downey (1992) question whether student learning can be used as a measure of effective instruction as good teaching is not that which necessarily produces the most learning. Learning styles may be inefficient as McKeachie (1997) observes when noticing that many students prefer teaching that enables them to listen passively—teaching that organizes the subject matter and prepares students well for tests. Senior (1999) notes that surveys often limit questions to low inference items such as "the classes started on time" referring to readily observable facts, while in "global" ratings, high inferential questions are ubiquitous. Teaching is a combination of high cognitive skills and improvisational performance, so evaluating teacher performance calls for items that require raters to make inferences based on pooled observations. Global, high-inference items often require knowledge of certain teaching techniques and the ability to recognize when they are being used and if they are effective or ineffective. Therefore, we can question whether untrained students have become qualified to rate teachers on high-inference items.

Generalizability of specific items and some of the factors they comprise is questionable when ratings are used across a variety of courses, instructors, students, and settings. Possible sources of bias, which is anything not under the control of the instructor, are very problematic, with variables needing to be controlled in personnel decisions (Cashin, 1995). Teachers are more likely to receive higher ratings in classes where students had prior interest or were taking courses as electives or for general interest, and there is a positive but low correlation between student ratings and expected grades. Humanities and arts courses receive higher ratings than math or science courses while it is reported that teachers of smaller classes tend to receive higher ratings (Hui & Leng, 2002). Group size can affect specific dimensions of effective teaching such as group interaction and instructional rapport.

Teacher Evaluation in Japanese Universities

Since the Second World War, the Japanese academic world has been strongly influenced by the United States, leading to the *University Council*, an advisory board to the Ministry of Education, requiring universities to apply themselves to the processes of self-monitoring and self-evaluation (Yonezawa, 2002). In 1994, 138 universities or approximately 20 percent were implementing class evaluation, up from 38 universities in 1992 (MEXT, 1996). In most cases teachers are being de-skilled as students are asked the extent to which classes meet their expectations, the efforts of teachers to make classes easy to understand, the use of teaching materials, and the characteristics of teachers such as enthusiasm and diction. The same Monbusho report published results of undergraduates' "wishes," noting that 65.7 percent of respondents wanted "easy to understand" classes with "useful content" (56.5 percent) while 36 percent wanted "easier credit approval," evaluation being mechanistic and reductionist. A later survey by the Ministry of Education shows that faculty evaluation at the Japanese universities has increased to 76 percent of 671 schools (University Council, 1998).

The prestigious Keio University was one of the first institutions to introduce evaluation in 1990. Kansai University established a similar system in 1994, asking students to respond to questions on interest aroused, ease of understanding, teachers' speaking style, and appropriate use of blackboards or audio-visual materials (Trends in Japan, 1997).

Are such student ratings applicable to Japanese culture? Okano and Tsuchiya (1999) note that there is strong informal communication, interdependence, and camaraderie among teachers in Japan, who believe that the informal sharing of experience among themselves is the most effective way of enhancing their individual professional development. Whereas in America the principal's leadership strongly affects school educational policies, Japanese teachers rate the influence of peers much higher in forming school policies and believe that what is expected of a principal is not exercising strong leadership but fostering cooperative consensus. As national universities are not well-organized communities but a congregation of extremely individualistic professors, there is little communication among the chairs of faculties, with lectures left entirely to the professors. Since the introduction of the Act of Tenure System (see Program for Educational Reform, August 5, 1997, Ministry of Education, Science, Sports and Culture) a selective tenure system to university faculty members is now in effect to "revitalize educational and research activities by raising liquidity of faculty members," (Monbusho, 1997) and teachers have suddenly been excluded from dialogue, debate, and critique on how education should change. Thus, the decision-making mechanism is not conducive to reform featuring a top-down organization.

The Study

While student evaluation is now becoming widely used in Japan, neither faculty nor students are informed in any concrete way as to its purpose, threatening consequential validity. Often, even the teachers do not receive any formative or summative feedback, and they aren't aware of administration procedures. Teachers are evaluated for promotion on scholarly output but may be putting their jobs at risk through failing to provide lessons that students claim to "want." Problematizing practice needs, as Pennycook (2001, p. 8) notes, "some sort of vision about what is preferable" to escape from unwanted labeling of merely "offering a bleak and pessimistic vision of social relations."

Research Questions

This study is an attempt to answer these research questions:

1. Do learners think evaluations are useful? Why or why not?
2. How should evaluation be subsequently used?
3. What would the students like to evaluate?

Method

The Instruments

The participants in this study belonged to three EFL classes, 40 students in each class, who were majoring in medicine, engineering, and law. Data for this study were collected in two stages using two different questionnaires.

Stage one
A week following the official administration of the teacher evaluations, in a lesson discussing positive or negative attributes and notions of "good" teaching, the students were asked if they would like to participate in "an evaluation of the evaluation." An open-ended questionnaire was given out comprising four questions. The students were informed about the purpose of the study, that answers would remain confidential, and that participation was voluntary; 89 students returned the questionnaire the following week for a return rate of 74 percent.

Stage two
A survey comprising a single open-ended question and 24 closed items was administered in two of the three classes, as the third class was unavailable that day. We wanted to allow students to provide their reasons for their opinions but the fifteen-week time constraints within a defined syllabus meant that interviews were impractical within classes of 40 students, yet we wanted to listen to them rather than only agreeing or disagreeing to a set of items. In the closed questions students were asked to circle the most appropriate answer on a seven-point agreement/disagreement continuum in which 1 indicates strong disagreement with the given statement and 7 strong agreement.

Responses were collected at the end of class: 59 out of 73 students filled in the questionnaire for a response rate of 81 percent. In order not to distort the quantitative data, the results of this small sample are shown as whole numbers. The sample was typical of *freshmen* classes at this national university.

The Procedure

Through coding, all the comments for each question were ordered into topics and further subcategorized. Key word analysis from paragraph to sentence generated a great deal of data as some students expressed more than one comment on a question. The data from the closed item survey were analyzed using SPSS v.11.0, generating descriptive statistics and an acceptable Alpha reliability score of .78.

Results and Discussion

1. Usefulness of Evaluation

As shown in Table 10.1, the majority of learners see evaluation as useful in terms of making lessons understandable, raising teachers' awareness of learner opinions, and encouraging change in conscious behavior. A number of students cited the "customer" analogy, stating that as they pay for lessons they have the right to point out poor teaching and concomitant need for remedial action. Students' comments were often framed in terms of effort required to make lessons understandable. As it is impossible to have lessons without learners, teachers should take learner's comments to heart while endeavoring to improve. Students commented that evaluation "is their voice" and that it is their chance to be heard. However, voice is of little use if no one is listening, and students expressed ambivalence as to whether teachers are learning or implementing change from comments.

Many students also acknowledged the uncertainty of change arising from evaluation, expressing doubt in terms of "if." Many students see evaluation as useful *if* teachers take comments to heart, or *if* they have the inclination to change. Doubts are expressed about chances of change if teachers do not read evaluations, so evaluation is useful only if teachers take them seriously. Furthermore, students saw usefulness in terms of depending on the teacher, or whether teachers care or not. Where evaluation was not very useful, students stated that student opinion is so varied as to be impractical, and a lack of guidance for teachers who receive a low appraisal is problematic. The few answers expressing lack of usefulness saw evaluation in terms of "bad" teachers not wanting to improve or reflect, and being too set in their ways.

Every respondent saw evaluation in terms of formative lesson improvement even though the official form was not distributed until the twelfth week of a fifteen-week semester. Although seen as useful, there seems to be a belief that improvement is only possible if the teacher has the will or inclination. This illustrates a widespread belief that ratings are seen only by teachers and are

---

Table 10.1: Do Learners Think Lesson Evaluations Are Useful? N = 89

Lesson evaluations are useful	51
Lesson evaluations are useful *if*	20
Lesson evaluations are not very useful	8
Lesson evaluations are not useful	4
Don't know	6
Total number of comments	89

Data taken from open-ended questionnaire

thus not subject to any hierarchical influence or pressure to improve. Only one student noted the necessity of guidance and that teachers can somehow improve by themselves.

2. How to Use Teacher Evaluation?

Table 10.2 shows that many saw usage in diagnostic terms of lesson evaluation for teacher reference, observation, reflection, change, and understanding. This is seen in terms of maintaining standards, enabling the teacher to get an idea of what students want and their points of view. Teachers should improve low scores, address weakness pointed out, and revise their thoughts to change or rethink their "ways."

Some students commented that there should be further feedback and discussion whereby teachers should solicit opinions from the students who should be encouraged to have the freedom to express views at any time. Evaluation needs to be used more strictly by all parties, and the university authorities should investigate the results with the "teacher in charge." A number of students wanted the results made public as not only teachers but students have the right, as noted in Spencer and Schmelkin's (2002) study, for future class/teacher selection. Therefore, to increase validity, student awareness of the importance of their input needs to be raised. Students also feel they should be free to submit suggestions at any time, with facilities available for them to address comments anonymously. As Ballantyne (1998) notes, it is important in the teacher/student relationship that the teacher is seen as a "real person" (p. 157) who makes errors, but who also takes comments on board. Teachers

Table 10.2: How Should Evaluation Be Used? N = 97	
For lesson improvement	19
For reference	14
For observing, reflecting	11
For deeper understanding	3
Should be made public	7
Students should express opinion	5
Free responses should be used	3
Authorities should be involved	3
Should be given at the start of the semester	1
Should be given at mid-point	19
Up to the teacher	6
To fire the teacher	1
To determine their salary	1
As now	3
Don't know	7
Total number of comments	97

Data taken from open-ended questionnaire

should tell students of changes made due to constructive feedback, or carry feedback over from one semester to the next, announcing at the beginning of a new course that they are trying a new approach based on comments of previous students. Acknowledgment often reinforces the importance of ratings and comments.

Abbot et al. (1990) argue that dissatisfaction can be alleviated if someone other than the teacher facilitates small group evaluation mid-semester to come to a consensus about the strengths of the class, areas for change, and how students would recommend change. The facilitator and teacher meeting to discuss findings is arguably more satisfactory than summative standardized methods of ratings.

Some students noted that they did not know how evaluations should be used as it was not their job or position to comment, while others sensed a futility in that teachers did not place value on learners' opinions or that the teacher's personality was in some way disagreeable. Students commented that usage of student evaluation is up to the teachers' discretion, and that teachers may not feel the need to do anything if comments represent just an individual student. Just one student freely stated that teachers should be dismissed or salary reduced, illustrating that learners have little comprehension of evaluation for summative purposes.

In Table 10.3, learner beliefs show 44 of the students disagree that evaluations are used in determining salary or to make decisions about promotion, and only seven agree that evaluations are used in teacher retention. Because of the serious implications for teachers, one would expect students to rate the teacher "leniently" (Centra, 1979) in salary, tenure, or retention decisions instead of "venting personal animosities" (Smith & Carney, 1990, p. 2) and thus leading to a higher mean average score. Students' knowledge of the evaluation process arguably affects its validity. If students are unaware of the rationale for evaluation, indifference is inadvertently encouraged, while if students are aware that ratings are used for personnel decisions, they generously rate teachers higher than if for only course improvement leading to a mismatch in perception between the students and management regarding the use of evaluation forms. Students are not aware of the hidden agenda in that they lack information about a crucial purpose of evaluation—retention or non-retention of teachers.

3. Learners' Views of What Should Be Evaluated

This open-ended question was administered along with the closed-item questionnaire and so 59 students responded. Table 10.4 shows that the students' largest concern was to understand content and the teacher's ability to communicate. As this evaluation was conducted in an English "conversation" class, the students commented on the amount of time the teacher speaks English, whether there is English throughout, and whether teachers enhanced learners'

Table 10.3: What Do Students Think Evaluations Are Used for? N = 59

To make decisions about teachers' promotion

1	2	3	4	5	6	7	Mean	S.D.
25	10	9	4	6	3	2	2.54	1.784

To make decisions about teachers' salaries

1	2	3	4	5	6	7		
29	11	4	6	7	1	1	2.29	1.641

To dismiss teachers

1	2	3	4	5	6	7		
32	8	8	4	5	1	1	2.14	1.559

To improve teaching

1	2	3	4	5	6	7		
0	4	2	11	17	13	12	5.17	1.404

To make course improvements

1	2	3	4	5	6	7		
1	2	3	9	21	11	12	5.17	1.392

Data taken from survey

ability to improve conversation skills through allowing learners to play a part or to contribute while having sufficient opportunities to speak English. Teachers' enthusiasm for the subject as demonstrated by being active, showing effort, trying hard, and being receptive, and the lesson being enjoyable, interesting, and fun were all important. Students believed that lessons would get a good form of evaluation if interest and curiosity are aroused. Classes are beneficial if content is meaningful or useful and if the objectives of the syllabus are reached. Only one student tied ease of the class to positive evaluation.

However, there is a need to research links between good teaching and good learning. We have a situation whereby certain classroom processes are regarded as worthy, leading to a prepackaged agenda with teachers' purpose being devised by students. If there are students who are not working hard to keep up with the class, should teachers be downgraded for failure of students to learn? As Scriven (1981) notes, teachers should provide the best possible environment without having to guarantee results no matter how little effort is produced by the students. The small number of "good teacher studies" in Japan listed similar attributes such as "kind," "friendly," "understandable," and "fun" (Hadley & Yoshioka-Hadley, 1996), which have clear implications: Doing one's best may not be enough to get glowing evaluations from students who are often using judgment criteria that are significantly different from the teacher's own. Worryingly, Shimizu (1995) suggests that foreign staff are evaluated differently from Japanese teachers.

Table 10.4: What Would You Like to Evaluate? N = 66	
Understandability	16
Teacher's method	12
Enthusiasm for the subject	9
Enjoyment	11
Usefulness of the content	7
Chances to participate	5
Kindness	2
Easiness of the content	1
Objectives of syllabus reached	1
The outcomes	1
Nothing	1
Total number of comments	66

Data taken from open-ended question in survey

Foreign expatriates are often valued more for personal characteristics such as friendliness. Hence, these teachers may be burdened with having to fulfill student expectations of being interesting, cheerful, and entertaining. This can be seen in part in Table 10.5 where twenty students feel that it's important that the teacher be amusing.

Kerridge and Mathews (1998) illustrate problems of asking students about teacher attributes using a parallel example of a patient in hospital who cannot evaluate medical science and so record perceptions of hotel decor, interpersonal skills of staff, food, and what services appear on time. By doing so, peripheral services are understood and evaluated rather than the core service. This can lead to an entire battery of subjective parameters appearing on ratings that students believe teachers must conform to and that actually have a different appeal for each student.

Scriven (1981) adds that style indicators have no reliable correlation with short- or long-term learning by students across a whole range of subjects, levels, and circumstances and so should not be used. The closed data (Table 10.5) were largely introduced to dispel some popular classroom folklore in Japan that teachers who use video receive high popularity ratings, as do teachers who give little homework.

Simmons' (1996) claim that students may judge a teacher as not "aesthetically acceptable" and "rendered less capable" of teaching seem to have been rejected in this study. However, 50 students thought that teachers should be evaluated on subject knowledge (p. 209). However this is just one knowledge base. Teachers also need practical knowledge; a repertoire of classroom techniques; and pedagogical knowledge, including the "ability to restructure content knowledge for teaching purposes and to plan, adapt and improvise." Arguably, there should be discussion beyond simplistic manifestations of knowledge as to how different kinds of knowledge, the core components, can benefit the learning experience.

Table 10.5: How Students Think Teachers Should Be Evaluated. N = 59

by personal appearance

1	2	3	4	5	6	7	Mean	S.D.
42	13	2	2	0	0	0	1.39	0.27

by how much they use AV materials

1	2	3	4	5	6	7		
28	15	6	6	1	2	1	2.1	1.459

by how amusing they are

1	2	3	4	5	6	7		
11	7	8	13	10	3	7	3.96	1.923

by how much homework they give

1	2	3	4	5	6	7		
20	8	10	10	9	1	1	2.78	1.641

by how interesting the textbook is

1	2	3	4	5	6	7		
8	3	8	10	11	11	8	4.32	1.916

by how punctually they start and finish class

1	2	3	4	5	6	7		
7	10	14	11	8	6	3	3.56	1.684

by how friendly they are

1	2	3	4	5	6	7		
7	3	3	12	16	14	4	4.44	1.735

by how much they know about the subject

1	2	3	4	5	6	7		
3	0	2	4	13	16	21	5.64	1.529

Data taken from survey

Some Implications

What Is Effective Teaching?

Often the primary concern in evaluation is learner satisfaction with instruction. Learners are viewed as consumers of the teaching process. Wachtel (1998) notes some of the caveats including a presumed consensus in evaluating effective teaching while there is no such agreement about what constitutes effective teaching. As teachers are subject to highly emotive "evaluation" and its implications for good teaching, there needs to be a system whereby teaching is not valued against mandated standards and low inference comments from students. To avoid bias, gathering evidence from different sources is vital, including peer appraisal and varied observational circumstances to allow for different classroom emphases. There is a need for a comprehensive, teacher-centered, teacher-led evaluation based on a hallmark of "good teaching." The teacher should be articulated through a structured multifaceted evaluation process. Since social conditions are constantly changing, education needs to be reconstructed accordingly. Unlike the common fixed instruction with homogenized lesson plans, curricula, and pedagogy, which neglects novel political, cultural, or ecological problems, there has to be pedagogical alternatives in terms of the students' needs and problems. As Morgan (1998) notes, students are not just entering a new culture of holidays, sports, and food, but also entering a new culture of politics, employment, and a social world where sophisticated forms of exclusion exist.

The governing definition of effectiveness is closely linked to *measurable* achievement so that discussion about the complex nature of effectiveness is discouraged. Arguably, evaluation leads to the hierarchy determining classroom practice and "desirable" teaching outcomes with sterile, narrowly defined competencies identifying the "good teacher" as one who expresses enthusiasm, smiles a lot, and displays interest. Instead of focusing on ends and means of education, we need to consider the conditions under which learners speak and how teachers can encourage language learners to become more communicatively competent. Instead of the "verified" effective teacher and the single-minded focus on these isolated components of effective teaching, we must look at the process of interaction and how learners are reorganizing a sense of who they are and how they relate to the social world. So far, moral aspects of effectiveness are removed from the evaluation procedure. Questions about justice, humanity, compassion, and their relationship to effective teaching lead to a necessity for empowerment (Pennycook, 2004) of learners through the provision of a critical analytical framework to help them reflect on their own language experiences and practices in the wider world. Engaging in needs analysis we should not think of students as "novices who must surrender their own language and modes of thought to the requirement of the target community" (Benesch, 1997, p. 729).

There is a need for a process whereby administrators are also subject to evaluation. Self-evaluation should also be introduced to encourage faculty efforts at professional development such as workshops and presentations aimed at improving teaching. Through quality assurance there needs to be negotiation between faculty and administrators about reasonable and acceptable standards, with systems in place to ensure that quality is regularly assessed and corrections made where necessary. Schools need to be open to change, encouraging innovation and facilitating communication. McKeachie (1997) adds that administrators have stereotypes about what good teaching involves with negative information likely to be weighted more heavily than positive. To avoid evaluation being a convenient weapon administrators can wield to prune overstaffing, ethical considerations need to be enshrined in a policy document whereby teachers who are subject to consistently poor evaluations have the chance to review and react to descriptions of unsatisfactory practice with guidelines or descriptions of practice providing time for improvement.

Richards (2001) recommends access to, and visibility of, administrative leaders who are receptive to teachers' suggestions and allow for shared decision-making with input from multiple sources, while Boore (1993) suggests widespread use of quality circles, initially introduced by Japanese manufacturers to improve the quality of their manufactured goods via human resource development, using available talents; regularly holding brainstorming sessions; and addressing problem-solving through information, idea gathering, coordination, and liaison. If, as some students noted, teachers should receive "good teacher" training, there is a need for a support system to be in place. Faculty need assistance in their effort to "improve," and in removing deeply held beliefs that faculty evaluation is not merely punitive, but is also diagnostic. One definition of quality involves "fitness for purpose" (Boore, 1993, p. 199) as many teachers use a conventional teaching method without considering underlying principles while students have tended to accept whatever pattern they have received as normal.

If we are to believe evaluation should benefit the system, administrators and teachers need to consider what is legitimate knowledge reflecting knowledge as tentative and problematic rather than instrumental. Teachers need to be flexible, adopting reflective thought because as Schon (1983) notes it is important to avoid practice becoming repetitive and routine.

Discussion Questions

1. How are EFL or ESL teachers evaluated in your professional context? Can teachers evaluate themselves or their peers?

2. Do students play any role in teacher evaluation in your professional context?

3. Does students' evaluation of teachers have any effect on pedagogical decisions and curriculum changes?

4. Do teachers receive any pedagogical feedback after their evaluations, and does this feedback affect their classroom practice?

5. Have a critical look at a current instrument used for teacher evaluation in your context, e.g., a multiple-choice questionnaire or a direct class-room observation, and see what approach to teacher effectiveness it reflects.

REFERENCES

Abbot, R., Wulff, D., Nyquist, J., Ropp, V., & Hess, C. (1990). Satisfaction with the process of collecting student opinions about instruction: The student perspective. *Journal of Educational Psychology, 82*(2), 201–206.

Ballantyne, C. (1998). Improving university teaching: Responding to feedback from students. In N. Zepke, L. Leach, & A. Viskovice (Eds.), *Adult learning cultures, challenges and choices in times of change* (pp. 155–165). Wellington, Australia: WP Press.

Benesch, S. (1997). Needs analysis and curriculum development in EAP: An example of a critical approach. *TESOL Quarterly, 30*(4), 723–738.

Boore, J. (1993). Teaching standards from quality circles. In R. Ellis (Ed.), *Quality assurance for university teaching* (pp. 194–211). Buckingham, UK: Open University Press.

Carr, W., & Kemmis, S. (1986). *Becoming critical. Education, knowledge and action research.* London: RoutledgeFalmer.

Cashin, W. (1995). Student ratings of teaching: The data revisited. In *IDEA paper No. 32* (pp. 1–9). Manhattan, KS: Kansas State University, Center for Faculty Evaluation and Development.

Cashin, W., & Downey, R. (1992). Using global rating items for summative evaluation. *Journal of Educational Psychology, 84*(4), 563–572.

Centra, J. (1979). *Determining faculty effectiveness.* San Francisco: Jossey-Bass.

d'Apollania, S., & Abrami, P. (1997). Navigating student ratings of instruction. *American Psychologist, 52*(11), 1198–1208.

Greenwald, A., & Gillmore, G. (1997). Grading leniency is a removable contaminant of student ratings. *American Psychologist, 52*(11), 1209–1217.

Hadley, G., & Yoshioka-Hadley, H. (1996). The culture of learning and the good teacher in Japan: An analysis of student views. *The language teacher, 20*(9), 53–55.

Hui, L., & Leng, G. (2002). Biases in student evaluation of teaching: The case of faculty of economics and administration, University of Malaya. In *Faculty of Economics and Administration working paper no. 2002-2003,* (pp. 1–19). Kuala Lampur: University of Malaysia.

Kerridge, J., & Mathews, B. (1998). Student ratings of courses in HE: Further challenges and opportunities. *Assessment and Evaluation in Higher Education, 23*(1), 71–83.

McKeachie, W. (1997). Student ratings: The validity of use. *American Psychologist, 52*(11), 1218–1225.

MEXT (Ministry of Education, Culture, Sports, Science, and Technology). (1996). *Japanese government policies in education, science, sports and culture 1995: Remaking universities: Continuing reform of higher education.* Printing Bureau, Tokyo: Ministry of Finance.

Monbusho (Ministry of Education, Science, Sports and Culture). (1997). *Program for educational reform (Revised on August, 5 1997).* Retrieved from www. mext.go.jp/english/news/1997/10/971002.htm

Morgan, B. (1998). *The ESL classroom: Teaching, critical practice, and community development.* Toronto: University of Toronto Press.

Okano, K., & Tsuchiya, M. (1999). *Education in contemporary Japan.* Cambridge: Cambridge University Press.

Pennycook, A. (2001). *Critical applied linguistics: A critical introduction.* Mahwah, NJ: Lawrence Erlbaum Associates.

Pennycook, A. (2004). Critical applied linguistics. In A. Davies & C. Elder (Eds.), *Handbook of applied linguistics* (pp. 1–30). Oxford: Blackwell.

Richards, J. (2001). *Curriculum development in language teaching.* Cambridge: Cambridge University Press.

Schon, D. (1983). *The reflective practitioner: How professionals think in action.* New York: Basic Books.

Scriven, M. (1981). Summative teacher evaluation. In J. Millman (Ed.), *Handbook of teacher evaluation,* (pp. 244–271). Beverly Hills, CA: Sage.

Seldin, P. (1993). The use and abuse of student ratings of professors. *The Chronicle of Higher Education, 39,* 40–43.

Senior, B. (1999, April 7–10). Student teaching evaluations: Options and concerns. In *ASC proceedings of the 35th annual conference* (pp. 251–260). San Luis Obispo, CA: California Polytechnic State University.

Shimuzu, K. (1995). Japanese college student attitudes towards English teachers: A survey. *The Language Teacher, 19*(10), 5–8.

Simmons, T. (1996). Student evaluation of teachers: Professional practice or punitive policy? *JALT Testing and Evaluation SIG Newsletter, 1*(1), 12–16.

Smith, M., & Carney, R. (1990, April). *Students' perceptions of the teaching evaluation process.* Paper presented at the annual meeting of the American Educational Research Association, Boston.

Spencer, K., & Schmelkin, L. (2002). Student perspectives on teaching and its evaluation. *Assessment and Evaluation in Higher Education, 27*(5), 397–409.

Trends in Japan. (1997, November 21). *Grading the teachers: More schools allowing student evaluation.* Retrieved from http://www.jinjapan.org/ trends98/honbun/ntj971121.html.

University Council. (1998). *A vision for universities in the 21st century and reform measures.* Tokyo: Ministry of Education.

Wachtel, H. (1998). Student evaluation of college teaching effectiveness: A brief overview. *Assessment and Evaluation in Higher Education, 23*(2), 191–213.

Yonezawa, A. (2002). The new quality assurance system for Japanese higher education: Its social background, tasks and future. *Research in University Evaluation, 2,* 23–33.

CHAPTER 11

An Exploration of Teaching Effectiveness: An Attempt to Define the Less Easily Definable

Deniz Kurtoğlu Eken

Introduction

Teaching effectiveness necessitates a theory of effective language teaching and a rich understanding of the key principles behind it. Such a theory can only be arrived at through an in-depth exploration of teaching from multiple perspectives. Based on this belief and the need to develop criteria for teaching effectiveness, an extensive research study examining the less easily definable aspects of teaching, such as the teacher's personal qualities and communication skills/interaction with students as well as what she calls, "affective-level" techniques, is presented. This leads to a discussion of the distinctive features of the effective teaching criteria and feedback and evaluation tools, a detailed account of the feedback received on the use of the criteria in the research context, and reference to its use in other similar contexts in Turkey.

The study was conducted over a two-year academic period between 1998–2000, the primary aim being an in-depth exploration of teaching effectiveness at Bilkent University School of English Language (BUSEL) in Ankara, where teacher training and development are key activities in promoting, evaluating, and maintaining teaching effectiveness. A core constituent of most training and development activities in BUSEL is classroom observation, carried out by trainers and academic managers for developmental purposes, for assessment, or for both. For assessment purposes, observers mainly used criteria set by Cambridge ESOL, and for developmental observations similar or more specific criteria focusing on one aspect of teaching, jointly decided on with the teacher observed, was used. Despite externally or internally set criteria, at the time of the research study, trainers at BUSEL often experienced situations where they found it difficult to comment on certain aspects of a lesson, feeling that there was something missing, but found it difficult to say exactly what it was. There were times when a trainer, after an observation, would say to his or her colleagues, "The lesson was O.K. Everything went according to plan, but there seemed to be something missing and I don't know exactly what it was." Similar experiences were also shared by other trainers in the group, and as a result it became necessary to explore these "emic" experiences with a view to having an enriched understanding of teaching effectiveness. As one of the trainers noted in an initial interview, if we could be more aware of what constitutes these experiences, we can be much more effective as teachers and trainers by giving more specific guidance to ourselves and to teachers (Teacher Trainer, TT8).

The study thus aimed to explore three research questions on teaching effectiveness:

- What accounts for the challenging experiences of BUSEL trainers regarding teaching effectiveness in classroom observations?
- What is the relationship between these challenging experiences and effective teaching?
- What form of training and development would be most beneficial in helping teachers to develop teaching effectiveness in the areas identified by the research?

Description

Over the decades there have been numerous studies and discussions on teaching effectiveness and the behaviors of successful teachers (Ornstein, 1990; Brookfield, 1990; Weimer, 1993; Engeström, 1994; Cullingford, 1995; Kyriacou, 1998). These have generated a wealth of definitions of effective teaching and the effective teacher, lists of effective teaching behaviors, and different frameworks and guidelines for teaching effectiveness. Azarov (1988) asserts that in effective teaching, much depends on individual characteristics of the creative personality and that teachers differ from each other not only in terms of the "stock" of techniques they use, but above all, by the manner in which these are implemented, which is marked by their individuality. As Hargreaves (1998, p. 835) also observes, good teachers are charged with "positive emotion" and their teaching is not just a matter of knowing their subject, being efficient, having the appropriate competences, or learning all the right techniques, but involves significant emotional understanding and emotional labor as well. Similarly, van Mannen (1995, p. 44) refers to "pedagogical tact" which occurs when the teacher "has the sensitive ability to interpret inner thoughts, understandings, feelings and desires of children from indirect clues such as gestures, demeanor, expression and body language." Although some of these concepts as well as others such as Gardner's (1993) interpersonal and intrapersonal intelligences and Goleman's (1995) emotional intelligence could relate in one way or another to BUSEL trainers' difficulties in identifying the less easily definable aspects of teaching, they did not appear to accurately or fully capture trainers' challenging experiences in classroom observations and hence led to a further need for the study.

Research Design

The research was designed as a case study based on naturalistic inquiry (Patton, 1987; Bogdan & Biklen, 1992) without any manipulation of or intervention on informants' experiences. The study was holistic in nature (Patton, 1987) as it aimed to account for trainers', teachers', and students' experiences with effective teaching as a whole. It was also descriptive, focusing largely on an exploration of informants' experiences and perceptions. There were three informant groups in the study: teacher trainers, teachers, and students in BUSEL. The first group of informants consisted of six British and two Turkish trainers, all with a minimum of three years of training experience. At the time of the study, half of the trainers were tutors on the Certificate for Overseas Teachers of English (COTE) Course, and the other half were tutors on the Diploma in Teaching English as a Foreign Language to Adults (DTEFLA) Course. The second informant group consisted of a total of 72 teachers, 32 with more than five years of teaching experience, 20 with three to five years, and 20 novice teachers, all teaching at a variety of levels. In the third and final group, there were 32 students who, at the time of the study, were at the pre-faculty level and also in their first year as a student in BUSEL. At the time of the study, levels at BUSEL consisted of Foundation (Beginners, Post-Beginners, and Pre-Intermediate), Intermediate, Upper-Intermediate, and Pre-Faculty. The length of the courses at different levels varied between eight and sixteen weeks. The normal tuition period for a student starting at Foundation Level was two years.

Data Collection

The data collection was carried out using five different instruments: individual interviews with eight teacher trainers, group interviews with 32 students, individual interviews with sixteen teachers, classroom observations with sixteen teachers, an analysis of 40 trainer feedback forms on observations, a teacher trainer questionnaire, and a video-based lesson observation and group discussion with the eight trainers.

Step 1. Individual Interviews with Trainers

The aim of these interviews was to explore trainers' perceptions of teaching effectiveness, their positive and also challenging experiences in classroom observations. The interviews were a combination of the standardized open-ended interview and the interview guide approach (Patton, 1987) in order to ensure a certain degree of systematicity as well as some flexibility in probing during the interview. The main question types used in the interview were a combination of experience, opinion, and belief questions (cf. Appendix A). The interviews were recorded with the permission of the trainers to allow for successful in-depth interviewing and reliable data. Later, they were also fully transcribed and a copy of the transcripts sent to the informants for data validation purposes.

Step 2. Individual Interviews with Teachers and Group Interviews with Students

The aim of the individual and group interviews was to explore teachers' and students' perceptions of teaching effectiveness, their positive and also negative experiences in teaching/learning, and to later see how the experiences they described related to the trainers' positive and challenging experiences in classroom observations. The questions used were therefore very similar (cf. Appendix A). These interviews were also recorded, fully transcribed, and later validated by the informants.

Step 3. Classroom Observations

The classroom observations were carried out with teachers who, at the time of the study, were participants on an in-service trainer training course on which I was a tutor. Therefore, the observations were conducted as part of the developmental course activities but later, with the teachers' consent, the data from the observations was also used for the purposes of this research. The instrument used in these observations was the same as the one all other trainers used in observations: a running commentary (a real-time observation tool providing a detailed account of the lesson through a description of the stages of the lesson, timing, and comments by the observer) and a general comments section consisting of "strong points" and "points to think about." The data from the observations was used for an analysis of teaching effectiveness in terms of what contributes to such effectiveness and what appears to hinder it.

Step 4. Document Analysis

With the permission of the teachers and trainers concerned, the data from written feedback forms (running commentaries and general comments sheets) on lessons observed by trainers over a period of six years in the context of COTE and DTEFLA training courses were analyzed in order to gain further insights on what contributes to teaching effectiveness and what hinders it.

Step 5. Questionnaire

This was a questionnaire for trainers based on the initial analysis of the data obtained. The questionnaire consisted of four sections, the first three of which were designed using the Likert scale, and the last section using an open-ended question. The items in the questionnaire were based on the initial analysis of the strong points identified in the classroom observations and the written feedback forms and on a selection of quotations from the interview data with trainers, teachers, and students (cf. Appendix B).

Step 6. Video-Based Lesson Observation and Group Discussion

In the final stage of the data collection process, trainers were asked to watch and comment on three different lesson extracts from the video *Looking at Language Classrooms* (Bampfield, 1997). The aim of this process was to get more specific data on actual lesson extracts from trainers on what aspects of lessons or teaching they may be finding difficult to comment on when they feel something is missing or lacking. The instrument trainers were asked to use was similar to the general comments sheet used in observations and consisted of three sections: strong points/positive points; points to think about/suggestions; and general comments related to the lesson/teaching. The video-based lesson observations were followed by a group discussion in which trainers discussed their views on the three lesson extracts with respect to former experiences they may have found challenging. The discussion was recorded and later fully transcribed for analysis purposes.

Findings

The data obtained from these procedures were analyzed qualitatively with the use of inductive analysis and quantitatively by using descriptive statistics. Internal reliability on the coding of data (e.g., interview transcripts) was also ensured with the help of an informed colleague.

The findings obtained from the study reveal that trainers' difficulties in trying to account for what may be missing in some observed lessons are closely related to the personal qualities of the teacher, the teacher's communication skills, and interaction with students, and to the teacher's use of what I have called "affective-level" techniques. The interview data with trainers, teachers, and students reveal that personal qualities refer to the general attitudinal qualities that the teacher has and displays as a teacher:

> When I came out of the lesson, I said 'Yes!!!' It was to do with the teacher's self-confidence, being interested in what she was doing, loving what she was doing, not just doing it for the sake of doing it—having a sense of satisfaction in what she was doing—being genuine, honest, open in dealing with students. (TT5)

The second area, communication skills and interaction with students, refers to more specific attitudinal qualities and skills that the teacher has and uses in order to establish and maintain effective communication with the students:

> I think as a teacher, you've got to be aware that you're dealing with a group of people that have feelings and that it's not just a class, just 20 people—it's 20 individuals who might be feeling ill or depressed or can't be bothered and that they're all different...and I think it's the human side that's really important. (Teacher 3)[1]

---

[1]   The informants were numbered randomly within their informant groups (i.e., 1–8 for trainers, 1–32 for students) to observe confidentiality in the presentation of data.

Finally, affective-level techniques are techniques and skills that the teacher uses as part of his or her teaching methodology in order to create a positive learning environment and to affectively involve students in the lessons:

> The teacher should do this job because s/he loves it not just to earn a living. You can tell very easily if the teacher loves what s/he is doing. For example, from the way s/he responds to your questions. Some teachers could explain something ten times to help you and they wouldn't feel forced to do it; they'd want to do it, but others would just give you a quick, evasive answer or would ask, 'Have you still not understood?' (Student Group 3)

The data obtained from the different observations and from the teacher trainer questionnaire reveal the same three main areas with respect to what may account for the challenges experienced by trainers in trying to define the less easily definable and support the data obtained from the interviews with trainers, teachers, and students. The quotations that follow were among those ranked highest in terms of their conceptual relation to trainers' experiences in trying to account for the less easily definable aspects in teaching effectiveness:

> [Times when I've felt something was missing are] times when I have not participated in the lesson at all and neither have many of my friends. You know, times when the teacher has taught the lesson, standing at the board, explaining things, etc., but then the lesson is over for both the teacher and the Ss. and no one has really participated. (Student Group 4)

> It has to do with interest and ability to teach—not ability in terms of knowing specific techniques and methods, but being able to feel the classroom atmosphere, understand Ss.' faces, even little expressions...If you don't have that interaction, that communication, and that atmosphere, you are not going to have optimum learning. (TT1)

With respect to teaching effectiveness, although on their own these qualities and skills cannot promote effective teaching, without them teaching cannot be effective either. Trainers' experiences with observed lessons where they felt *something or some things were missing* fully support this:

> Probably the lack of genuine feeling, shall I say—or lack of feeling in reacting to students perhaps...just carrying out the lesson sort of automatically...and in the end you feel that there's something lacking, that there isn't this genuine interest in students' reactions and their contributions and you can see an opportunity to communicate, an opportunity to interact has been missed. (TT5)

In this sense, the personal qualities of the teacher, the teacher's communication skills and interaction with students and affective-level techniques are at the heart of effective teaching with the affective thread running through all components of effective teaching: knowledge of the language, knowledge of teaching methodology, lesson planning and preparation, lesson presentation, and lesson management. The findings also suggest that teaching effectiveness in the three key areas discussed can be developed and improved by building on the qualities and skills that a teacher already possesses through activities such as these commonly expressed ideas by trainers: watching different lessons of different teachers on video, having developmental observations with a trainer, carrying out self- and peer observations, all followed by discussions on strong areas related to personal qualities, communication skills, and affective-level techniques as well as areas to develop, focusing particularly on the interaction between the teacher and the students.

Most important, the findings necessitated a reexamination of the classroom observation and evaluation tools and criteria in BUSEL, leading to the development of a new set of criteria for the enhancement and evaluation of teaching effectiveness (cf. Appendix C). Although there is a certain amount of overlap among the five effective teaching areas presented, once again considering the complex nature of teaching and learning, this is both natural and desirable. As can be observed from the criteria, personal qualities of the teacher, the teacher's communication skills and interaction with students, and the affective-level techniques discussed, act as an affective thread embedded in and running across all five areas. The sections highlighted in bold in the criteria in Appendix C refer to the qualities and skills that appear to be *most* closely related to the less easily definable. Although there could be other qualities and skills within each area, these stand out as the main qualities and skills also cross-validated through a triangulation of the data obtained. The effective teaching criteria is *not* a checklist but should be used as a guide and a reference document for both analytical and holistic reflection, discussion, and feedback on teaching effectiveness at an individual level (i.e., through self-observation and reflection) as well as at a shared level (i.e., peer observation, formal observation, three-way observation, team teaching, learner observation), before and after lessons and observations. All qualities and skills are equally important and are not presented in any order of priority, hence the use of bullet points.

Trainers and academic managers at BUSEL continued to use the running commentary, which was an effective tool, but academic managers totally abandoned the discrete point checklists, which at the time were in use for the purposes of probation observations, and fully adopted the new effective teaching criteria in the pre- and post-observation stages of both assessed and developmental observations along with a new feedback and evaluation tool designed by the author. The way this tool worked was that *after* an observation, while reflecting back on the lesson and their running commentary, the observer would note down both strong points and suggestions within each of the five categories of effective teaching by making use of the skills and qualities presented in the new effective teaching criteria. What is of great importance here was that there was no required number of points that needed to be mentioned within each category and that what would be presented in the feedback would be presented because it was relevant and appropriate. The observer then summarized the feedback in the general comments section and, in the case of assessed observations, gave a holistic grade. Similarly, the teachers who were observed reflected back on the lesson by using a guided feedback tool and were also encouraged to refer to the effective teaching criteria to support this reflection process before the post-observation discussion as well as in pre-observation planning. Although the trainers continued to use the existing evaluation tools for the externally accredited Cambridge ESOL courses they were working on (as some forms naturally had to be filled in), they used the new effective teaching criteria as a guide and a reference document for both analytical and holistic reflection on the lesson and to support their feedback processes in the observations they carried out.

Distinctive Features

There are three key features that distinguish this evaluation study from others. First and foremost, the study stemmed from a genuine need to explore teaching effectiveness in terms of some less easily definable aspects of teaching considering their potential effect on the evaluation of teaching effectiveness by trainer observers. Second, the study was holistic and descriptive in nature, aiming to explore and discover, rather than to prove or disprove hypotheses. What was more important here was the involvement of multiple informant groups and the use of multiple data collection procedures. Third and most important, the findings obtained from the study led to the development of a new set of research-based effective teaching criteria for BUSEL, both holistic and analytical, but far from a checklist mentality and fully suitable for all types of observations and discussions on teaching effectiveness. The feedback on the use of the criteria proved to be highly positive and in addition to its use in BUSEL, the criteria on effective teaching were later also adopted by three other institutions in Turkey. These were among the commonly mentioned strengths of the criteria by trainers, academic managers, and teachers.

- The new criteria provide more support and ideas for both the teacher and the observer; are user friendly; and provide guidance in planning, reflection, and action points.
- It is easier to be positive in one's reflection and/or feedback because of the wider coverage.
- Giving strategies is appreciated by the teacher and encourages the observer to reflect; it is therefore more developmental.
- Division of main areas and presence of adjectives is very helpful.
- It is both analytical and all encompassing.
- The criteria describe in such a way that there is no room for subjective interpretation—it is easier to standardize with such descriptive criteria.

- It is more honest and fair with no serious anomalies in the weighting of areas.
- It will make observers/assessors fit their feedback to the lesson, i.e., the lesson will be taken on its own merits and not judged against very restricted and restrictive criteria.

Caveats

There are two main limitations of the study. The first of these concerns the analysis of the data from the classroom observations and written feedback forms on observed lessons. This was based on an analysis of the "strong points" in the lessons and did not involve an analysis of any "negative" aspects. This was due to the fact that when the informants agreed to have their feedback analyzed, they were reassured that the analysis would focus only on the positive aspects and strong points in their lessons and not on "weak" areas. However, since multiple data collection procedures were used in the study, I was able to compensate for this limitation in the interviews with all informants and in the video-based observation and discussion with trainers. A second important limitation is related to the fact that the study was conducted in one educational context only and that the findings obtained may not be generalizable to other ELT institutions. However, in the light personal communications with different trainers and teacher colleagues in the field, the fact that the feedback on the criteria was highly positive and the criteria and processes were later also used in three other contexts in Turkey, and based on positive feedback received on the research study after several presentations at national and international venues, it is believed that the research and findings presented here will be of informative and practical value to other professionals and practitioners in the field.

Recommendations

At the macro-level, it is essential to incorporate personal qualities of the teacher, the teacher's communication skills and interaction with students, and affective-level techniques as a strand or a thread running through course syllabi and activities on all teacher training courses. For years teacher training practices have focused successfully on teaching techniques and methodology but not equally on the less easily definable aspects of teaching effectiveness. Although in most training courses there are sessions on, for example, teacher beliefs, student motivation, learning styles and strategies, these have been few in number and also presented as one-off sessions rather than as themes explored throughout the courses. It is believed that themes such as these, as well as effective teaching, teacher motivation, communication skills and interaction with students, affective-level techniques, and student psychology, need to be incorporated into courses, both as sessions in their own right and as threads to be explored systematically through different areas of input and with respect to different student populations.

At the micro-level, one of the most important activities is to encourage teachers to carefully consider who their students are both as a group and as individuals in the planning choices they make to cater better for their needs and interests. This can be done by asking teachers to consider what has been called "affective-level aims" (techniques and skills the teacher uses as part of his or her methodology to create a positive learning environment and to affectively involve students in the lesson) along with cognitive ones. Affective-level aims such as, "In this lesson, I would like to pay particular attention to Mert and involve him more in the lesson in order to raise his self-esteem" should be as legitimate and acceptable as cognitive-level aims. In addition, particularly in post-observation discussions, it would be very useful to explore the teacher's "interactive decisions"—that is, decisions that teachers make as they are teaching according to the specific dynamics of the lesson, since such decisions, "enable teachers to assess students' response to teaching and to modify their instruction in order to provide optimal support for learning" (Richards & Lockhart, 1994, p. 84). It is also essential that comments related to the personal qualities of the teacher, the teacher's communication skills and interaction with students, and affective-level techniques be incorporated into both written and oral feedback given to teachers on their lessons. In order to do this successfully, it is important that observers do not take certain qualities and skills for granted and sensitively focus on these three areas as much as they focus on the successful implementation of teaching methods and techniques. This is certainly very challenging since mentioning points related to personal qualities and skills, in particular, can be very threatening for the teacher if raised as critical points. But with a supportive style and the use of sensitive, non-threatening language, one can successfully raise a teacher's awareness of how crucial such qualities and skills are in effective teaching and discuss strategies for developing them further. Finally, having one-to-one tutorials with teachers either on training courses or in informal developmental contexts might prove to be very useful in exploring teacher's beliefs and motivation. Such an activity would allow the trainer to work with a teacher in a non-threatening environment, especially if the teacher is feeling particularly unconfident. Discussions in a tutorial might also give the trainer the opportunity to suggest different developmental activities to the teacher, especially if the teacher appears to need considerable support and guidance regarding teaching effectiveness: keeping a diary either for their own self reflection or interactively, by sharing it with the trainer or a peer; involving their students in observing some of the lessons with simple yet revealing observation tasks (Kurtoğlu Eken, 1999); and carrying out three-way observations involving their own, their students', and a peer's reflections on the same lesson (Richards, 1998).

Conclusion

This study has attempted to investigate the need to develop criteria for teaching effectiveness through an exploration of the less easily definable aspects of teaching. Findings of the study reveal that the challenging experiences trainers experienced in situations in which they found it difficult to comment on certain

aspects of the lesson or the teaching, feeling that there was something missing but found it difficult to say exactly what it was, relate to three main areas
of teaching effectiveness: the personal qualities of the teacher, the teacher's
communication skills and interaction with students, and to the teacher's use of
affective-level techniques. The qualities and skills within each of these areas were
incorporated as a thread running through a newly designed set of both holistic
and analytical criteria used in several educational settings in Turkey, in addition
to its successful implementation in the research context. One of the biggest aims
of teacher training practices needs to be an exploration of teachers' potential
with teachers themselves and equipping them with tools and processes that allow for a rich investigation and evaluation of their own teaching. It is believed
that this study has demonstrated an example of such an approach by involving
teachers in research that aims to explore criteria for teaching effectiveness and
by proposing a series of macro- and micro-level training and development
activities, as well as processes that aim to build on the strengths of teachers by
placing them at the heart of all explorations. This is where all future direction
lies—that without the involvement and ownership of teachers we cannot have
healthy practices in research, training and evaluation.

Discussion Questions

1. To what extent can you relate to the challenging experiences presented
   in the article? Reflect and discuss with reference to one or more of the
   quotations used from the student, teacher, or trainer data provided.

2. How would you answer the two questions provided in the extract in
   Appendix A? Reflect and share your views with a partner.

3. What is distinctive about the effective teaching criteria presented in the
   article? Which points does the author emphasize regarding the nature
   of the criteria and the process for their use?

4. To what extent do you believe the effective teaching criteria presented
   by the author are applicable in other teaching contexts? Why? Why
   not?

5. In your view, which of the micro-level activities or processes discussed
   in the Recommendations section could best support a teacher who is
   experiencing difficulties with his/her communication and interaction
   with students? Discuss.

6. In her discussion of micro-level recommendations, the author argues
   that, "Affective-level aims…should be as legitimate and acceptable as
   cognitive-level aims." To what extent do you agree with this point?
   Why? Why not?

REFERENCES

Azarov, Y. (1988). *Teaching: Calling and skills.* Moscow: Progress Publishers.

Bampfield, A. (1997). *Looking at language classrooms.* Cambridge: Cambridge University Press.

Bogdan, R. C., & Biklen, S. K. (1992). *Qualitative research for education: An introduction to theory and methods.* Boston: Allyn and Bacon.

Brookfield, S. D. (1990). *The skillful teacher: On technique, trust and responsiveness in the classroom.* San Francisco: Jossey-Bass.

Cullingford, C. (1995). *The effective teacher.* London, New York: Cassell.

Engeström, Y. (1994). *Training for change.* Geneva: ILO.

Gardner, H. (1993). *Multiple intelligences: The theory in practice.* New York: Basic Books.

Goleman, D. (1995). *Emotional intelligence: Why it can matter more than IQ.* London: Bloomsbury.

Hargreaves, A. (1998). The emotional practice of teaching. *Teaching and Teacher Education, 14*(8), 835–854.

Kurtoğlu Eken, D. (1996). Through the eyes of the learner: Learner observations of teaching and learning. *ELT Journal, 53*(4), 240–248.

Kyriacou, C. (1998). *Essential teaching skills.* Cheltenham: Stanley Thornes.

Ornstein, A. (1990). *Strategies for effective teaching.* New York: Harper Row.

Patton, M. Q. (1987). *How to use qualitative methods in evaluation.* Newbury Park, CA: Sage Publications.

Richards, J. C. (1998). *Beyond training.* Cambridge: Cambridge University Press.

Richards, J. C., & Lockhart, C. (1994). *Reflective teaching in second language classrooms.* Cambridge: Cambridge University Press.

van Mannen, M. (1995). *The tact of teaching: The meaning of pedagogical thoughtfulness.* New York: The State University of New York Press.

Weimer, M. (1993). *Improving your classroom teaching.* Newbury Park, CA: Sage Publications.

APPENDIX A: Extract from Interview Schedule for Teacher Trainers, Teachers, Students

Question 2: Can you think back to a time or times when you have come out of a lesson as a trainer/teacher/learner thinking and feeling, "Yes!!!"; a lesson after which you felt really happy and satisfied. Can you please describe why you believe you felt like that and what contributed to this "Yes!" feeling.

Question 3: How about the opposite scenario? A time or times when you have come out thinking and feeling something or some things were missing and you did not feel the, "Yes!!!". Can you again describe why you felt like that?

APPENDIX B: Extract from Teacher Trainer Questionnaire

<u>SECTION C</u>: The following extracts are taken from interviews with teachers and students on **teaching effectiveness**. Based on your views and experience, how closely does each description/account reflect your perception of what it is that may be creating difficulty for you in identifying what was missing in the lesson(s) observed? Please read each extract carefully and circle the number that best represents your view.

What a STUDENT said...	fully related			not related at all
1. You can understand if a smile is genuine or not. You can also understand if the teacher just goes in to teach and that's it. You know, a teacher who goes into class and starts teaching right away. S/He has to have some communication and interaction with Ss. For example, asking them about how they feel, how they are, etc. S/He should also be able to understand the Ss.' moods and teach accordingly.	4	3	2	1

APPENDIX C: Effective Teaching Criteria

Area	Qualities and Skills
Knowledge and awareness	• knowledge of and about the language • knowledge of relevant teaching methods/strategies • understanding of relevant language/skill/concept/content • **knowledge about the class (e.g., level, abilities, interests, needs, class dynamics)** • **knowledge about individual students (e.g., names, interests, affective needs, cognitive needs, learning styles, study habits)** • **awareness of students' progress and potential difficulties**
Planning and preparation	• general preparation for the lesson • lesson aims and objectives (e.g., relevant to course aims, **appropriate to students' needs**, clear, realistic) • how the lesson fits in the whole picture with respect to course aims and previous and future lessons/how it relates to previous and future learning re. language/skill/concept/content • materials and resources (e.g., well-chosen/well-prepared, relevant to lesson/aims, appropriate to the level and students) • choice of techniques/teaching strategies (e.g., **appropriate to students' needs and interests**, **motivating**, varied, balanced, principled) • choice of activities/tasks (e.g., **appropriate to students' level**, **motivating**, varied, balanced, principled) • **incorporation of knowledge about students and class and sensitivity to students' needs/level of language** • lesson plan (e.g., clear, organized, consideration of aims, class profile, anticipated problems and strategies, staging, timing, interaction patterns)
Rapport and communication with learners (attitude/manner & interpersonal skills)	• **general attitude/manner (e.g., confident, pleasant, enthusiastic, positive, fair, smiling)** • **attitude toward students (e.g., understanding, positive, caring, patient, approachable, supportive, interested)** • **ability to build a good relationship with students (e.g., using students' names, knowledge about students, awareness of how students feel, empathetic)** • **ability to motivate students to learn (e.g., expressing genuine interest in students, listening actively to students, reacting and responding to students, involving different students in the lesson, valuing students' contributions, using humor)** • **ability to build trust (e.g., genuine interest in students,** sound knowledge of the language, **helping students to see the value of learning, being open and receptive)** • **ability to build individual communication with students (e.g., awareness of students' strengths, needs, interests)** • **giving praise and encouragement** • **expressing confidence in students' knowledge and abilities**

Area	Qualities and Skills
Lesson presentation	• **ability to encourage participation and involve students** (e.g., **nominating students, using humor, expressing confidence in students, giving students time to think, giving students equal opportunities to participate**) • **making use of students' existing knowledge, previous learning** (e.g., elicitation, prediction work) • giving students time to think • encouraging independent learning (e.g., raising students' awareness of and promoting the use of different learning strategies, study skills, encouraging students to use dictionaries, encouraging students to make use of academic support facilities) • providing challenge for students (e.g., encouraging students to think critically, asking students to justify answers) • giving instructions (e.g., clear, staged, checked if necessary) • elicitation/questioning techniques (e.g., varied, challenging, motivating) • accuracy in presentation (e.g., language used, concept presented, explanation given) • **use of personalization** (e.g., language, topic) • encouraging students to use English as much as possible • **encouraging students to interact with each other** • use of voice (e.g., ability to project, clarity, audibility, **enthusiasm**) • body language (e.g., reflects interest, confidence, eye contact with whole class) • catering for a variety of learning styles and abilities • use of teaching aids and materials (e.g., whiteboard, OHP, pictures, realia, task sheets) • using a variety of techniques and strategies • effective exploitation of materials and tasks • use of IT to support learning processes
Lesson management	• **flexibility and ability to adapt lesson to students' needs and interests** • lesson development and flow (e.g., clear aims, smooth transitions, coherence between stages) • **monitoring of students' work and providing support where necessary (e.g., encouraging students to think, challenging students, probing for right answers, guiding but not doing the work for the students)** • **involving different students in the activities** • **error correction techniques (e.g., supportive, encouraging, constructive, unobtrusive, appropriate, principled)** • checking of learning and feedback (e.g., systematic, focused, **involving different students**, varied, giving students time to respond) • staging of activities/tasks • pace (e.g., varied, **engaging**, snappy) • timing of the activities and the lesson • physical organization of the room (e.g., seating arrangements, lights) • control and handling of discipline

The sections in bold are **not** in bold in the actual criteria. They have been presented in bold here only to highlight the qualities and skills **most closely** related to the less easily definable.

CHAPTER 12

Faculty Attitudes toward Three Methods of Evaluating Teacher Effectiveness

Peter Davidson

Introduction

As is common at many tertiary institutions around the world, faculty at Zayed University (ZU) in the United Arab Emirates are evaluated in three main areas: teaching effectiveness, research and scholarly activities, and contributions to the university and the wider community. This study investigated teachers' views regarding the three methods used at ZU to evaluate teachers' performance: student evaluation of teaching (SET), classroom observations that are carried out by administrators, and teaching portfolios that are submitted each year. These research questions were formulated:

1. To what extent do faculty think the ZU evaluation process is an effective means of evaluating teaching effectiveness?
2. To what extent do faculty think SET, the Teaching Portfolio, and Classroom Observations are effective tools to evaluate teaching?

Previous Research

The majority of studies that have examined faculty attitudes toward teacher evaluation have focused primarily on their views of SET questionnaires. According to Costins, Greeough, & Menges, (1971, p. 511), teachers think that "student ratings are unreliable, that the ratings will favor an entertainer over the instructor who gets his material across effectively, that ratings are highly correlated with expected grades (a hard grader would thus get poor ratings), and that students are not competent judges of instruction since long-term benefits of a course may not be clear at the time it is rated." However, as noted by Schmelkin, Spencer, and Gellman (1997), most of what has been written about the attitudes that teachers and students have toward SET is largely anecdotal.

It should be noted, however, that there is a small but growing body of research that has examined the attitudes that teachers have toward SET. The results of these studies indicate that faculty have mixed attitudes toward the usefulness, validity, and reliability of SET. A number of studies have indicated that while some teachers view SET as potentially useful, other teachers do not think that it is useful (Ory & Braskamp, 1981; Hamdy et al., 2001; Mertler, 1999; Rich, 1976; Ryan, Anderson, & Birchler, 1980; Schmelkin et al., 1997; Simpson & Siguaw, 2000; Davidson, 2004). Franklin and Theall (1989) found that many teachers did not have the knowledge or skills necessary to analyze and use SET data effectively, and they surmised that teachers who did not find student ratings useful tended to have less knowledge about SET than teachers with more positive attitudes towards SET. Yao, Weissinge, and Grady (2003) found that faculty who received very high ratings from students were more likely to make use of SET data. They also found that the use of SET data was different according to academic rank, academic field, class size, and class level, with junior faculty and those teaching graduate classes more likely to make use of SET data. Similarly, Rich (1976) also found that younger faculty were more likely to have positive attitudes to SET than older faculty, but he found no relationship between academic rank, gender, or academic field, and attitudes to SET.

The research has also revealed that only a small number of faculty modify their teaching based on data generated by SET, and these modifications are generally quite minor (Hamdy et al., 2001; Nasser & Fresko, 2002; Ryan et al., 1980; Schmelkin et al., 1997; Sojka, Gupta, & Deeter-Schmelz, 2002; Spencer & Flyr, 1992). Interestingly, in one study (Davidson, 2004) in which faculty were identified as having very negative attitudes to SET (with only 21.4 percent indicating SET was effective, only 16.5 percent indicating that students were capable of rating teachers, and only 8.7 percent indicating that students took it seriously), 56.3 percent indicated that they had modified their teaching in some way based on their SET scores, and only 17.5 percent of the teachers responded that they had taken no action based on SET ratings.

Other studies have revealed that teachers are concerned about the validity and reliability of data generated by SET (Carson, 2001; Dent & Nicholas, 1980; Nasser & Fresko, 2002; Simpson & Siguaw, 2000; Sojka et al., 2002; Davidson, 2004). Teachers have also doubted whether students take SET seriously, and they have expressed their concern over the ability of students to rate their teaching in a fair and objective manner (Avi-Itzhak & Kremer, 1986; Hamdy et al., 2001; Nasser & Fresko, 2002; Ryan et al., 1980; Davidson, 2004), although in one study (Dent & Nicholas, 1980) more than 70 percent of faculty felt that students were capable of rating their teaching. Franklin and Theall (1989) found that that teachers who questioned the ability of students to rate teaching had less knowledge about SET than teachers with more positive attitudes toward SET.

Faculty opinion is also split on whether data from SET questionnaires should be published in order to assist students when selecting courses. Ory and

Braskamp (1981) found that 40 percent of faculty thought students should have access to SET data, compared to 62.5 percent who felt that students should have access to evaluative data generated from student group interviews, and 71.8 percent who felt students should have access to students' written comments. In a study by Howell and Symbaluk (2001), faculty felt that publishing student ratings would result in instructors lowering standards, be an invasion of privacy, be viewed as a threat and a potential source of punishment, influence students expectations of instructors, and bias how students would rate a particular instructor in the future. One disturbing finding from the research is that some faculty believed that other teachers lowered standards by giving less coursework and/or easier exams, or engaged in other inappropriate behavior, in order to raise their SET ratings (Nasser & Fresko, 2002; Ryan et al., 1980).

SET has the potential to be an effective tool to assist administrators in evaluating teaching effectiveness, but only if it is valued by teachers and students. A review of the literature indicates that teachers generally have somewhat negative attitude toward SET. As Callahan (1992) notes, teachers generally accept SET, but they do not approve of it. However, research also suggests that, while faculty certainly have concerns about the validity and reliability of data generated by SET and are concerned about students' ability to rate their teaching in a fair and objective manner, they are more predisposed to SET than the anecdotal evidence would suggest, generally finding SET to be reasonably effective and useful. In other words, teachers are not opposed to SET per se, but they may be opposed to the way it is administered and what is done with the results. Davidson (2004, p. 384) surmises that the attitudes that teachers have toward SET are influenced by these variables:

- teachers' attitudes toward students
- teachers' attitudes toward evaluation in general
- the quality of the SET questionnaire that is administered
- the purpose of SET
- how often SET is implemented
- teachers' previous experience with SET
- teachers' previous SET results
- the type and orientation of the institution
- the country the institution is in
- the amount of experience the teacher has
- the subject the teacher teaches

In the only study that has examined faculty perceptions of different tools used to collect data to evaluate teaching effectiveness, Ory and Braskamp (1981) compared faculty attitudes toward three methods of gathering evaluative data from students, namely SET questionnaires, open-ended written comments, and group interviews. The student group interviews were found to be the most comprehensive source of evaluative data, followed by SET questionnaires and then open-ended questions. The researchers also found that faculty felt evaluative data was more accurate, trustworthy, useful, comprehensive, believable, and valuable when used for self-improvement rather than for promotion. How credible faculty thought the evaluative data were depended on the purpose for which the data were used—for example, they felt that written comments were less credible than SET questionnaires when used for promotion, but more credible when used for self-development. Another interesting finding from this study was that the faculty expressed a desire to be evaluated by more than one particular method, with a third of faculty indicating that they would like to be evaluated by their peers.

Method

A Faculty Survey was distributed to all faculty on both the Dubai and Abu Dhabi campuses at the end of the Spring 2002 semester. The survey consisted of four sections that sought to determine teachers' attitudes toward SET (referred to at ZU as the *Student Evaluation of the Learning Environment*, or SELE for short), the Teaching Portfolio, Classroom Observations, and the Evaluation Process in general. The survey consisted of closed questions using a five-point Likert scale, as well as open-ended questions. It was decided to distribute hard copies of the survey as opposed to electronic copies because the electronic program *Perception* that was available at the time was not fully operational. It was also hypothesized that a higher response rate would be obtained by using hard copies. The response rates to the Faculty Survey from the two campuses are presented in Table 12.1.

Mean scores for the five-point Likert scale questions on the survey were calculated. As such, a mean score of 3 is neutral, a mean score of 5 is the highest possible positive score, and a mean score of 1 is the lowest possible negative score. In addition, the percentages for each of the five options on the Likert scale for each question was also calculated. The percentages for the options "strongly agree" and "agree" were then added together, as were the options "strongly disagree" and "disagree," in order to create two broader categories "generally agree" and "generally disagree" for ease of analysis and comparison. The responses to the open-ended questions were collated and categorized.

Table 12.1: Faculty Survey Response Rates

	Total # faculty	# surveys returned	Response rate
Dubai	146	52	35.6%
Abu Dhabi	132	42	31.8%
Total	278	94	33.8%

Findings and Discussion

Faculty Attitudes toward SELE

As can be seen from Table 12.2, the majority of ZU faculty who completed the Faculty Survey did not have very positive attitudes toward the SELE. Question 8, which asked faculty if they felt that the SELE was an effective tool with which to measure their teaching effectiveness, received a low mean score of 2.34, with the majority of respondents (56 percent) disagreeing with this statement. With regard to the usefulness of the SELE (Q.7), again a low mean score of 2.78 was achieved, with only a third of respondents indicating they felt that it was useful.

In response to Question 5, the majority of respondents (54.3 percent) expressed concern about the reliability of the data generated by the SELE (mean = 2.38), and in Question 6, an even higher percentage (62.8 percent) expressed concern about the validity of the data generated by SELE, which obtained a mean score of 2.26. When asked if they thought students were capable of rating faculty in a fair and objective manner (Q. 1), only 28 percent of respondents agreed, 55.9

Table 12.2: Faculty Attitudes toward SELE

Key:
n = number of respondents   SA/A = Strongly Agree/ Agree
D/SD = Disagree / Strongly Disagree

Question	n	mean	SA/A	Neutral	SD/D
1. Students in general are capable of evaluating faculty in a fair and objective manner.	93	2.49	28.0%	16.1%	55.9%
2. Students in general read each question on the SELE Q carefully and spend sufficient time reflecting before answering.	92	2.17	14.1%	17.4%	68.5%
3. Students in general take the SELE Q seriously.	91	2.73	31.9%	24.2%	44.0%
4. Students need training on how to complete the SELE Q before it is implemented.	94	4.02	68.1%	17.0%	14.9%
5. The ZU SELE generates statistically reliable data about my teaching effectiveness.	94	2.38	23.4%	22.3%	54.3%
6. The ZU SELE generates valid data about my teaching effectiveness, i.e., it measures what it is intended to measure.	94	2.26	23.4%	13.8%	62.8%
7. Despite the limitations of SELE, it generates useful data about my teaching effectiveness.	94	2.78	33.0%	23.4%	43.6%
8. The SELE is an effective tool with which to measure my teaching effectiveness.	91	2.34	23.1%	20.9%	56.0%
27. I receive my SELE results in a timely manner.	84	3.00	39.3%	27.4%	33.3%

percent disagreed, and this statement generated the low mean score of 2.49. In contrast, however, when faculty were asked if they felt students needed training on how to complete the SELE before it was implemented (Q. 4), the relatively high mean score of 4.02 was achieved, with the majority of respondents (68.1 percent) agreeing with this statement, and only a minority (14.9 percent) disagreeing. Faculty opinion on whether students take the SELE seriously (Q. 3) was split, with 31.9 percent responding that students do take it seriously, 44 percent responding that they do not take it seriously, and about a quarter of faculty remaining neutral. However, only 14.1 percent of respondents felt that students read each question on the SELE questionnaire carefully and spent sufficient time reflecting before answering (Q.2), with the majority (68.5 percent) disagreeing with this statement, resulting in the lowest mean score (2.17) of the Faculty Survey.

Faculty were also asked to identify those potential areas of bias that they thought significantly affected their SELE ratings (see Table 12.3). One variable stood out above all others, with nearly 80 percent of respondents indicating that they thought the grade students expected would significantly influence their SELE ratings. This was followed by the subject they teach (64.9 percent), their gender (51.1 percent), the number of students in the class (50.0 percent), the time of day the lesson took place (47.9 percent), which program they taught on (41.5 percent), and the status of the course (40.4 percent). Approximately a quarter of respondents identified two other variables, ethnic background and nationality, as potentially influencing student ratings, and age was identified by a more modest 22.3 percent of respondents. One other variable, the campus you teach on, was identified as affecting SELE scores, but only by less than 9 percent of respondents.

Table 12.3: Areas of Potential Bias in SELE as Identified by Faculty

9. Tick those areas below that you think significantly influence your SELE ratings.

Q. #	Area of potential bias	Total #	%	Rank
9.1	your gender	48	51.1%	3
9.2	your age	21	22.3%	10
9.3	your ethnic background	23	24.5%	8 =
9.4	your nationality	23	24.5%	8 =
9.5	the campus you teach on, i.e., Dubai or Abu Dhabi	8	8.5%	11
9.6	the subject you teach	61	64.9%	2
9.7	the time you teach, i.e., morning or afternoon	45	47.9%	5
9.8	the status of your course, i.e., compulsory or elective	38	40.4%	7
9.9	which program you teach in, i.e., Readiness, GE, Majors	39	41.5%	6
9.10	the number of students in your class	47	50.0%	4
9.11	the grade your students expect	74	78.9%	1

Faculty Attitudes toward the Teaching Portfolio

Respondents felt that the Teaching Portfolio (see Table 12.4) was a marginally more effective tool with which to measure teaching effectiveness than the SELE (Q. 13), achieving a mean score of 2.80, but with only 27.2 percent agreeing that it was effective, 40.2 percent indicating they thought it was ineffective, and a relatively high percentage (32.6 percent) remaining neutral. When asked if they received sufficient guidance on what to include in their Teaching Portfolio (Q. 14), the opinion of the respondents was evenly divided among the three categories. However, 53.8 percent indicated that sample Teaching Portfolios would also be useful (Q.15), and half of the respondents indicated that a training session on compiling a Teaching Portfolio would also be useful (Q. 16).

When asked how much time they devote to writing and compiling their Portfolios (see Table 12.5), responses varied considerably from less than two hours (5.6 percent) to more than ten hours (27.8 percent). Similarly, the number of

Table 12.4: Faculty Attitudes toward Teaching Portfolios

Question	n	mean	SA/A	Neutral	SD/D
13. The Teaching Portfolio, as it is used at ZU, is an effective tool with which to evaluate my teaching effectiveness.	92	2.80	27.2%	32.6%	40.2%
14. Sufficient guidance is provided on what to include in the Teaching Portfolio.	93	3.01	34.4%	34.4%	31.2%
15. Samples of different Teaching Portfolios would assist me in compiling my portfolio.	93	3.54	53.8%	26.9%	19.4%
16. A training session on Teaching Portfolios would assist me in compiling my portfolio.	92	3.41	50.0%	29.4%	20.7%

Table 12.5: Time Spent and Length of Teaching Portfolio

17. On average how many hours do you devote to writing and compiling your Teaching Portfolio at ZU? (n = 90)

< 2	2–4	4–6	6–8	8–10	> 10
5.6%	15.6%	17.8%	17.8%	15.6%	27.8%

18. On average how many pages do you include in the Appendices of your Teaching Portfolio at ZU? (n = 87)

< 20	20–40	40–60	60–80	80–100	> 100
43.7%	12.6%	24.1%	5.8%	8.1%	5.8%

pages faculty included in the Appendices of the Teaching Portfolio also varied considerably from less than 20 pages (43.7 percent), to more than 100 pages (5.8 percent). Nearly a quarter of respondents indicated that they included between 40 and 60 pages in their Appendices.

Faculty Attitudes toward Classroom Observations

Classroom Observations (see Table 12.6) were seen by those faculty that responded to the survey as a more effective tool with which to measure teaching effectiveness than both the SELE (mean = 2.34) and the Teaching Portfolio (mean = 2.80), achieving the slightly higher mean score of 3.14 (Q. 20). However, almost a third of respondents indicated that they did not think Classroom Observations were an effective evaluative tool with which to measure teaching effectiveness. For Question 21, most respondents (42.2 percent) felt that the number of classroom observations was sufficient, but nearly a third of respondents were neutral, and nearly another third felt that the number of observations was not sufficient for an observer to make informed decisions about a teacher's effectiveness. Nearly half of the faculty responded that a common ZU Classroom Observation instrument would contribute to better standardization of the observation process (Q. 22), with approximately a quarter disagreeing with this statement.

Faculty Attitudes toward the Evaluation Process in General

With regard to the evaluation process overall (see Table 12.7), more than 50 percent of respondents indicated that they were well informed of the evaluation process (Q. 26), with just more than a quarter indicating that they were not. However, most respondents (44.7 percent) felt that the process used to evaluate ZU faculty was not an effective means of evaluating teaching effectiveness

Table 12.6: Faculty Attitudes toward Classroom Observations

Question	n	mean	SA/A	Neutral	SD/D
20. Classroom observations, as conducted at ZU, are an effective tool with which to measure my teaching effectiveness.	93	3.14	44.1%	24.7%	31.2%
21. Two classroom observations for probationary faculty) and one for non-probationary faculty are sufficient for an observer to make informed judgments regarding teaching effectiveness.	90	3.20	42.2%	28.9%	28.9%
22. A common ZU Classroom Observation Instrument with specified criteria would contribute to better standardization of the observation process.	91	3.22	49.5%	25.3%	25.3%

Table 12. 7: Faculty Attitudes towards the Evaluation Process

Question	n	mean	SA/A	Neutral	SD/D
24. The evaluation process at ZU, based on SELE, the Teaching Portfolio, and Classroom Observations, is an effective means of evaluating my teaching effectiveness.	85	2.73	27.1%	28.2%	44.7%
25. The evaluation process at ZU is carried out in a fair and equitable manner.	85	2.53	25.9%	24.7%	49.4%
26. I am well informed of the evaluation process.	84	3.54	52.4%	21.4%	26.2%

(Q. 24), with 27.1 percent indicating that it was an effective process. What is of concern is that almost a half of respondents felt that the evaluation process at ZU is not carried out in a fair and equitable manner (Q. 25), with just more than a quarter responding that they felt the process was fair and equitable.

When asked what percentage of the evaluation process should be allocated to each of the three evaluative tools (see Table 12.8), 58 faculty responded, specifying that the Teaching Portfolio should be weighted the highest with 40.7 percent, followed by Classroom Observations (27 percent) and SELE (20.8 percent). When asked specifically what other tools or methods might be used to evaluate teaching effectiveness, 63 faculty (67 percent) did not respond. The 31 faculty that did respond to this question proposed these additional evaluative tools: peer observation (4); student performance (4); performance appraisal interview (4); samples of students work (3); self-evaluation (2); peer review (2); more frequent observations (2); manager's report (2); and one for each of the following: materials written by teachers; peer interview with class; informal class visits; creativity in teaching; publications; classroom research; research; team work; attendance; punctuality; collegiality; resume; peer supervision; research; ongoing meetings;

Table 12.8: Faculty Preferred Weightings for Overall Teaching Evaluation

28. When evaluating Teaching Effectiveness for the purpose of Merit Pay increases, how much weighting in terms of percentage should be allocated to each of the following components: (n=58)

Component	%
SELE	20.8%
Teaching Portfolio	40.7%
Classroom Observations	27.0%
Other - specify* _____	11.3%**

*Other included: performance appraisal interview, managerial report, student performance, publications, classroom research, university service, team work, attitude, attendance, punctuality, collegiality, community service, research.

**21 faculty indicated other, with an average weighting of 31.1 percent.

teacher workbooks (of lesson plans, sample tests); community service; university service; and developmental achievement.

Differences across the Two Campuses

Given the small sample size, there were only very small differences in the average responses between the two campuses with regard to the questions about the SELE and Classroom Observations. There were, however, some differences by campus in response to Question 9 which asked faculty to identify those variables that they felt might bias SELE ratings. Both campuses agreed that expected grade and subject taught were the two variables that were most likely to influence SELE ratings. Similar percentages of faculty from both campuses identified gender, number of students per class, ethnic background, nationality, age, and campus taught on. There were, however, differences between the two campuses with regard to three other variables, namely time of lesson (Dubai = 40.4 percent, AD = 57.1 percent), which program you teach in (Dubai = 30.8 percent, AD = 54.8 percent), and status of the course (Dubai = 28.9 percent, AD = 54.8 percent). More Abu Dhabi respondents on average identified more areas of potential bias (45.7 percent) than Dubai respondents (37.3 percent).

There were also a number of minor differences between the results of the two campuses (mean score differences larger than 0.25) with regard to the questions about the Teaching Portfolio. The Abu Dhabi respondents indicated that they thought the Teaching Portfolio was less effective (m = 2.60) than their counterparts in Dubai (m = 2.98). A higher percentage of respondents in Abu Dhabi than in Dubai also felt that not enough guidance was provided on what to include in the Teaching Portfolio, and more of them felt that a sample Teaching Portfolio and a training session would be useful. Interestingly, there were also large differences in the number of pages that faculty on the two campuses include in the Appendices of their Teaching Portfolios. Just under a third of Dubai respondents indicated that their Appendices were less than 20 pages, compared with 59 percent of Abu Dhabi respondents. Moreover, 27 percent of Dubai faculty indicated that their Appendices were longer than 60 pages, compared with only 10.3 percent of Abu Dhabi faculty.

A number of minor differences were also found between the results of the two campuses (mean score differences larger than 0.25) with regard to the overall evaluation process. Dubai respondents were neutral about the effectiveness of the evaluation process (m = 3.06), with 40.4 percent either strongly agreeing or agreeing that it was effective, compared with the Abu Dhabi respondents who appeared more negative (m = 2.32), with 0 percent strongly agreeing and only 10.5 percent agreeing that the evaluation process was effective. This may partly be explained by the fact that Abu Dhabi respondents also indicated that they were less informed about the evaluation process (m = 3.12) compared with their Dubai counterparts (3.61).

Conclusion

The findings of this study indicate that, while teachers' attitudes toward evaluating teacher effectiveness may not be as negative as the anecdotal evidence suggests, there is little agreement among teachers as to how to most effectively measure teachers' performance. The results of this study also show that teachers think that classroom observations are the most effective way to evaluate teachers' performance, followed by teaching portfolios and SET. Given the multidimensional nature of teaching, evaluating faculty is a complex, and often contentious, issue. Teachers are obviously concerned about the validity and reliability of faculty evaluation due to the fact that the evaluative data are used to inform important decisions such as passing probation, contract renewal, tenure, promotion, and merit or performance-related pay. It is advisable, therefore, for institutions to consider adopting a range of different evaluative tools in order to capture the complexity of teaching and to provide teachers with sufficient opportunities to demonstrate their teaching effectiveness. It is unlikely, however, that all faculty will be totally satisfied with faculty evaluation regardless of what evaluative tools are implemented. The reality is that some faculty will be resistant to any form of faculty evaluation. However, whatever method is used to evaluate faculty performance, it is essential that the evaluative process is structured, fair, reliable, consistent, and as objective as possible.

Discussion Questions

1. In your opinion, what are the most effective ways to evaluate teachers' performance?

2. What role should student evaluation of teaching (SET), classroom observations, and teaching portfolios play in faculty evaluation?

3. What other evaluative tools might be used to evaluate teachers?

4. To what extent do teachers try and manipulate SET ratings from their students?

5. Should SET responses from students be anonymous? Why? Why not?

6. What should be included in teaching portfolios?

7. How can teachers use evaluative data to help them develop professionally?

References

Avi-Itzhak, T., & Kremer, L. (1986). An investigation into the relationship between university faculty attitudes toward student rating and organizational and background factors. *Educational Research Quarterly, 10*(2), 31–38.

Callahan, J. P. (1992). Faculty attitudes towards student evaluation. *College Student Journal, 26,* 98–102.

Carson, L. (2001). Gender relations in higher education: Exploring lecturers' perceptions of student evaluations of teaching. *Research Papers in Education, 16*(4), 337–358.

Costins, F., Greeough, T., & Menges, R. J. (1971). Student ratings of college teaching: Reliability, validity, and usefulness. *Review of Educational Research, 41*(5), 511–535.

Davidson, P. (2004). An investigation into teachers' and students' attitudes towards student evaluation of teaching. In P. Davidson, M. Al-Hamly, M. A. Khan, J. Aydelott, K. Bird, & C. Coombe (Eds.), *Proceedings of the 9th TESOL Arabia Conference: English Language Teaching in the IT Age, Vol. 8* (pp. 374–388). Dubai: TESOL Arabia.

Dent, P. L., & Nicholas, T. (1980). A study of faculty and student opinions on teaching effectiveness ratings. *Peabody Journal of Education, 25,* 135–147.

Franklin, J., & Theall, M. (1989). *Who reads ratings: Knowledge, attitude, and practice of users of student ratings of instruction.* Paper presented at the Annual Meeting of the American Educational Research Association, San Francisco. (ED 306 241)

Hamdy, H., Williams, R., Tekian, A., Benjamin, S., El Shazali, H., & Bandaranayake, R. (2001). Application of "vitals": Visual indicators of teaching and learning success in reporting student evaluations of clinical teachers. *Education for Health, 14*(2), 267–271.

Howell, A. J., & Symbaluk, D. G. (2001). Published student ratings of instruction: Revealing and reconciling the views of students and faculty. *Journal of Educational Psychology, 93*(4), 790–796.

Mertler, C. A. (1999). Teacher perceptions of students as stakeholders in teacher evaluation. *American Secondary Education, 27*(3), 17–30.

Nasser, F., & Fresko, B. (2002). Faculty views of student evaluation of college teaching. *Assessment and Evaluation in Higher Education, 27*(2), 187–198.

Ory, J. C., & Braskamp, L. A. (1981). Faculty perceptions of the quality and usefulness of three types of evaluative information. *Research in Higher Education, 15*(3), 271–282.

Rich, H. E. (1976). Attitudes of college and university faculty toward the use of student evaluations. *Educational Research Quarterly, 1*(3), 17–28.

Ryan, J. J., Anderson, J. A., & Birchler, A. B. (1980). Student evaluation: The faculty responds. *Research in Higher Education, 12*(4), 317–333.

Schmelkin, L. P., Spencer, K. J., & Gellman, E. S. (1997). Faculty perspectives on course and teacher evaluations. *Research in Higher Education, 38*(5), 575–592.

Simpson, P. M., & Siguaw, J. A. (2000). Student evaluations of teaching: An exploratory study of the faculty response. *Journal of Marketing Education, 22*(3), 199–213.

Sojka, J., Gupta, A. K., & Deeter-Schmelz, D. R. (2002). Student and faculty perceptions of student evaluations of teaching: A study of similarities and differences. *College Teaching, 50*(2), 44–49.

Spencer, P. A., & Flyr, M. L. (1992). The formal evaluation as an impetus to classroom change: Myth or reality? *Research/Technical Report.* Riverside, CA.

Yao, Y., Weissinger, E., & Grady, M. (2003). Faculty use of student evaluation feedback. *Practical Assessment and Evaluation,* 8/21. Retrieved October 7, 2003, from http://edresearch.org/pare/getvn.asp?v=8&n=21

PART 4:

Tools for Evaluating Teacher Effectiveness

Part 4 offers tools that could be considered in teacher evaluation programs.

Brandt (Chapter 13) examines the issue of self-evaluation in teacher evaluation and appraisal. Through an overview of reflection in teacher education, she explains how self-awareness of teaching can be increased through self-talk. She also addresses issues that need to be considered if self-evaluation is to be used as part of the overall assessment of a teacher trainee's performance.

In Chapter 14, Taylor and Sobel report on an innovative standards-based evaluation tool that can be used for developmental and mentoring purposes, enabling teachers to better meet the needs of their diverse teaching populations.

Alwan (Chapter 15) takes a new look at an old topic and discusses how teaching portfolios can be used to evaluate public school teachers. She examines the large-scale use of the teaching portfolio in the context of teacher evaluation in public UAE schools. Alwan concludes by providing a number of invaluable recommendations on how to most effectively introduce teaching portfolios in other teaching contexts.

CHAPTER 13

Giving Reflection a Voice: A Strategy for Self-Evaluation and Assessment in TESOL Teacher Preparation

Caroline Brandt

Introduction

This chapter reports on the development and application of a self-evaluation strategy in training pre-service teachers who are learning to teach EFL/ESL to adults. The strategy was initiated and trialed during longitudinal qualitative research into short, intensive pre-service training courses, leading to the award of an internationally recognized certificate.

The research questions initially focused broadly on the experiences of course participants. The final questions, however, were emic, arising during the course of the study itself and focused on trainees' learning-related concerns. Two field-work phases, including a case study, led to the identification of critical issues in the assessment of pre-service teachers on such courses. These issues were considered in light of recent research that suggested that learning in an adult context is an awareness-raising process, involving autonomously reflecting on how learning has occurred, staying open to alternative perspectives, engaging in dialogue, finding personal meanings, becoming aware of unspoken assumptions, and enhancing and maintaining self-esteem and confidence (Mezirow, 1990; Brookfield, 1994), and that evaluation and assessment in such a context should reflect such understandings.

The critical assessment issues and current understandings of adult learning were considered in relation to a strategy involving tape-recording self-talk, which facilitated trainees' reflection on their experiences. Themes were identified in these recordings, leading to the development of written personal narratives. The process was observed to allow trainees potentially to make a significant contribution to their evaluation.

The term *self-talk* is borrowed from psychology where it refers to subvocal speech articulation, the activity of silently talking to oneself, internal dialogue, or inner speech (Morin, 1993, p. 223). Morin notes that some writers distinguish between "self-talk," which is silent, and "private speech," which refers to speech self verbalized out loud by adults (Flavell, 1966, in Morin, 2004, p. 2). However, the term *self-talk* is deliberately retained here as a strategy that depends on—and harnesses—the fluency of extensive internal dialogue, rather than the briefer "private speech" that adults may engage in. *Self-talk* is a term also found in relation to performance enhancement in sports psychology, involving the conscious manipulation of self-talk in favor of affirmations, and as such should be distinguished from the term as it is used here.

Self-evaluation is understood to refer to the capacity to make judgments about the "worth" of one's performance and identify one's strengths and weaknesses, with the aim of improving learning outcomes. The term reflects the fact that it is trainees themselves who are contributing to their own formative evaluation, and it is distinct from summative assessment, understood in this context to refer to final judgments and decisions made by tutors.

Description

The Research Context

Much of the provision of international initial training in teaching ESOL is carried out through centralized organizations based in the U.K. Such organizations take responsibility for syllabus design, which is then implemented by tutors in local centers. The syllabus is typically objective driven, encompassing both teaching skills and language awareness development, normally specified in the form of course components, topics or units, syllabus content descriptors, and course objectives or learning outcomes. These courses are usually delivered through a combination of input, tutorials, feedback, supervised teaching practice, and guided observation of experienced teachers. They tend to be about 120 hours long. One of the main advantages of this model is that it seeks to improve the standardization of courses taken and passed by several thousand people each year in centers around the world.

Assessment and Achievement

Assessment on such courses is usually continuous, and there are no formal examinations. Achievement that exceeds the criteria may be distinguished by award of a pass A or B. These courses tend to be viewed as high stakes, in the sense that trainees often make a significant personal investment, with the expectation of achieving a grade that will enable them to find related employment upon completion.

In accord with current thinking and so-called best practice regarding initial and ongoing teacher training, trainees are usually expected to demonstrate the ability to identify their own strengths and weaknesses, to take steps to remedy the latter, and to carry out effective self-evaluations of their own teaching (Scrivener, 1994, pp. 195–199). Such learning outcomes are of particular relevance to this study.

Research Methodology and Outcomes

A twelve-week, part-time course provided the context for the case study. Outcomes took the form of twenty statements, which prompted the question: To what extent did these statements have broader applicability—that is, to other course participants, in other centers, in other parts of the world, at other times? To answer this, the twenty statements provided the focus for the development of questionnaires used to elicit further data in Phase 2, the aim being to triangulate and enable the rejection, substantiation, modification, or supplementation of Phase 1 outcomes.

In Phase 2, access to a large number of potential respondents around the world was sought. However, piloting the questionnaires, with 21 open-ended questions (including an "any other comments?" question), indicated that they required from 60 to 90 minutes to complete. This created difficulties that were addressed by co-opting by email a network of 22 professional contacts, who were asked to identify further potential respondents and act as their point of contact. This was found to be powerfully generative as secondary and tertiary level contacts emerged, providing access to 237 contacts and resulting in the receipt of 72 completed questionnaires. The approach developed, termed *generative networking* (Brandt, 2004), was further exploited in relation to the strategy described here.

Phase 2 outcomes led to the identification of 26 critical issues in the preparation of TESOL teachers. Issues considered "critical" were those supported by both fieldwork phases. These included seven that were directly related to assessment.

Critical Issues in the Assessment of the Pre-Service Adult ESOL Teacher

The seven critical issues related to assessment are (the original numbering, in which issues were assigned a number from 1–26, has been retained):

Critical Issue 2
Trainees' need for a second Teaching Practice tutor, should the first relationship be poor. This led trainees to seek information concerning tutors' preferences, to facilitate corresponding performance modification.

Critical Issue 3
Trainees finding it difficult to comply with their tutors' expectations, when they do not agree with, like, or feel confident using the behavior or technique that tutors expect them to demonstrate.

Critical Issue 4

Trainees having to demonstrate key techniques in limited time for assessment purposes; and finding that teaching "practice" actually means "assessment," because all teaching practice is assessed, with little or no opportunity to teach unsupervised.

Critical Issue 13

Inconsistency in expectations among tutors in interpreting course objectives and judging related performance.

Critical Issue 22

Trainees' need for immediate performance feedback on failing lessons contrasted with tutors' preference to delay such feedback in case of subsequent improvement.

Critical Issue 23

Final grades are felt accurately to reflect actual performance, but not potential.

Critical Issue 26

Trainees and tutors feeling under pressure and short of time. Limited opportunity for experimentation, reflection, and revision.

These issues were established after the completion of Phase 2. However, a few trainees attending the case study course struggled to complete it. The case of one such trainee both illustrates her difficulties with aspects of the experience and explains the origin of the strategy.

Distinctive Features

Wendy's Experience: The Origin of the Strategy[1]

Wendy nearly failed to complete the course. In an interview in the early stages she described some of the difficulties she faced: "I [have] to take on board an enormous amount all at once, and I can't do it....I need to see the whole thing in its entirety and its flow. I hate it when I'm expected to accept something when I can't see the reasons for it, when I can't understand WHY." Wendy needed both order and understanding. She disliked being asked to accept without question someone else's knowledge and ideas. To address such needs, she tape-recorded a description of the day's events and her reaction to them. When questioned about the reasons for this decision, Wendy stated that she "wanted some

---

[1] Names have been changed to ensure anonymity.

record of the words furiously rushing through [her] head, and to try to slow them down." The process helped her to organize her thoughts, and became, for her, a regular event.

As part of the broader enquiry, Wendy was interviewed three times during the course. The second interview took place in Week 5, and here she described the value of her recordings: "If I hadn't started [to make recordings] I know I wouldn't have survived....Talking to myself like that—I know it sounds quite nutty—but it keeps me going." Four other trainees volunteered to take a similar approach. A pilot study was initiated and the strategy was developed, a derivative of the main enquiry focus.

Strategy Development

The pilot study began in the second half of the case study course, when Teaching Practice groups had been allocated different tutors. The five trainees (four women and one man) made an average of fourteen recordings each during the second half of the course. Four used a tape recorder, and one used speech recognition software. The group quickly realized that its tape recordings held value in relation to their development. Instead of making and then abandoning the recordings, one member started listening to earlier recordings and making notes. She identified themes and summarized aspects of her recordings under headings. The other four trainees were asked to take a similar approach. Headings that emerged included: Nerves; Finding ideas; My Teaching Practice group!; and Being observed. These notes formed the basis of written personal narratives, prepared once in Week 8 and again at the end of the course.

The group met at the end of the course at my request to discuss the process of making recordings and preparing personal narratives. Trainees observed that the process "provided evidence of progress which made me feel good"; "allowed me to work through aspects of the course in my own way"; "improved my self-confidence"; "gave me the courage to challenge some aspects of the course."

With trainees' agreement, themes and narratives were retained for subsequent investigation. One gave permission for the retention and transcription of all her recordings. The intention was to show these to tutors at a later stage with a view to establishing their potential value. This was carried out after the completion of Phase 2, by approaching a number of selected tutors who had responded to the questionnaire. Eleven agreed to participate and were provided with a description of the self-talk strategy. They were asked to read the transcript of one trainee's recordings, all themes and narratives, and answer a brief questionnaire.

Analysis of tutors' responses suggested the process "encouraged private reflections and critical evaluation upon experience"; "was likely to provide trainees with an opportunity to vent." Tutors also felt that the outcomes "provided evidence of private reflection and development"; "enabled trainees to demonstrate learning from their reflections, particularly when.... someone had changed their plan as a result of some insight"; "potentially gave trainees the opportunity to become involved in their own assessment." However, they expressed concern regarding the transfer from *private* self-talk to *public* themes and narratives, discussed on p. 209.

Adult Learning

Tusting and Barton (2003) provide a comprehensive overview of recent research into adult learning and suggest that adult educators should "encourage exploratory rather than controlled forms of learning, where the learner is empowered to follow their own interests and desires in the learning process, in ways that relate meaningfully to the practices in which they are engaged" (Tusting & Barton, 2003, p. 36). They propose seven supporting inferences, drawn from the extensive body of research they reviewed:

1. Adults have their own motivations for learning. *Learners build on their existing knowledge and experience.*
2. Adults have a drive toward self-direction and toward becoming autonomous learners.
3. *Adults have the ability to learn about their own learning processes and can benefit from discussion and reflection on this.*
4. Learning is a characteristic of all real-life activities in which people take on different roles and participate in different ways.
5. *Adults reflect and build on their experience. Reflective learning is generated when people encounter problems and issues in their real lives and think about ways of resolving them.*
6. *Reflective learning is unique to each person, since it arises out of the complexities of their own experience. A great deal of learning is incidental and idiosyncratically related to the learner: It cannot be planned in advance.*
7. *Reflective learning enables people to reorganize experience and "see" situations in new ways.*
   (Tusting & Barton, 2003, p. 36). (italics added)

Central to several of these inferences is the notion of reflection. Of particular relevance in this study is the notion that adults build on their knowledge and experiences, and that they often solve problems by a unique and personal process of reflection.

Reflection

Dewey (1933) saw reflection as a special form of problem solving, as an active and deliberate holistic cognitive process, involving sequences of interconnected ideas that take account of underlying beliefs and knowledge. Since then, reflection has been the subject of much discussion (for example, see Schön, 1987; Eraut, 1994; & Boud & Walker, 1998). There is evidence to suggest that reflection allows time for learners to personalize (Rogers, 1969), reprocess (Vygotsky, 1978), and absorb material (Tobin, 1987), and that good learners are reflective learners (Ertmer & Newby, 1996). Common to all these writers are the notions that learning and reflection are interrelated, and that reflection requires a recapturing of experience in which the person thinks about it, mulls it over, and evaluates it (Loughran, 1996). Thus, Loughran argues, reflection helps develop the habits, skills, and attitudes necessary for teachers' self-directed development.

The notion that teachers should be reflective practitioners became widely accepted in teacher education circles in the 1980s and 1990s (see, for example, Wallace, 1991; Brookfield, 1995). It was argued in particular that teachers should be responsible for their actions, and that teacher training should "transcend mere training in the use of specific behavioral competencies" (Korthagen, 1993).

Engaging in reflection, however, requires certain skills and conditions. Boud, Keogh, and Walker (1985) suggest that reflection requires open-mindedness and motivation, while other writers have suggested that self-awareness is a critical factor (Atkins & Murphy, 1998).

Self-Awareness through Self-talk

Definitions of *self-awareness* vary according to the field of enquiry but frequently relate to the notion of organisms having knowledge of themselves as contextually situated subjects, which can affect behavior. A key aspect of most definitions of self-awareness is the notion that only by knowing oneself can we know others. Trainees are required to demonstrate high levels of self-awareness. A novice is expected to monitor his or her performance in Teaching Practice and as part of a group, and adapt it according to the recommendations of experienced practitioners, while also providing colleagues with feedback. Little adaptation is possible unless the individual has a degree of awareness of his or her public self and actions. This is because, as research has shown, individuals' self-awareness affects their ability to incorporate feedback into their self-perception (Fletcher & Baldry, 2000). Morin (2004, pp. 1–2) defines self-awareness as "the capacity to become the object of one's own attention...where the individual actively identifies, processes, and stores information about the self. It is an awareness of one's own mental states...and public self-characteristics...." Drawing on research in social experimental psychology, psychiatry, and neurology, Morin argues that self-awareness is mediated by self-talk or inner speech. It has a behavioral shaping function: "not only do we use inner speech frequently: it shapes our thoughts, feelings and behaviors in a great variety of ways. For instance it has been shown that inner speech plays a decisive role in self-regulation...in problem-solving...and in planning...." (Morin, 1993, pp. 223–224). Critically,

Morin has suggested that inner speech may have a role in the acquisition of information about oneself:

> One potential function of inner speech is its role in self-awareness and the acquisition of self-information....When one talks to oneself one can verbally identify, process and store data about one's current physical and mental states as well as past or present behaviors. One view of consciousness...suggests that a person becomes aware of a mental state when the individual generates a higher-order thought about that state. This position is congruent with the present proposal: we become self-aware when we engage in self-talk (higher-order thought) about our current mental states and personal characteristics. (Morin, 2004, p. 2)

The relationship, he argues, is probably bidirectional: inner speech depends on self-awareness while the converse applies. Unless we are self-aware, we are likely to have little to say to ourselves (Morin, 2004, pp. 2–3). Other writers agree that self-awareness is necessary for self-talk. For example, Vocate (1994, p. 7) observes that "In self-talk, the self is both the source and the object of interaction....The distinctive attributes of self-talk, given this definition, are: (a) self-awareness...; (b) its dialogical nature—addressing the self as the object of one's talk...."

Our definition of self-awareness may now be refined to include the mediating function of language. Self-awareness may therefore be seen as the *language-mediated* capacity to become the object of one's own attention.

The strategy described here gives voice and visibility to self-awareness, which, it is argued, is a critical component of reflection. In so doing, the strategy can contribute toward prevention of this potential problem:

> If left unsocialized, individual reflection can close in on itself, producing detached, idiosyncratic teachers. Because reflection is not an end in itself, but for the purpose of action, communal dialogue is essential. Many different voices are necessary. (Valli, 1997, p. 86)

Weaving the Strands: Critical Issues, Strategy Process and Outcomes, and Course Assessment Criteria

In relation to the seven critical issues, the process broadly develops and reinforces self-awareness and reflection. It appeared to have improved trainees' self-confidence as it provided positive evidence of progress, led to personalization, increased debate or dialogue, and offered opportunities for ongoing self-evaluation. For tutors, the data potentially offered both feedback on their own performances as well as a rich source of trainee data that could contribute toward dialogue and assessment. In relation to the assessment criteria, the strategy process and outcomes provided opportunities for trainees to develop abilities to identify their strengths and weaknesses, to take steps to remedy the latter, and to carry out effective self-evaluations of their teaching. The relationships between these ideas are explored in Table 13.1.

Table 13.1: Relationship among Critical Issues, Strategy Process and Outcomes, and Assessment Criteria

Critical Issue (in brief)	Advantages of strategy process to trainee	Application of strategy outcome (written personal narratives)	Course assessment criteria
#2: Need for second TP tutor and information about him/her.	Awareness of tutors' preferences; consideration of alternative responses: to challenge or comply.	Creates opportunity for clarification between trainees and tutors.	Enables trainees to develop their capacity to: • identify their strengths and weaknesses
#3: Difficulty complying with counter-intuitive expectations.	Reflection on expectations may lead to greater understanding and acceptance of tutors' expectations and their relevance.	Explanations of behavior may become clearer to tutors, leading to greater understating of trainees' reasons for action or inaction.	• take steps to remedy weaknesses • carry out effective self-evaluations of their teaching
#4: Having to demonstrate key techniques in limited time.	Process can reinforce personal learning, improve self-confidence, and balance use of TP for assessment by tutors.	Visible evidence for tutors that could contribute to improved objectivity in assessment.	
#13: Inconsistency in expectations among tutors.	Inconsistencies may be placed into perspective. Allows trainees to give vent to any inequities.	Provision of feedback to tutors ideally leading to open and frank discussion, reconciling inconsistencies and differences.	
#22: Need for immediate performance feedback on failing lessons.	Process should trigger integration of developmental and performance feedback from tutors.	Improve relations and authenticity between trainee and tutor.	
#23: Grades accurately reflecting performance, not potential.	Opportunity to reflect on and articulate potential, future, teaching strategies.	Narratives likely to provide strong evidence of potential which can be included in final grade or report.	
#26: Pressure and limited opportunity for reflection.	The process, if integrated into a program, would encourage in-built reflection time.	Narratives likely to reveal reflection skills which can be included as topic for assessment.	

Good evaluation (and good assessment) should help trainees to reconsider old understandings, make new connections, and develop transfer strategies. Good evaluation is closely related to, not divorced from, learning. Earl and LeMahieu (1997, in Thaine, 2003, p. 13) note:

> If people learn by constructing their own understanding from their experiences, assessment is not only part of learning, it is the critical component that allows the learners and their teachers to check their understanding against the views of others, and against the collective wisdom of the culture....The alternative is for learners to be passive and uncritical recipients of disconnected (and often conflicting) ideas, without the skills to challenge or judge for themselves.

The strategy described here offers opportunities for trainees to scrutinize their own understandings and progress, and increase ownership of their learning, while concurrently encouraging them to share responsibility for learning with their tutors. Learning in such a context can become mutual and reciprocal. Mutuality requires communication, as Harris & Bell (1994, p. 88) suggest: "...assessing without communication is of doubtful value: communication between the teacher and the learner is an essential part of the learning process and should be on a regular basis."

The evaluation of teaching should include helping the novice teacher to articulate his or her reflections as part of a teaching and learning dialogue. For such changes to take place, however, teacher education will ideally reflect an understanding of classroom cultures where learning and learners are at the center. Attention to helping teachers reflect on their knowledge, beliefs, and their performance and its effect is but one aspect of such a culture.

Caveats

This discussion raises a number of issues worthy of further investigation:

♦ **While the process of arriving at written personal narratives may lead to self-evaluation, the two should not be equated.** Trainee self-evaluation is a process whereby trainees reflect on the effectiveness of their knowledge, beliefs, and their performance and its effect, and make judgments or changes in order to develop themselves. Self-evaluation however does not take place until these reflections, observations, and judgments about one's own performance are *operationalized;* that is, put into practice in the form of an iterative process of setting or reconsidering goals; preparing action plans for the achievement of goals; and reviewing progress and monitoring whether actions have been compatible with goals.

♦ **Self-evaluation is a formative, not a summative, activity.** Outcomes of the present research suggested that formative evaluation and summative assessment frequently conflict on such courses, as tutors are required to adopt two roles: that of tutor and that of assessor. Establishing activities that are clearly identified as either formative or summative may be one way to assist the tutor to distinguish his or her changing function as the course progresses.

♦ **Reliability and validity matter.** Should the strategy be found to lend itself to assessment, in order to improve validity there will be a need to ensure that trainees are familiar with the criteria against which they are being asked to evaluate their performance. This should prove straightforward as such criteria are normally clearly specified in the syllabus of such courses. The case of reliability may prove more challenging. Trainees' ability to evaluate accurately their own performance cannot be guaranteed but could be included as an aspect of early learner training, being supported by the constant feedback, which is a feature of such courses.

♦ **In the current circumstances, if the personal narratives were to be used toward trainees' final assessment, what trainees wrote would change.** The personal narratives have a potential role in summative assessment. Indeed, they would have the advantage of increasing trainees' involvement in their final assessments. However, trainees preparing personal narratives for assessment purposes may feel compelled to manipulate what is written, particularly within the current context, because the course ethos tends to foster dependency, compliance, and, as one trainee described it, a "just tell me what you want me to do and I'll do it" culture. It may be that this culture would need to undergo a radical shift before personal narratives could be relied on to make an authentic contribution toward assessment.

♦ **The self-talk strategy is an intervention.** Any strategy that aims to manage the individual and personal process of reflection is an intervention, and with interventions come risks. An immediate consideration at this stage is the need for clear parameters to delineate the uses that would be made of the narratives and to establish their audience (peers, tutors, or both groups?) as the shift is made from *private* self-talk to *public* narrative.

♦ **The strategy will not appeal to all.** Some trainees may prefer not to engage in this strategy. In accord with the view of the adult learner as ideally "empowered to follow their own interests and desires in the learning process, in ways that relate meaningfully to the practices in which they are engaged" (Tusting & Barton, 2003, p. 36), the strategy would be presented as one option among several leading to similar outcomes.

♦ **Reflection could become merely one of many goals to accomplish in an already demanding course.** Strategies to help new teachers to reflect can take on a life of their own, becoming yet another hurdle and detracting from the central purpose of assisting novice teachers to become more aware of themselves and their actions. The preparation of themes and personal narratives from tape recordings was reportedly time consuming. Although speech recognition software reduced this problem for one trainee as it largely eliminated the need for transcription, she had, prior to the start of the course and for another purpose, invested many hours in training her computer to recognize her voice. As technological advances are made, however, such software may prove to be of real value. For the moment, one solution may lie in offering the strategy as one alternative among others.

Conclusion

I have argued that adult learning in a learning-to-teach context ideally will encompass reflective practice, and it was suggested that one of the conditions required for effective reflective practice is self-awareness. Self-awareness, however, is enhanced by self-talk. The strategy proposed here both recognizes this and engages self-talk in order to foster, facilitate, and make visible reflective practice. As such, it is another strategy in a range of strategies currently available to enable the integration of reflective practice into a curriculum, including, for example, keeping a journal and maintaining a portfolio. It is suggested that one of the outcomes of the strategy, the personal narratives, could contribute toward both trainees' self-evaluation and the assessment of trainees' overall performance on the course, and could form part of trainees' portfolios, which are intended to capture the complexity of teaching and present a more rounded and valid view of a teacher's performance.

The strategy may also have applications in other contexts, as in the case of practicing, experienced teachers, and teacher trainers, as part of ongoing professional development or evaluation.

As I hope will be evident, this is an innovative strategy for trainee self-evaluation and assessment. The strategy should not be seen in isolation, but should be viewed as contributing to ongoing professional development, with the potential to sustain best practice over a trainee's post-course teaching career. Further research is called for, not only to address the issues but also to determine the overall value of the strategy for trainees, tutors, and potentially the experienced teacher. It is hoped that such challenges will be taken up and explored by other researchers in the field.

Discussion Questions

1. What are the ethical implications of the self-talk strategy as it is described in this chapter?

2. In what other educational contexts do you think the self-talk strategy could be effective?

3. How might you adapt the self-talk strategy to suit your own context?

4. Should skills of reflection be assessed in an adult learning context, and if so, how would you make such assessment fair?

5. Should tutors assume a responsibility for developing reflection skills in their adult learners?

REFERENCES

Atkins, S., & Murphy, K. (1998). Reflection: a review of literature. *Journal of Advanced Nursing, 18*, 1188–1192. In P. Moore, *Effectiveness of reflective learning. Development of professional practice research training fellowships: Occasional papers.* Bangor, Wales: Health Professions.

Boud, D., Keogh, R., & Walker, D. (1985). *Reflection: Turning experience into learning,* London: Kogan Page.

Boud, D., & Walker, D. (1998). Promoting reflection in professional courses: The challenge of context. *Studies in Higher Education, 23*(2), 191–206.

Brandt, C. (2004). Using generative networking to gather qualitative data. In P. Davidson, K. Bird, M. Al-Hamly, J. Aydelott, C. Coombe, & M. A. Khan (Eds.), *Proceedings of the 9th international TESOL Arabia conference: English language teaching in the IT Age.* TESOL Arabia: Dubai.

Brookfield, S. D. (1994). Significant personal learning. In D. Boud & V. Griffin (Eds.), *Appreciating adults learning: From the learners' perspective.* London: Kogan Page.

———. (1995). *Becoming a critically reflective teacher.* San Francisco: Jossey-Bass.

Dewey, J. (1933). *How we think.* Boston: D. C. Heath.

Earl, L., & LeMahieu, P. (1997). Rethinking assessment and accountability. In C. Thaine (2003). Diaries, theory, practice and assessment: The teacher educator as reflective practitioner. *University of Cambridge ESOL Examinations, Research Notes,* Issue 14, November 2003.

Eraut, M. (1994). *Developing professional knowledge and competence.* London: Falmer Press.

Ertmer, P., & Newby, T. (1996). The expert learner: strategic, self-regulated and reflective. *Instructional Science, 24,* 1–24.

Fletcher, C., & Baldry, C. (2000). A study of individual differences and self-awareness in the context of multi-source feedback. *Journal of Occupational & Organizational Psychology, 73*(3), 303–320.

Harris, D., & Bell, C. (1994). *Evaluating and assessing for learning,* London: Kogan Page.

Korthagen, F. A. J. (1993). Two modes of reflection. *Teaching and Teacher Education, 9*(3), 317–326.

Loughran, J. (1996). *Developing reflective practice: Learning about teaching and learning through modeling.* London: Falmer Press.

Mezirow, J. (1990). How critical reflection triggers transformative learning. In J. Mezirow & Associates, *Fostering critical reflection in adulthood. A guide to transformative and emancipatory learning,* San Francisco: Jossey-Bass.

Morin, A. (1993). Self-talk and self-awareness: on the nature of the relation. *Journal of Mind and Behaviour, 14*(1), 223–234.

———. (2004). Developing self-awareness with inner speech: Theoretical background, underlying mechanisms, and empirical evidence. Submitted for publication. Retrieved May 13, 2004, from   http://www2.mtroyal.ab.ca/~amorin/InnerSpeech.htm

Rogers, C. (1969). *Freedom to learn: A view of what education might be.* Columbus, OH: Merrill.

Schön, D. A. (1987). *Educating the reflective practitioner: Towards a new design for teaching and learning in the professions.* San Francisco, Jossey-Bass.

Scrivener, J. (1994). *Learning Teaching.* Oxford, UK: Heinemann.

Tobin, K. (1987). The role of wait time in higher cognitive learning. *Review of Educational Research, 57*(1), 69–75.

Tusting, K., & Barton, D. (2003). *Models of adult learning: A literature review.* National Research and Development Centre for Adult Literacy and Numeracy. London: Institute of Education.

Valli, L. (1997). Listening to other Voices: A description of teacher reflection in the United States. *Peabody Journal of Education, 72,* 68–89.

Vocate, D. R. (Ed.). (1994). *Intrapersonal communication: Different voices, different minds.* Mahwah, NJ: Lawrence Erlbaum Associates.

Vygotsky, L. (1978). *Mind in society, the development of higher psychological processes.* Cambridge, MA: Harvard University Press.

Wallace, M. J. (1991). *Training foreign language teachers: A reflective approach.* Cambridge: Cambridge University Press.

CHAPTER 14

Diversity-Responsive Assessment Tool: Assessing and Mentoring Effective Teaching in Multilingual, Multicultural Classrooms

Sheryl V. Taylor and Donna Sobel

Introduction

Accountability is a primary purpose in the teacher evaluation process. As recipients of public funds responsible for educating all students, universities and schools must ensure that each classroom is in the care of a competent teacher (Danielson, 2001). Teacher quality and effectiveness are inextricably tied to the work of schools, which is student learning (Schalock & Imig, 1999). The process of educational observation and supervision must support and prompt excellence in instruction for *all* learners, in particular English language learners. Today, nearly every state in the United States is engaged in a standards-based reform as evidenced by the development of statewide academic goals and guidelines for students as well as teachers (Claycomb & Kysilko, 2000). The *ESL Standards for Pre-K–12 Students* (TESOL, 1997) specified academic, social, and cultural goals for English language learners. These standards identified characteristics of high-quality programs intent on meeting the needs of English language learners.

Competent teachers today must understand, value, and know how to accommodate learners' experiences based on language, culture, race, ethnicity, ability, economic background, gender, and religion (Escamilla & Nathenson-Mejia, 2003; Taylor & Sobel, 2003a; Snow, 2000) in order to meet standards set by groups such as The National Council for Accreditation of Teacher Education (NCATE) and The National Board for Professional Teaching Standards (NBPTS). As we seek to reform educational practice for all learners, we must understand and capitalize on the dynamic relationship between standards for students and standards for teaching (Cloud, 2000).

Part of the challenge in identifying quality standards for teachers is distinguishing quality in the act of teaching. NCATE (1995) standards require that teachers "acquire and learn to apply the professional and pedagogical knowledge and skills to become competent to work with all students" and to create meaningful learning experiences for them (p. 17–18). NBPTS (1998) delineates four areas related to the knowledge base needed by ESL teachers and twelve teaching standards for teachers wanting certification in English as a new language. The four areas addressed include knowledge of (a) students, (b) language development, (c) culture, and (d) subject matter. The teaching standards specify creating positive learning environments, using instructional resources, providing meaningful learning experiences, using a variety of assessment methods, and understanding that there are multiple paths to knowledge. Moreover, both the NCATE and NBPTS standards have been adapted by state departments of education to guide requirements for teacher licensure and an added endorsement in a specialization area. We report on a standards-based tool developed to assess and mentor teachers' performance to meaningfully address the needs of learners with diverse backgrounds and abilities in multilingual, multicultural, and inclusive classrooms.

Context

Set within the western United States, the School of Education at the University of Colorado at Denver and Health Science Center (UCDHSC) is an urban teacher education program that reflects an urban mission, specifically, to ensure that teachers are skilled in working with diverse populations (Guyton & Byrd, 2000). The School of Education is situated in the heart of downtown Denver and provides leadership to support individuals from diverse backgrounds, communities, and organizations. In collaboration with partner schools, districts, and community agencies, the school: (1) offers degree programs in graduate and undergraduate initial teacher licensure, master's and doctoral levels; (2) conducts collaborative decision-making regarding course design and teacher evaluation; and, (3) supports models of instructional and learning excellence for all students, in particular, students from diverse populations.

Similar to many teacher educators and supervisors across the United States and elsewhere, the faculty in the School of Education are challenged to prepare, support, and evaluate teachers who can meet the demands of standards-based reform as they concurrently meet the educational needs of an increasingly diverse population in the classroom. While there is a critical need in the United States to recruit teachers of color and teachers from culturally diverse background and abilities, certainly all teachers must work effectively with learners in multilingual, multicultural, and inclusive classrooms in the nation's schools. Townsend (2002) cautions that "culturally responsive school reform must center on teacher expectations that are consistent with students' capabilities" (p. 228). Yet, it becomes near impossible to assess diversity-responsive teaching in a reliable and valid manner without basic agreement in the field or among faculty and school administrators about (1) how best to prepare teachers to teach in classrooms with diverse student populations (Cohran-Smith, 2004; Sleeter, 2001; Taylor & Sobel, 2003a); (2) how to recognize diversity-responsive teaching practices (Cochran-Smith & Lytle, 1993; Taylor & Sobel, 2002); and, (3) how to conduct collaborative dialogue about practice (Cochran-Smith & Lytle, 1993). Regrettably, such dialogue regarding diversity-responsive teaching practice is difficult, uncomfortable, and foreign to many educators (Sobel, Taylor, & Anderson, 2003a, 2003b).

While numerous studies have reported on teachers' perceived competence and attitudes regarding diversity issues in the classroom (Garmon, 2004; Middleton, 2002; Sleeter, 2001; Sobel, Taylor, Kalisher, & Weddle-Steinberg, 2002; Taylor & Sobel, 2001, 2003), few data support or distinguish effective classroom teaching practices (Sheets, 2003; Taylor & Sobel, 2002). The processes of educational observation and supervision need to occur to support and promote excellence in instruction for all learners. Objective, differentiated observation instruments as well as exemplars that substantiate quality teaching performance are especially needed in the area of diversity-responsive teaching. Customized guides focused on observing, assessing, and mentoring teachers' abilities to meet the diverse needs of all students offer one way to serve this need. We describe a standards-based assessment tool used to evaluate and mentor pre-service and inservice teachers' abilities to meaningfully address issues of a diverse learner population in multilingual, multicultural, and inclusive classrooms.

Description

The need for an assessment tool that focuses on diversity-responsive teaching is an outgrowth of a seven-year longitudinal investigation (Sobel et al. 2002; Taylor & Sobel, 2001, 2002, 2003a, 2003b) and our work as university faculty who regularly coach and supervise teachers during their school internship and practicum experiences. Coming from the perspective of teacher educator researchers in the respective fields of Second Language Education (Taylor) and Special Education (Sobel), we saw a clear need for research and organizational support of teachers' instructional practices regarding learners who are linguistically, culturally, and academically diverse. Conclusions from our baseline investigation (Taylor & Sobel, 2001) concur with assertions made by Schultz, Neyhart, and Reck (1996) and Webb-Johnson, Artiles, Trent, Jackson, & Velox (1998) for future research needed to understand how teachers' beliefs are integrated within their classroom teaching practices and behaviors. However, to date, most teacher education research has not been designed to investigate the assumption that teachers' learning or experiences with learners in culturally diverse contexts will result in better teaching of learners with diverse backgrounds and abilities.

Prompted by an identified need to focus on teacher education outcomes regarding factors of diversity, we began collaboration on the development of an observation tool. After reviewing various observation tools, we drafted a tool that aligned with the School of Education mission, and focused on diversity-responsive teaching practices and behaviors. A group of highly experienced "critical friends" who reviewed the tool called for expanded clarification of terminology, minor editorial revisions, and resounding agreement for such a tool. Concurrent to our drafting of the preliminary observation tool, a large school district near Metropolitan Denver (Boulder Valley School District [BVSD], Boulder, Colorado) was finalizing district evaluation standards and criteria for classroom teaching that aligned with state teaching standards (Colorado Department of Education, 2000), and requested our help to customize their standards with classroom observation criteria.

Hence, our work began with district representatives to refine our observation tool for evaluating diversity-responsive teaching and to operationalize the district's diversity teaching standard (e.g., *The teacher shall demonstrate competency in valuing and promoting understanding of diversity* see Table 14.1). The charge was two-fold: (a) meet the requirements of the district evaluation standard and (b) evaluate and support teachers' development in diversity-responsive teaching. Our collaboration resulted in a refined tool which was adopted by the district administration (See Table 14.2), piloted with district principals and teachers, and published (Kozleski, Sobel, & Taylor, 2003; Sobel, Taylor, & Anderson, 2003a, 2003b).

Regardless of the need for such an observation tool, tools are only as good as they are reliable. Reliability, the consistency of scores obtained from a measurement technique, is generally indicated by a high reliability coefficient as a result of fairly stable or consistent scores across multiple administrations of the measurement (Goodwin, 2001; Hughes, 2003). There are several different types of reliability; the types that are particularly relevant here are interrater reliability and interrater agreement. To obtain preliminary estimates of interrater reliability and interrater agreement, we conducted a preliminary reliability study using the "diversity-responsive assessment tool."

Serving as "expert" raters in a preliminary reliability study using the "diversity-responsive assessment tool," we employed the tool to independently rate the teaching practices and behaviors implemented by a classroom teacher in a videotaped teaching segment. The teaching episode was videotaped in a general education classroom at a professional development school that partners with the School of Education. The school profile mirrors many of the challenges faced by urban schools in the United States today, including: 40 percent of students are from minority ethnic/racial backgrounds, close to 15 percent of the students are English language learners, 15 percent of the students are identified with special education needs, and the school has a 29 percent mobility rate. The teacher in the videotape has 24 years of teaching experience, a Master's degree in Elementary Education, and additional licensure in Literacy.

After viewing the segment, we independently rated and scored the teacher's behaviors and practices using the tool. Our analysis focused on looking at the

Table 14.1:
Standard 2: The Teacher Shall Demonstrate Competency in Valuing and Promoting Understanding of Diversity

The licensed teacher is dedicated to making academic achievement a reality for all students and acts on the belief that all students can learn. The teacher is responsive to the needs and experiences each student brings to the classroom, including those based on race, ethnicity, gender, sexual orientation, disability, age, religion, socio-economic status, and linguistic differences.

Criteria	Indicators
A. Demonstrates skill and competency in the design and application of inclusive instructional approaches, assessment techniques, and curriculum content.	1. Employs a variety of assessment methods to obtain information about students' learning and development to support student achievement among groups that show gaps in achievement. 2. Demonstrates knowledge of multicultural education and incorporates contributions and perspectives of diverse groups of people in curriculum and content in all subject areas. 3. Makes multicultural concepts an integral part of classroom. 4. Makes appropriate modifications and accommodations to ensure that every student is successful. 5. Identifies specific interventions to support increased student achievement among groups and reduce differences in patterns of achievement. 6. Uses grouping strategies to enhance student achievement and promote non-like group interaction.
B. Reinforces and models the district's strategic priority of valuing and promoting understanding of diversity.	1. Understands and implements the non-discrimination policy of no tolerance for discrimination and harassment. 2. Models principles of an inclusive democracy such as majority rule with individual rights and due process. 3. Reinforces respect for the rights and responsibilities of citizens in a democracy. 4. Works well with and treats with dignity and respect all individuals regardless of race, ethnicity, gender, sexual orientation, disability, age, or religion. 5. Encourages students to work cooperatively, enabling social and intellectual interactions and meaningful relationships to develop across diverse groups in the classroom. 6. Maintains a safe and culturally responsive classroom.
C. Continues to increase knowledge of equity and diversity issues and recognizes their effect on student achievement.	1. Understands implications of teacher attitudes and beliefs about diversity for student achievement. 2. Practices and exhibits commitment to principles of equity and diversity.
D. Acknowledges that parent and community involvement in the education of students is key to achievement.	1. Involves all parents, with particular outreach to parents who are underrepresented members of the community, in school-planned activities. 2. Broadens understanding of cultural differences in school/parent relationships that can lead to misunderstandings. 3. Welcomes parents and community members into the classroom and encourages volunteering.

extent of a match between raters as we assigned scores and rated the teacher's practices and behaviors (Taylor & Sobel, 2004). This preliminary study of reliability resulted in 80 percent agreement between the two raters in the scores assigned to the teacher's performance or behavior. Despite these promising outcomes, we recognize the need for subsequent research in order to verify the results of the preliminary study and have conducted a follow-up study including 40 raters using the tool to assess teaching practices and behaviors in the same videotaped teaching segment. A final report of the analysis is anticipated shortly (Sobel & Taylor, 2004).

Distinctive Features

The call for teacher accountability has been clearly made by U.S. legislators at the national and state level, educators from universities and school districts, and profoundly concerned parents and community leaders. Good teaching is responsive instruction in which educators provide instructional strategies and curriculum consistent with students' experiences, linguistic and cultural perspectives, and developmental needs. Today, all teachers will be held accountable to demonstrate such responsiveness. Given that approximately 39 percent of the teachers had students in their classrooms with limited English proficiency and only one-quarter of those teachers received training to work with these learners (U.S. Department of Education, 1997), educators must be extended feedback and clear guidance for professional development in the area of standards-based teaching that is responsive to the challenges of students with increasingly diverse backgrounds and needs (Taylor & Sobel, 2003a).

An observation tool such as the "diversity-responsive assessment tool" provides one component of a differentiated accountability plan for teachers given that good teachers are good for a variety of reasons, and we want the evaluation data to reflect each teacher's individual strengths" (Peterson, Wahlquist, Bone, Thompson, & Chatterton, 2001, p. 41). Moreover, observation tools that reflect a standard for performing competently help supervisors recognize demonstrable elements of diversity-responsive teaching. The "diversity-responsive assessment tool" illustrates key elements of innovative standards-based assessment.

Consisting of two major sections, the standards-based tool aligns with each of the four criteria and the seventeen indicators identified in the BVSD diversity standard (see Table 14.2). Section one focuses on direct classroom observation with skill indicators in the two areas of (A) instructional approaches, assessments, techniques, and curriculum, and (B) valuing and prompting an understanding of diversity. Section two prompts guided questions for conversation relevant to the areas of (C) the teacher's knowledge of equity and diversity issues and their impact on student achievement, and (D) parent and community involvement in the education of students as key to their achievement.

Table 14.2: Standards-Based Assessment Tool
for Diversity-Responsive Teaching.

DIVERSITY-RESPONSIVE ASSESSMENT TOOL

TEACHER: _____ SCHOOL: _____

SUBJECT AREA: _____ GRADE: _____

OBSERVER: _____ DATE(S) OF OBSERVATION: _____

STANDARD: The teacher shall demonstrate competency in valuing and promoting
understanding of diversity.

SECTION #1: DIRECT CLASSROOM OBSERVATION
<u>Directions</u>: The observer and observee should collaboratively determine which section(s) of the
tool should be selected as areas of focus. It may be that some items, particularly section #1A and
section #3 is completed by the observee, while section #2 is completed by the observer. Those reflections, observations, and conversations should focus on the following diversity factors: culture,
ethnicity/race, gender, language, ability/learning, religion, socio-economic status, age, and sexual
orientation.

A. Demonstrates skill and competency in the design and application of inclusive
   instructional approaches, assessments, techniques, and curriculum.

Evidence:
1. Describe the environmental print displayed about the room that demonstrates a valuing of
   diversity (i.e., visual supports, posters, banners, etc.).

2a. Describe grouping strategies that enhance student achievement and promote non-like group
    interaction (i.e., ability level, gender, etc.).

2b. Sketch the room with attention to the instructional arrangements.

BACK OF ROOM	What conclusions would you draw from this arrangement?
FRONT OF ROOM	

3. Describe specific instructional materials that illustrate valuing and promoting the understanding of diversity factors (i.e., multicultural literature, manipulatives).

4. How is the teacher adapting the lesson for individual students (i.e., differentiating instruction regarding diversity factors across content, delivery or evaluation)?

Student (identified by name or clothing, i.e., color of shirt)	**Explicit illustration that reflects a valuing of diversity factors**

Please rate each item with the scale: 1 = little to no competency observed; 2 = fair to adequate competency observed; 3 = strong competency observed		
5. Demonstrates appropriately needed "distribution of attention" to all students. Teacher attends to students in a manner that demonstrates respect for students' diverse abilities and experiences.	1 2 3	Comments:
6. The teacher ensures that all students understand and can carry out the procedures for instructional activities.	1 2 3	Comments:
7. The teacher makes instructional content relevant, linked to students' practical experiences, attends to learning styles, multiple modes of delivery, and checks for understanding.	1 2 3	Comments:

B. Reinforces and models the district's strategic priority of valuing and promoting understanding of diversity.

Evidence:
1. Works well with and treats with dignity and respect all individuals regardless of race, ethnicity, ability, language, gender, sexual orientation, age, or religion.

Tally the specific teacher comments and interactions directed towards each student.

Student	Praise	Question	Feedback	Direction Giving	Redirection	Other

2a. Describe the types of student-to-student and student-to-teacher interactions.

2b. What does the teacher do to encourage social and intellectual interactions and promote meaningful relationships to develop across diverse groups in the classroom?

Please rate each item with the scale: 1 = little to no competency observed; 2 = fair to adequate competency observed; 3 = strong competency observed		
3. Establishes and maintains consistent positive standards for classroom behavior that are equitable for all students. The teacher demonstrates the ability to change and adapt his/her classroom plan after reflecting on changing student and classroom needs.	1 2 3	Comments:
4. Makes the physical and psychological environment safe and conducive to learning. The teacher uses the physical and psychological environment as a resource to facilitate learning. Provisions are made to accommodate all students.	1 2 3	Comments:

SECTION #2: GUIDED QUESTIONS FOR CONVERSATION

C. Continues to increase knowledge of equity and diversity issues and recognizes their effect on student achievement.

Evidence:

1a. Teacher identifies specific examples of what he/she has personally engaged in that demonstrate commitment to principles of equity and diversity.

a.

b.

c.

1b. How did those experiences increase your understanding regarding the implications of teacher attitude and beliefs about diversity for student achievement?

2. Teacher articulates the specific goals that he/she has set aimed at personally increasing knowledge of equity and diversity issues and the resulting effect on student achievement.

a.

b.

c.

> D. Acknowledges that parent and community involvement in the education of students is key to achievement.

Evidence:

1. Teacher articulates concrete examples (i.e., newsletter, phone log, home visits, content-sharing documentation, mentors, field trips, guest speakers) of ways he/she has involved all parents, with outreach to parents who are underrepresented members in the community.

   a.

   b.

   c.

2. Teacher identifies concrete examples that illustrate efforts that welcome parents and community members into the classroom and encourage volunteering.

   a.

   b.

   c.

SECTION #3: ANALYSIS AND RECOMMENDATIONS

◆ Areas of Strength:
◆ Suggestions for continued attention to students' diversity factors:

With the call for quality-teaching performance in the area of diversity-responsive teaching, teachers and their supervisors continue to be challenged by the day-to-day planning and delivering of instruction that is responsive to the diverse backgrounds and needs of learners in the classroom. Despite descriptions of characteristics and practices that are culturally responsive (Ladson-Billings, 2001; Villegas & Lucas, 2002), teachers ask for specific examples of teaching practices and behaviors that meet the needs of students in linguistically and culturally diverse classrooms. Moreover, supervisors continue to struggle with effective ways to evaluate and support teachers as they strive to meet standards and address learners' needs.

Using the diversity-responsive assessment tool, supervisors and teachers are prompted to consider nine components relevant to diversity responsiveness (i.e., Section One: classroom observation; and, Section Two: guided questions to prompt conversation). These components focus on specific aspects of instruction and include:

- *Environmental print.* Descriptions of print and displays around the room that demonstrate a valuing of diversity.
- *Grouping strategies.* Provide guidelines for identifying grouping strategies that enhance student achievement and promote non-like group interaction (i.e., language, ability level, gender, etc.).
- *Instructional materials.* Description of specific instructional materials that illustrate valuing the understanding of diversity factors (i.e., multicultural literature, manipulatives, etc.).
- *Lesson adaptations.* Articulate the continued process of accommodating for individual strengths and needs (i.e., differentiating instruction regarding diversity factors across content, delivery, and evaluation).
- *Distribution of attention.* Descriptions of ways the teacher attends to students in a manner that demonstrates respect for students' diverse abilities and experiences.
- *Evidence of student understanding.* Identification of ways the teacher ensures that all students understand and can carry out instructional activities.
- *Positive standards for classroom behavior.* Description of consistent positive and equitable standards for classroom behavior.
- *Personal growth toward principles of equity and diversity.* Description of ways teacher increases knowledge of equity and diversity issues relevant to student achievement.
- *Parent and community involvement.* Articulation of ways teachers involve all parents, outreach to underrepresented parents, community members (i.e., newsletter, phone log, home visit).

Since its early development, the "diversity-responsive assessment tool" has been guided by feedback from stakeholders including experienced teachers, pre-service teachers, principals, administrators, supervisors, and teacher educators. The stakeholders concurred that a tool such as this can contribute to meeting teaching standards focused on demonstrating a valuing of diversity (Kozleski, Sobel, & Taylor, 2003; Sobel, Taylor, & Anderson, 2003a, 2003b). Principals and teachers noted that using the tool spurred new conversations focused on cultural awareness-raising. For example, one teacher noted how the tool served as a script: "This [tool] served as an excellent set of conversation prompts for teachers. Another use might be peer coaching. I could see myself using this [tool] with student teachers so they could actually hear me articulate the values and beliefs that guide my work in the classroom that they will be working in." Another teacher explained how the tool could aid in her own understanding: "There are so many differing perspectives about these issues. This tool helps to get us all thinking and discussing with some common language those important issues."

These type of assessments send a serious message about standards to administrators, teacher educators, and teachers. Second, each of the evidence indicators delineated under sections one and two guides teachers toward the district's vision of essential teaching and learning. Third, it helps individual teachers meet the standards. The ultimate goal of the district standard is not to sort "good" versus "poor" teachers, but rather to enable all teachers to demonstrate competency in valuing and promoting understanding of diversity. Finally, an assessment such as this one ensures all students equal access to and the benefits of quality education. Focused observation, assessment, and mentoring of teachers' abilities to provide diversity-responsive instruction contribute to enhanced access for all students.

Caveats

Evaluating and supporting teachers' skills to address the diverse backgrounds and needs of students in today's classrooms are ongoing challenges facing administrators, supervisors, and teacher educators in U.S. school districts and universities. With the number of school-age learners who use a language other than English in U.S. schools having increased 68 percent since the mid-1990s (TESOL, 1997), teachers today are called on to serve an evermore diverse student population. However, many teachers lack the training necessary to carry out these new roles. How do we as supervisors go about assessing teachers' competence and concurrently supporting their professional development in this area? The "diversity-responsive assessment tool" offers one way to focus on teachers' practices and teacher education outcomes relevant to learners and factors of diversity. Yet, there are caveats and considerations as we look at contextual, programmatic, and personnel factors in order to make assessment decisions regarding teachers' performance.

An instrument used to evaluate and support teachers' performance must be relevant for the given educational context. It must align with program expectations, goals, and professional teaching standards. Such alignment requires careful review and candid reflection by program administrators, faculty, and stakeholders. In the case of the "diversity-responsive assessment tool," we made a continued effort throughout its development to align the tool with the School of Education mission that also corresponds closely with our own goals as researchers and teacher educators. Once collaboration with BVSD began, our efforts to customize and align the tool with district standards were time consuming but rewarding because of our shared commitment to teaching that is responsive to students' diverse backgrounds and needs.

In order for the diversity-responsive assessment tool or any instrument to be used successfully, there must be buy-in from key stakeholders. Ideally, the supervisors evaluating teachers will have reflected introspectively on their own commitment to learners of diverse backgrounds and abilities. It is imperative that supervisors and university faculty examine our philosophy and practice to determine if we are "walking the talk" or just "talking the talk." Such critical reflection should be encouraged at the individual level and coordinated at the program level (e.g., faculty inservice). Moreover, it is essential for the supervisor to have had successful, ongoing experiences delivering teaching that is responsive to students' of diverse backgrounds and needs. Without such experiences, the supervisor will lack confidence and credibility with classroom teachers.

Individuals using the tool for evaluation and mentoring purposes need to be skilled at quickly assessing the teacher's proficiency. A highly competent supervisor needs to engage a variety of strategies to assess the teacher's performance, explain the outcomes, and construct effective learning processes for the teacher's professional development. If concerns are identified, the supervisor needs to describe clear and concrete exemplars the teacher can implement to improve his or her instruction relevant to diversity responsiveness. When the teacher asks, "But, how else could I respond to the students' diverse backgrounds and needs? What else could I be doing to support these learners?" the supervisor must be prepared with a ready supply of examples to articulate what the teacher is doing and what must be improved. The supervisor must be committed to conversations that support purposeful improvement of practice through collaborative dialogue about practice (Cochran-Smith & Lytle, 1993).

Last, teachers as stakeholders need time to review and discuss the tool prior to its implementation. Before teachers are evaluated, they should be provided an overview of the expectations and performance-based assessments. In our pilot study, stakeholders reported that review and discussion of the tool aided their understanding of the new diversity standard and essential issues related to culture, language, and other factors of diversity with respect to classroom instruction. Stakeholders also indicated an enhanced ability to self-analyze their own practice as a result of having reviewed the tool. Hence, we encourage supervisors to use the tool for informative and instructional purposes with teacher-stakeholders prior to implementing the tool for evaluative purposes.

Conclusion

Recent policy changes and redesign efforts by professional organizations and university schools of education across the United States have led to the creation of performance-based assessments. These assessments align with national, state, and district teaching standards and aid in determining teachers' proficiency to meet the standards. Clearly, all teachers will be held accountable to meet diversity-related standards, thereby demonstrating responsiveness to learners' diverse backgrounds and needs. As such, teachers are expected to provide instructional strategies and curriculum consistent with students' life experiences, linguistic and cultural perspectives, and developmental needs.

The diversity-responsive assessment tool offers a standards-based and customized assessment guide focused on observing, assessing, and mentoring teachers' abilities to meaningfully address the diverse needs of learners in multilingual, multicultural, and inclusive classrooms. With few data supporting or distinguishing effective teaching that is responsive to students' diverse backgrounds and needs, we predict that assessment guides grounded in performance-based assessment such as the diversity-responsive assessment tool will become part of a support system that can signal when a teacher excels or needs extra help. Moreover, tools that clearly and concretely reflect a teaching standard for performing competently help supervisors recognize demonstrable elements of responsive teaching.

Together, school districts and universities share the responsibility to address teacher standards. Both school districts and universities need tools that assess teacher standards and encourage substantive discussions about diversity-responsive teaching. Given that teachers continue to ask for clear examples of teaching practices and behaviors that successfully meet the needs of students in linguistically and culturally diverse classrooms, the nine components addressed in the tool direct teachers and supervisors to the "nuts and bolts" of comprehensive teaching that can demonstrate a competency in valuing and promoting understanding of diversity. With 80 percent of teachers reporting that they feel ill equipped to teach diverse populations (Futrell, Gomez, & Bedden, 2003), a standards-based assessment tool such as the diversity-observation assessment tool gives a serious message to administrators and teachers about the need to guide and enable teachers to demonstrate competency in teaching that is responsive to students' diverse backgrounds and needs.

Discussion Questions

1. Consider the stakeholders in your current teaching context. In what ways do you hold them accountable? As a teacher, to whom are you accountable? In what ways are your teaching practices and subsequent learning outcomes held accountable?

2. Locate the professional teaching standards that guide teachers in your professional field (e.g, TESOL standards). What attributes, dispositions, and characteristics are delineated in these teaching standards? In what ways do the standards impact your work? What steps do you take to ensure that you meet the teaching standards on a regular basis?

3. Locate and bring a sample of an observation tool that is currently being used by a program, school, or district for the purpose of evaluating and operationalizing a teaching standard for teachers of English language learners. After a thorough review of the tool, analyze the extent to which the application of the tool evaluates the teacher's ability to meet the standard. What potential does the tool—and subsequent discussion—offer for the teacher's professional development toward meeting the standard?

4. All teachers teach students with a range of diverse backgrounds and abilities. Consider and explain the ways that you identify English language learners' backgrounds and abilities. Articulate the ways you plan for and teach in such a way to address a wide range of learner backgrounds and abilities.

5. Identify considerations and potential challenges that teachers of English language learners face with designing grouping arrangements (e.g., small groups, pairs, whole class, etc.).

6. Provide examples of a lesson where the teacher made instructional content relevant, linked to English language learners' practical experiences, attends to learning styles, multiple modes of delivery, and checks for understanding. Consider how you do this or could do this in your teaching context.

7. Articulate specific steps and actions that teachers can take to increase their knowledge of cultural issues and the impact of culture on equity issues relevant to teaching English language learners from a variety of cultural backgrounds and/or with a range of diverse abilities.

REFERENCES

Claycomb, C., & Kysilko, D. (2000, Spring). The purposes & elements of effective assessment systems. *The State Education Standard*, 7–11.

Cloud, N. (2000). Incorporating ESL standards into teacher education: Ideas for teacher educators. In M. A. Snow (Ed.), *Implementing ESL standards for pre-K-12 students through teacher education* (pp. 1–32). Alexandria, VA: Teachers of English to Speakers of Other Languages.

Cochran-Smith, M. (2004). The problem of teacher education. *Journal of Teacher Education, 55*(4), 295–299.

Cochran-Smith, M., & Lytle, S. (1993). *Inside/outside: Teacher research and teacher knowledge.* New York: Teachers College Press.

Colorado Department of Education. (2000). *Performance-based standards for Colorado teachers.* Denver, CO: Author.

Danielson, C. (2001). New trends in teacher evaluation. *Educational Leadership, 58*(5), 12–15.

Escamilla, K., & Nathenson-Mejia, S. (2003). Preparing culturally responsive teachers: Using Latino children's literature in teacher education. *Equity & Excellence in Education, 36*(3), 238–248.

Futrell, M. H., Gomez, J., & Bedden, D. (2003). Teaching the children of a new America: The challenge of diversity. *Phi Delta Kappan, 84*(5), 381–85.

Garmon, M. A. (2004). Changing preservice teachers' attitudes/beliefs about diversity: What are the critical factors? *Journal of Teacher Education, 55*(3), 201–213.

Goodwin, L. D. (2001). Interrater agreement and reliability. *Measurement in Physical Education and Exercise Science, 5*(1), 13–34.

Guyton, E., & Byrd, D. (Eds.). (2000). *Standards for field experiences in teacher education.* Reston, VA: Association of Teacher Educators.

Hughes, A. (2003). *Testing for language teachers.* Cambridge: Cambridge University Press.

Kozleski, E. B., Sobel, D. M., & Taylor, S. V. (2003). Embracing and building culturally responsive practices. *Multiple Voices, 6*(1), 73–87.

Ladson-Billings, G. (2001). *Crossing over to Canan: The journey of new teachers in diverse classrooms.* San Francisco: Jossey-Bass.

Middleton, V. A. (2002). Increasing preservice teachers' diversity beliefs and commitment. *The Urban Review, 34*(4), 343–361.

National Board for Professional Teaching Standards. (1998). *English as a new language standards for national board certification.* Southfield, MI: Author.

National Council for Accreditation of Teacher Education. (1995). *Standards, procedures and policies for the accreditation of professional education units.* Washington, DC: Author.

Peterson, K. D., Wahlquist, C., Bone, K., Thompson, J., & Chatterton, K. (2001). Using more data sources to evaluate teachers. *Educational Leadership, 58*(5), 40–43.

Schalock, D., & Imig, D. (1999). *Shulman's Union of Insufficiencies + 7: New dimensions of accountability for teachers and teacher educators.* Washington, DC: AACTE.

Sheets, R. H. (2003). Competency vs. good intentions: Diversity ideologies and teacher potential. *Qualitative Studies in Education, 16*(1), 111–120.

Schultz, E., Neyhart, T. K., & Reck, U. M. (1996). Swimming against the tide: A study of prospective teachers' attitudes regarding cultural diversity and urban teaching. *Western Journal of Black Studies (20)*1, 1–7.

Sleeter, C. E. (2001). Preparing teachers for culturally diverse schools: Research and the overwhelming presence of whiteness. *Journal of Teacher Education, 2*(2), 94–106.

Snow, M. A. (2000). *Implementing ESL standards for pre-K-12 students through teacher education.* Alexandria, VA: Teachers of English to Speakers of Other Languages.

Sobel, D. M., & Taylor, S. V. (2004). *Recognizing diversity-responsive teaching practices: A reliability study of the "diversity-responsive assessment tool.* Unpublished, University of Colorado at Denver & Health Sciences Center.

Sobel, D. M., Taylor, S. V., & Anderson, R. E. (2003a). Shared accountability: Encouraging diversity-responsive teaching in inclusive contexts. *Teaching exceptional children, 35*(6), 46–54.

———. (2003b). Teacher evaluation standards in practice: A standards-based assessment tool for diversity-responsive teaching. *The Teacher Educator, 38*(4), 285–302.

Sobel, D. M., Taylor, S. V., Kalisher, S., & Weddle-Steinberg, R. (2002). A self-study of diversity issues: Preservice teachers' beliefs revealed through classroom practices. *Multiple Voices, 5*(1), 1–12.

Taylor, S. V., & Sobel, D. M. (2001). Addressing the discontinuity of students' and teachers' diversity: A preliminary study of preservice teachers' beliefs and perceived skills. *Teaching and Teacher Education, 17*(4), 487–503.

———. (2002). Missing in action: Research on the accountability of multicultural, inclusive teacher education. *Essays in Education, 2* (summer), 1–21. Retrieved from www.usca.edu/essays/vol22002/taylor.pdf

———. (2003a). Rich contexts to emphasize social justice in teacher education: Curriculum and pedagogy in professional development schools. *Equity and Excellence in Education, 36*(3), 249–258.

———. (2003b). Paradise envisioned? Paradise realized? What do preservice teachers in an initial teacher education program grounded in PDSs say about their preparation to address issues of students' diversity? In press, *Teaching & Change* [On-line serial].

———. (2004). Interrater agreement and reliability study of diversity-responsive assessment tool. Unpublished raw data.

TESOL. (1997). *ESL standards for pre-K-12 students.* Alexandria, VA: Author.

TESOL/NCATE Program Standards (2003). *Standards for the accreditation of initial programs in P-12 ESL teacher education.* Alexandria, VA: Author.

Townsend, B. (2002). Testing while black: Standards-based school reform and African American learners. *Remedial and Special Education, 23*(4), 222–230.

United States Department of Education. (1997). *To assure the free appropriate public education of all children with disabilities: 19th annual report to Congress on the implementation of the Individuals with Disabilities Education Act.* Washington, DC: U.S. Department of Education.

Villegas, A. M., & Lucas, T. (2002). Preparing culturally responsive teachers: Rethinking the curriculum. *Journal of Teacher Education, 53*(1), 20–32.

Webb-Johnson, G., Artiles, A. J., Trent, S. C., Jackson, C. W., & Velox, A. (1998). The status of research on multicultural education in teacher education and special education. *Remedial and Special Education, 19*(1), 7–15.

CHAPTER 15

Teacher Voice in Teacher Evaluation: Teaching Portfolios in the United Arab Emirates

Fatma Alwan

Introduction

Teaching Portfolios (TPs) have been in use for teacher evaluation in higher educational institutions in the United Arab Emirates (UAE) for some time, but were almost unknown in the public education sector until recently. This chapter discusses the rationale behind using TPs for teacher evaluation and the measures to be taken to ensure successful implementation of the practice. First, a description of the context is presented to familiarize the reader with the working conditions in UAE public schools, followed by an account on how the innovation came into existence. The recommendations listed at the end are based on empirical research as well as on published literature. They are meant to guide those who wish to start a similar project. I offer them as guidelines to counter, or at the very least, ameliorate the imperfections and gaps that I found associated with the practice at its early stages.

Teacher Evaluation in the UAE: The Status Quo

The majority of the EFL teachers in the UAE come from Arab countries, including Egypt, Syria, Lebanon, Jordan, Palestine, Tunisia, and Sudan, and their contracts are renewed on an annual basis. Generally, the first year of the teacher's work in the UAE has a critical consequence on gaining tenure. At the beginning of the year, new recruits are familiarized with the system and coached throughout the year by supervisors. Intensive follow-up of newly recruited teachers ensures that low-performing teachers are released from service by the end of the year. In subsequent years, the evaluation report is a decisive element as to whether or not the annual contract is renewed.

Currently, teacher evaluation in the UAE is carried out by two evaluators—the school principal and the subject supervisor—who participate jointly in writing an annual confidential appraisal report for each teacher. Several attempts have been made to improve the quality of the practice. For instance, the criteria for evaluation have been reviewed several times to cover as much as possible all the areas of the teacher's work (Al-Nayadi, 1989). Classroom observation has always been the major component on which teacher evaluation was based, and consequently, the final appraisal report. But how effective is classroom observation as the sole basis for teacher evaluation? This has, and continues to be, a controversial issue.

The Ministry of Education (MoE) is aware that relying on classroom observation as the sole measure in evaluation has serious drawbacks. While it is recognized that teachers give their best during the observed class, it is believed that they are likely to resort to traditional ways of teaching in other lessons when they are not observed. They are also thought to perform exceptionally well when the supervisor's visit is planned. What is more, during the post-observation conference, some teachers seek to get credit for oral reports of their achievements without providing solid evidence. These ratings are unreliable since different ratings, as Gersten (2001) observes, are given by different supervisors when the teacher is transferred to another school and the difference seems to be higher when the teacher is transferred to another educational district (Alwan, 2004).

Contextual Constraints: Are They Considered When Evaluating Teachers?

But if teachers were initially well qualified, why do they resort to traditional ways of teaching? And how can we make sure that teachers are given credit for what they do? The stressful working conditions have a lot to do with this, and they are discussed in the section that follows. Educational research in the UAE indicates that there is a general dissatisfaction with regard to the working conditions of teachers in public school (Altraifi, 1999; Ghareeb, 1996). Overall there are various curricular restraints associated with the materials, the exams, and teaching methods in a context where there is a lack of support and resources (Ghareeb, 1996). On the other hand, teachers carry out various administrative tasks in addition to their instructional duties. As a result, all these constraints have dire consequences on teachers when considering evaluation.

In the first place, various curricular constraints have contributed to making the teacher's working environment very demanding. EFL teaching materials in public schools often fail to meet students' needs and do not match the allotted time. The nature of the text-based exam adds to this restriction (Loughrey et al., 1999). Parallel to these demands remains the problem of the lack of curricular resources and support. Taken as a whole, these multifaceted factors have contributed to the problem regarding teachers using traditional teaching techniques. In addition, since the exams are text based and time pressures are ever existent, teachers inevitably tend to focus mainly on that which is covered on the exam (Altraifi, 1999).

Furthermore, as noted by Altraifi (1999), teachers are burdened with administrative tasks that consume their time at school. Besides instruction, teachers carry out instruction-related tasks of writing lesson plans, preparing supplementary materials and exams, checking written work, marking exams, and the like. Additionally, they do other administrative tasks such as preparing report cards, advising students, solving problems, supervising activities, invigilating exams, supervising buses and field trips, attending meetings, and pursuing professional development, to mention a few. Added to these are frustrations associated with the demands of supervision in the area of professional development, while provision for in-service training is lacking (Al-Nayadi, 1989; Ghareeb,1996).

Unfortunately, neither the school principal nor the supervisor can become aware of all aspects of the teachers' performance. In reality, while principals are overburdened with administrative issues, the supervisors are absent from schools most of the school year. Considering that both are responsible for evaluating teachers, one can only wonder how reliable their evaluation of teachers is. Consequently, an additional person, who knows the teacher very well, needs to take charge in teacher evaluation. This person is the teacher. But how can self-evaluation be incorporated into teacher evaluation?

Description

Some grievances I collected during my work experience as a supervisor show that teachers have every reason to seek more control over the evaluation of their teaching. Bearing in mind that teacher assessment is a high-stakes issue; teachers have to be invited to take part in the process. But how can teachers have a voice in this issue? The answer is to introduce portfolio assessment. In many respects, teaching portfolios (TPs) allow teachers to take part in their own evaluation. This section describes how I introduced this innovation in the schools where I am a supervisor, then in my local educational district, and how they were eventually adopted statewide for formative evaluation.

An Innovation in Teacher Evaluation in the UAE: The Case of Teaching Portfolios

As a supervisor of EFL teachers, I began using TPs in some of my schools on a gradual basis for two years (1999 to 2001). I believed that in this way I was making teachers partners in teacher evaluation, as TPs were useful in providing a wider scope of the teacher's work that I was not paying attention to because, like other supervisors, my visits to the schools were limited to one or two per month. Subsequently, portfolios served the purpose in giving me a clearer idea of the teachers' accomplishments while I was away from the school. They were also useful tools for collecting formative data to guide the discussion when negotiating the final evaluation reports with the school principals. Based on solid evidence in TPs, I was able to negotiate better ratings for teachers because anyone who doubted the ratings could easily refer to the teachers' portfolios.

In the academic year 2001–02 I proposed using portfolios as tools of supervision for formative evaluation on a larger scale in the Ajman Educational District along with three other English supervisors who embraced the innovation. The first purpose behind the use of portfolios was to get teachers to provide evidence of completed activities that were usually credited without proof of completion, and to keep other documents required for follow-up ready for review (such as annual plans, analysis of students' results, and remedial or curriculum enrichment activities administered to students). The second purpose was to back up the evaluation process recommended by the MoE, which was thought to be lacking in reliability (Loughrey et al., 1999). This was clear to the senior supervisor of English, and the EFL supervisors in all districts, since they realized that many teachers seemed to get different ratings when they were transferred to other educational districts (Gersten, 2001).

To be able to maintain conformity among teachers, I worked out a list of what was supposed to be included in portfolios based on the MoE's criteria for evaluation listed in the teacher's cumulative register, which is a booklet for recording classroom observation reports and other supervisory visits of individual teachers. The list was reviewed by the team of supervisors of English in the district, and an extensive letter was sent to all the schools in the district. The teachers were asked to submit evidence that documented their work for that year only and present it formally by the end of the year by including it in a portfolio. They were also encouraged to showcase their accomplishments during the supervisors' visits to the schools. Throughout the year, several teachers discussed their portfolios with their supervisors. The supervisors reported the success of portfolios in terms of their usefulness in many areas.

In the beginning, as this had been an in-house initiative, several teachers who have been known for their competence and long years of service asked to be exempt from the project and their wishes were respected. Still, they made available for review the basic requirements of annual and daily plans and papers produced as a proof of professional development. Later on, they were encouraged to showcase the evidence in a portfolio. The fact that the initiative was a local one made it possible for supervisors to maintain a relaxed atmosphere in which they accepted whatever was displayed regardless of the quality. There was no training provided at this point as the TP required was only a collection of documents and simple guidelines were sufficient, although some teachers consulted us with regard to evidence required and criteria of organisation. In retrospect, it would have been better to provide training to teachers at this stage on how to develop a TP.

The following year, in September 2002, the MoE announced the use of TPs as a means of assessment to complement traditional annual teacher assessment (Bird & Owais, 2004). Since then TPs has become part of teacher evaluation throughout the country. This change was sudden for the majority of the schools in the Emirates as they did not have a prior experience with TPs. Bird and Owais (2004, p. 356–357) explain that the MoE portfolio serves two purposes:

> The first is to improve teaching by encouraging teachers to set their own goals, and to self-evaluate these, to encourage professional development practices, to organize records and evidence of and reflection on good practices....The second is to provide an evaluation tool that is formative, fair and balanced.

In spite of the clear requirement for reflection stated in the MoE guidelines, teachers had difficulty abiding by the requirements (Alwan, 2003c, 2004). Unfortunately, there was no initial training to familiarize teachers with the practice. Currently, however, teachers are trained on how to develop and maintain a TP. They are also taught some theory around the benefits of TPs.

Distinctive Features

Teaching portfolios exhibit documents that are indicative of the teacher's work (Alwan, 2003a; Bullock & Hawk, 2001; Shulman, 1998). When used for evaluation, they have to be organized around a defined set of criteria (Green & Smyser, 2001). Teachers may keep all their work in one portfolio but should prepare another one to present for evaluation purposes. The artifacts in the presentation portfolio should be accompanied by a written reflection (Bailey, Curtis, & Nunan, 2001; Campbell, Cignetti, Melenyzer, Nettles, & Wyman, 2001). It is argued that TPs have an advantage over classroom observations in that they document larger sections of teaching (Shulman, 1998). This makes them capture the teacher's professionalism (Alwan, 2003a; Bailey et al., 2001; Campbell et al., 2001). However, TPs should not be used exclusively for evaluation; rather, they should take a complementary stance along with other assessment tools (Tucker, Stronge, Gareis, & Beers, 2001). Basically, it is advisable that teachers seek feedback from their colleagues before submitting TPs for review (Bailey et al., 2001; Shulman, 1998). It is also agreed that evaluators have to exercise caution when reviewing portfolios when the evaluation is a decisive element in making employment decisions (Tucker et al., 2001; Pitts, Coles, & Thomas, 2001). Researchers assert that maintaining a TP has positive effects on teachers in terms of reflecting on their work (Bullock & Hawk, 2001; Lyons, 1998). Teachers are encouraged to pursue professional development and obtain evidence of this to be able to give concrete proof that they have done so (Alwan, 2003a).

Studies on Using Teaching Portfolios for Evaluation

Several studies have been conducted to investigate the use of TPs for evaluation in teacher education programs, but there is less research on the use of portfolios for evaluating practicing teachers' performance. A recurring theme in discussions of TPs, however, is related to issues of validity and reliability. Tucker et al. (2001)

report findings of a study to evaluate the use of portfolios in teacher evaluation in the United States. The main findings indicate that portfolios are useful tools that complement other tools of evaluating teaching as they help administrators in making distinctions regarding the quality of individual teacher performance. However, the researchers attest that the results of their investigation "were least definitive regarding the input of portfolios on professional development" (Tucker et al., 2001, p. 4). They argue that portfolios do not contribute to improving teaching practices or changing instructional techniques. While having strong face validity, they recommend more research be carried out to investigate content validity and reliability of portfolios as performance assessment tools.

Klenowski (2000) reports a case study on the use of portfolios for evaluating student teachers in which she collected qualitative and quantitative data from various higher education institutions in Hong Kong. Her findings outline principles for using portfolios when facing difficulties in managing the introduction of innovations in an educational context that bears similar characteristics to that of the UAE in terms of resistance to change (Alwan, 2003c). Depending on an analysis of the research data and findings, the researcher describes six principles that underpin the use of portfolios for assessment purposes, of which three apply to practicing teachers. First, portfolios demonstrate whether the teacher has developed professionally over time. Second, they encourage reflection. And third, they enable self-evaluation.

Snyder, Lippincott, & Bower, (1998) reported findings of a study of experienced teachers keeping portfolios while in a Master's of Education course. Their action research was based on the dual function of portfolios in evaluation and in supporting teacher development through reflection. Over two years and with a sample of eighteen candidates, they followed two cohorts of students through their professional preparation year. Their findings highlight the benefit of portfolios that result from reflection. The process of maintaining a TP indicated growth opportunities to the teacher. The effectiveness of portfolios was enhanced by two innovations: first, the introduction of a portfolio entry that requires reflection on growth over time; and second, the integration of research and theory. Participants, despite struggling with deep reflection, started to include more realistic evidence to signify improvement in their performance. This resulted in improving the validity of portfolios as assessment tools on that program.

In the field of evaluating practicing teachers' performance, Peterson, Stevens, & Mack (2001) report research findings that highlight the disadvantages of using portfolios for in-service teacher evaluation. The researchers studied teacher evaluation systems in five school districts in Utah. They concluded that a more compressed form of a portfolio is more valid for teacher evaluation. As I see it, the reported disadvantages were not only due to the huge size of the portfolio but also to two other factors. First, the evaluations were carried out by a panel of evaluators who did not know the teacher in person; and second, TPs were used for summative evaluation, a purpose that several people have raised concerns about (Pitts et al, 1999, 2001 & 2002). The results of evaluation when using portfolios are more valid when the evaluators know the teacher personally (Snyder et al, 1998) and when evaluation is formative and seen from a constructivist perspective.

Pitts et al. (1999, 2001, & 2002) report a series of studies in the U.K. that have been carried out in an attempt to enhance the reliability of portfolios as assessment instruments when used for summative evaluation. The researchers aimed at assessing the reliability of evaluation results that were made based on TPs developed by trainers during a training program. Three studies were conducted with three different cohorts on a voluntary basis. In each of the studies there were eight experienced evaluators. In the first study, the evaluators viewed and rated portfolios each on their own twice, with an interval of one month. The findings of Pitts et al. (1999) indicate that while the reliability of individual evaluators' ratings were moderate, inter-rater reliability indicated that portfolios are not reliable assessment tools for summative judgements. This weak reliability is a result of assessors making individual judgements separately. In the second study (Pitts et al., 2001), the assessment criteria were defined and the evaluators were briefed. The group of evaluators assessed the portfolios separately on two occasions with a one-month interval. The study revealed similar findings to the previous one; that inter-rater reliability was weak concluding that portfolios were not reliable as assessment instruments for summative evaluation. In the third study (Pitts et al., 2002), portfolio raters carried out independent assessment at first. Then, after two months, they met in random pairs to discuss and reassess the portfolios in which they used six criteria for assessment. The results of this study confirmed their previous findings that open discussions among assessors make their implicit beliefs and values explicit. Since portfolios have a narrative nature, discussions between assessors on the one hand, and between assessors and those being assessed on the other hand, improve the reliability of portfolio assessment.

Finally, I investigated teachers' perceptions of TPs with regard to validity and reliability, as well as with implementation issues in two qualitative case studies. The first study (Alwan, 2003b) was conducted toward the end of the first semester when TPs were introduced in the academic year (2002–03). In a secondary school, the EFL staff, the school principal, and the EFL supervisor were interviewed individually. The second case study (Alwan, 2003b) was partially about portfolio assessment and included all the teachers in one secondary school using an open-ended questionnaire and a focus group interview. The findings indicated that, in spite of the positive effects on professional development, as an evaluative tool TPs were less effective than other tools that were used to evaluate teachers.

Caveats

There is no doubt that TPs can have a significant effect on a teachers' professional development (Braskamp & Ory, 1994). This was also the case within the context of UAE public schools (Alwan, 2004). However, certain measures have to be taken to improve the reliability and validity of TPs as assessment tools (Alwan, 2003c). Feedback from the EFL teachers, as well as from teachers of other subjects, indicated that portfolio assessment had its weaknesses not only from a practical perspective but also from an ethical standpoint. Therefore, several procedures need to be taken when introducing TPs as an innovative tool for evaluating teaching effectiveness to enhance their benefits and eliminate their shortcomings. The following are caveats that may help augment the effectiveness of the practice.

Enhance Benefits

Teachers can benefit from the self-reflective process while documenting their work (Bailey et al., 2001). Additionally, and more important, they can benefit from expert advice by discussing their documented work with others. Therefore, it is recommended that a discussion with the teacher around the contents of the TP be initiated. When using TPs for evaluation, face-to-face interviews can pinpoint areas of deficiency in performance or aspects that can be improved on, as well as areas of distinguished performance that may be made public. In addition, peer-coaching serves as a good long-term process of reflection-on-action (Schon, 1998). Based on my observations, when teachers share their work with others they become more aware of what needs to be improved regarding specific aspects of their work. Generally, teachers accept criticism from colleagues more than they do from evaluators as peer criticism does not have negative consequences on their appraisal results.

Overcome Problems of Size with Selection

Too much attention to an impressive appearance and size of the TP was found to be a major problem with this innovation (Alwan, 2003b, 2003c). This deprived portfolios of their representative nature and shifted attention from quality to quantity. With competition, portfolios became arenas for exhibition and showing off, which resulted in the documentation or irrelevant and trivial evidence. Therefore, selection is recommended. Teachers should be advised to exhibit selected samples of their work that they find to be of high quality rather than all what they have. Setting à limit on the number of artifacts would be a practical idea for both teachers and evaluators. More important, the criteria of organization need to be clear too. Including a reflective report with every artifact may help in making the contents of the portfolio more representative of the effectiveness of the teachers' performance (Braskamp & Ory, 1994; Janesick, 2001).

Set a Timeline for Portfolio Reviews

The issue of lack of secure places for storage of portfolios meant they were kept with the teachers all the time. In addition, curricular demands made teachers postpone documenting their work till they were officially asked to submit their portfolios. In this case developing the TP was an endless process. As a result, TPs were not accessible when required and teachers, more often than not, requested an extension of time to be able to complete its contents. As Bird and Owais (2004) conclude, TPs are worth the time they require. It is therefore recommended to set specific dates for teachers to present their TPs for review.

Make Documentation Resources Available to Teachers

Another concern in developing TPs is that of resources to be used for preparing the documents that are to be showcased. It goes without saying that compiling evidence of teaching activities requires various facilities to make documentation feasible and reduce the demands on teachers (Curtis, 2000). In addition to this, attention to the aesthetic quality of the documents is an inevitable drawback since TPs create an atmosphere of competition among teachers (Alwan, 2003b, 2003c). Surprisingly, in the context of UAE public schools, other issues created tension as well. For instance, whether or not to type the artifacts was an issue, and whether to use colorful attractive paper was another (Alwan, 2003c, 2004). This resulted from a misconception that evaluators would compare portfolios. Thus it is recommended to provide teachers with standard services, not only to overcome this misconception and reduce the demands on teachers, but also to maintain standardization. Examples of such services are photocopying machines, stationery, photography equipment, scanners, and computers.

Provide Defined Assessment and Organization Criteria and Make Teachers Aware of Them

Various misunderstandings also occur when there are no defined assessment criteria, resulting in representative samples of work that are unconnected (Shulman, 1998). This was the case in this context as well. While there were defined criteria for the organization of the portfolio, many teachers organized their TPs in different ways as they appeared to be uninformed of the official circular from the MoE (Alwan, 2003c). While ineffective communication channels might have had a hand in this, evaluators should make sure that teachers know what they are required to do by either offering orientation workshops or checking TPs as early as possible when the innovation is initially introduced.

Eliminate Affective Issues

Issues of teacher evaluation are very sensitive and any innovation related to it creates tension among teachers (Alwan, 2004). Portfolios may mar teachers' self-perceptions. For instance, in the two case studies mentioned (Alwan, 2003b, 2003c), when teachers compared their portfolios with their colleagues, some of them were affected negatively by the realization that others worked more on certain areas than they did, such as writing materials to supplement textbooks or attending professional development activities. As a result, they worked harder in an attempt to expand the content of their TPs to compete with others. As informants in both studies reported while commenting on practices in the various educational districts, some teachers took unethical stances by borrowing the work of others and displaying it as their own. Others attended professional development activities and left as soon as they got the certificates of attendance. The competitive atmosphere added to the overall tension, and TPs were blamed for this. These problems might be avoided if a limited number of artifacts is required whereby teachers select the contents that best represent their work.

Promote Collaboration to Eliminate Competition

As mentioned earlier, competition was found to be a major drawback when TPs were first introduced in the UAE public schools. This drawback might have been due to the public nature of portfolios. Researchers assert that some professionals feel uncomfortable when sharing their weaknesses or goals for improvement with others and consider them private matters (Wildy & Wallace, 1998). Bearing in mind that collaboration and mentoring are essential elements in compiling TPs for evaluation as feedback from peers aids in improving the content (Bailey at al, 2001), teachers need to take advantage of feedback from colleagues. Hence, a supportive climate is needed for teachers to be able to share their concerns, weaknesses, and goals for improvement (Green & Smyser, 2001). It is advisable, therefore, to designate mentors in schools to help their peers in organizing their portfolio.

Improve Trustworthiness of Portfolio Assessment with Standardization

From the point of view of evaluators, portfolios are difficult to deal with. In addition, several researchers question the validity and reliability of approaching portfolios in measurement terms (Doolittle, 1994). Shulman (1998) doubts the objectivity of portfolio assessment and concedes that TPs are unmanageable as assessment instruments. In addition, Oakley (1998) stresses the halo effect that evaluators are subject to when they become impressed by parts of the TP and, as a result, fail to recognize potential drawbacks in some other parts. Peterson et al. (2001) note that some teachers may only select simple material for their TPs because they lack the skills to select materials that may be more representative of their performance. As a result, it is difficult to judge performance from such artifacts. Curtis (2000, p. 43) argues that documenting the three-dimensional teaching events in paper is nothing more than producing an "edited version rather than the complete picture."

While standardization is considered a problematic area by some (e.g. Shulman, 1998; Lyons, 1998), Doolittle (1994) considers the opposite to be true. He justifiably explains that comparability between teachers is sought with standardization as it is a positive tribute in portfolio assessment. It is true that variability in contents and non-uniformity of TPs imply difficulties in judging standards of teachers and subjectivity is a potential threat. However, Doolittle (1994) declares that because any form of teacher evaluation is inevitably subjective, subjectivity is not an issue. What is important is how to make portfolio assessment more valid and reliable. Therefore, he recommends a "Likert-type evaluation form, of predetermined qualities, based on the mandated items" (Doolittle, 1994).

Conclusion

There is no doubt that portfolios have a fundamental effect on teachers' professional development. Using them for assessment, however, creates various problems associated with the process of compilation of exhibits as well as with the implementation of the practice. Nevertheless, using TPs for teacher evaluation is a winning situation for teachers and evaluators alike, regardless of the difficulties associated with portfolio evaluation. There is no doubt that portfolios give teachers a voice in their own assessment. When portfolios are used for evaluating teacher effectiveness, teachers can highlight aspects of their work that they wish their assessors to focus on. Further, aspects of work that are not covered by classroom observation can be captured in a portfolio. The main issue to take into consideration is to require a standard, manageable portfolio that includes artifacts that are organized around predefined standardized evaluation criteria. Another major issue is the reflection that is to accompany each selected document. For TPs to be successful, training is a priority. These four issues (size, organization criteria, reflection, and training) are major considerations for the success of the practice. Additionally, evaluators should also keep professional portfolios because those who have not lived the experience are not in a good position to make judgments about others' portfolios.

Discussion Questions

1. With regard to the context of the case reported, to what extent is the teacher evaluation system described similar to or different from that in your context?

2. What is the rationale given for including self-evaluation as a part of teacher evaluation?

3. Identify the purposes for using teaching portfolios in the UAE context. Could this type of initiative be used in your own context? Why? Why not?

4. What advantages do teaching portfolios have over other forms of teacher evaluation?

5. Why is reflection important in the teaching portfolio process?

6. Issues that are major considerations for the success of using portfolios for teacher evaluation are identified here. What are they? Are there other issues in your context that need to be considered?

References

Al-Nayadi, M. A. (1989). *Educator's perceptions of the teacher evaluation system in the United Arab Emirates.* Doctoral Dissertation, The George Washington University. Michigan: UMI.

Altraifi, J. S. (1999). *The perceptions of women teachers in the United Arab Emirates of the conditions under which they work.* Doctoral Dissertation, University of Wales, Cardiff, UK. (Unpublished).

Alwan, F. (2003a). Teaching portfolios: A Magna Carta for teacher evaluation. *TESOL Arabia Perspectives, 10*(3), 36–45.

———. (2003b). *Teacher's roles in leading innovations and managing educational change in the United Arab Emirates.* (Unpublished paper).

———. (2003c). *Using teaching portfolios for evaluating EFL teachers in the UAE: Validating a floating concept.* (Unpublished paper).

———. (2004). *Teacher evaluation: A Star Academy approach?* Paper presented at the 8th International CTELT Conference, Dec., 2004. Sharjah, United Arab Emirates.

Bailey, K. M., Curtis, A., & Nunan, D. (2001). Teaching portfolios: Cogent collages. In D. Freeman (Ed.), *Pursuing professional development: The self as source* (pp. 223–236). Boston: Heinle & Heinle.

Bird, K., & Owais, A. (2004). The teaching portfolio. In P. Davidson, M. Al-Hamly, M. Athar Khan, J. Aydelott, K. Bird, and C. Coombe (Eds.), *Proceedings of the 9th TESOL Arabia Conference: English language teaching in the IT age, Vol. 8* (pp. 353–360). Dubai: TESOL Arabia.

Braskamp, L., & Ory, J. C. (1994). *Assessing faculty work: Enhancing individual and institutional performance.* New York: Jossey-Bass.

Bullock, A. A., & Hawk, P. (2001). *Developing a teaching portfolio: A guide for preservice and practicing teachers.* Upper Saddle River, NJ: Merill/Prentice-Hall.

Campbell, D., Cignetti, P. B., Melenyzer, B. J., Nettles, D. H., & Wyman, R. M. (2001). *Portfolio and performance assessment in teacher education.* Boston: Allyn and Bacon.

Curtis, A. (2000). CPD: Portfolios I. *English Teaching Professional, 16*, 41–43.

Doolittle, P. (1994). Teacher portfolio assessment. *Practical assessment, research and evaluation, 4*(1).

Gersten, B. (2001). A systematic approach to teacher evaluation. Workshop: Ministry of Education and Youth. Sharjah, UAE.

Ghareeb, K. (1996). *INSET in the United Arab Emirates, An Evaluation and recommendations for future development.* Master's Dissertation, Centre for English Language Teacher Education, University of Warwick. (Unpublished).

Green, J. E., & Smyser, S. O. (2001). *The teacher portfolio: A strategy for professional development and evaluation.* Boston: Scarecrow Press.

Janesick, V. J. (2001). *The assessment debate: A reference handbook.* Santa Barbara, CA: ABC-CLIO.

Klenowski, V. (2000). Portfolios: Promoting teaching. *Assessment in Education,* *7*(2), 216–236.

Loughrey, B., Hughes, A., Bax, S., Magness, C., Aziz, H., Badry, R., Alwan, F., Abbas, R., Araishi, M., & Al Samadi, K. (1999). *English language teaching in the UAE evaluation report.* Roehampton Institute: University of London. (Unpublished).

Lyons, N. (1998). Constructing narratives for understanding: Using portfolio interviews to scaffold teacher reflection. In N. Lyons (Ed.), *With portfolio in hand: Validating the new teacher professionalism* (pp. 103–119). New York: Teachers College Press.

Oakley, K. (1998). The performance assessment system: A portfolio assessment model for evaluating beginning teachers. *Journal of Personnel Evaluation in Education, 11,* 323–341.

Peterson, K. D., Stevens, D., & Mack, C. (2001). Presenting complex teacher evaluation data: Advantages of dossier organization techniques over portfolios. *Journal of Personnel Evaluation in Education, 15*(2), 121–133.

Pitts, J., Coles, C., & Thomas, P. (1999). Educational portfolio in the assessment of general practice trainers: Reliability of assessors. *Medical Education, 33,* 515–520.

———. (2001). Enhancing reliability in portfolio assessment: Shaping the portfolio. *Medical Teacher, 23*(4), 351–356.

Pitts, J., Coles, C., Thomas, P., & Smith, F. (2002). Enhancing reliability in portfolio assessment: Discussion between assessors. *Medical Teacher, 24*(2), 197–201.

Schon, D. A. (1998). *The reflective practitioner.* London: Avebury, Ashgate Publishing Limited.

Shulman, L. (1998). Teacher portfolios: A theoretical activity. In N. Lyons (Ed.), *With portfolio in hand: Validating the new teacher professionalism* (pp. 23–37). New York: Teachers College Press.

Snyder, J., Lippincott, A., & Bower, D. (1998). Portfolios in teacher education. In N. Lyons (Ed.), *With portfolio in hand: Validating the new teacher professionalism* (pp. 123–142). New York: Teachers College Press.

Tucker, P. D., Stronge, J. H., Gareis, C. R., & Beers, C. S. (2001). Research base for portfolios in teacher education. Retrieved December 22, 2002, from http://edtech.connect.msu.edu/searchaera2002/viewproposaltext. asp?propID=408

Wildy, H., & Wallace, J. (1998). Professionalism, portfolios and the development of school leaders. *School Leadership and Management, 18*(1), 123–140.

CONTRIBUTORS

Mashael Al-Hamly is an Associate Professor at the Department of English Language and Literature at Kuwait University. She has a Ph.D. in Computer-Assisted Language Learning from the University of East Anglia, UK. Dr. Al-Hamly teaches English Language and Linguistics to undergraduate and postgraduate students as well as to the community-center adult learners at Kuwait University. She has published in regional as well international journals in the areas of testing, using computers in learning foreign languages, and translation studies.

Fatma Alwan has experience in TEFL as a teacher, supervisor, and a curriculum writer in the Ministry of Education, UAE. She has an Ed.D. in TEFL from Exeter University, UK. Her main interests lie in the following areas of research: (1) improving learning outcomes and instruction using NLP, (2) teacher training, (3) teacher evaluation, (4) curriculum issues, and (5) educational change.

Caroline Brandt has a Ph.D. in TESOL from the University of East Anglia, UK, and is currently Assistant Professor with the Petroleum Institute in Abu Dhabi, United Arab Emirates, where she teaches communication skills to undergraduate engineers. Caroline has worked in ELT for more than 22 years in diverse institutions in Europe, the Middle East, and the Asia-Pacific region. Her research interests include critical pedagogy, qualitative research methods, and teacher education and development. She is the author of *Success on Your Certificate Course in English Language Teaching: A Guide to Becoming a Teacher in ELT/TESOL* (2006).

Lyn Bray has extensive experience teaching migrants and overseas students in Australia, including programs in workplace education, vocational preparation, and foundation studies. She has also taught in the Philippines, Indonesia, China, Laos, and the United Arab Emirates. As a teacher educator, she has trained English teachers at a summer school in Romania, developed a program for a Sudanese community school in Adelaide, and lectured in TESOL at the University of South Australia, where she is currently undertaking Ph.D. studies.

Peter Burden is an Associate Professor at Okayama Shoka University in Japan where he has taught English for fifteen years. His research interests include student and teacher perceptions of classroom events and how these perceptions are often not shared. He has published a number of articles on the use of students' Mother Tongue in English classes.

Jill Burton is associate professor of applied linguistics in the School of Education, University of South Australia, Adelaide. She supervises research students in TESOL, and researches, edits, and writes on reflective practice, teacher learning, and classroom discourse. She has just completed a 21-volume of *Case Studies in TESOL Practice* as series editor for TESOL Publications, Inc.

Liying Cheng (Ph.D.) is an Associate Professor and a Director of the Assessment and Evaluation Group (AEG) at the Faculty of Education, Queen's University. Her primary research interests are the impact of testing on instruction and the relationship between assessment and instruction in classrooms. Her recent evaluation project is the program evaluation of the Bachelor of Education program (B. Ed.) for the Alternative Teacher Accreditation Program for Teachers with International Experience (ATAPTIE).

Christine Coombe has a Ph.D. in Foreign/Second Language Education and Testing from The Ohio State University. She is currently on the English faculty of Dubai Men's College and works as an Assessment Leader for the Higher Colleges of Technology. She has spent 14 years living and working in the Arabian Gulf. Christine is co-editor of the *Assessment Practices* volume in the TESOL Case Studies series (with Nancy Hubley).

Andy Curtis has an M.A. in Applied Linguistics and a Ph.D. in International Education from the University of York, UK. He has worked on professional development with 10,000 language educators in more than 20 countries. He has also co-edited two books: one on language testing and one on color, race, and language teaching; co-authored one book on teacher professional development; and published 35 book chapters, refereed articles, and papers.

Peter Davidson teaches composition at Zayed University in Dubai, having previously taught in New Zealand, Japan, the UK, and Turkey. He recently co-edited *Teacher Education and Professional Learning: Insights from the Arabian Gulf, Vocabulary Teaching and Learning in Another Language,* and *Assessment in the Arab World.* He is particularly interested in vocabulary teaching and learning, language testing, and teacher evaluation.

Deniz Kurtoglu Eken (Ph.D.) is the Director of the School of Languages at Sabanci University in Turkey. She has worked as an EFL teacher, an M.A. lecturer, and a trainer on many training programs, including UCLES and British Council courses. Since 1997, she has also been designing and running diploma and certificate programs in trainer training, which is her main area of expertise. Her research interests include supervisory practices and qualitative research.

Dorit Kaufman is director of the Professional Education Program at Stony Brook University, State University of New York (SUNY). Her research interests include native language attrition and narrative development in children, teacher education, content-based instruction, and constructivist pedagogy. She received the R. Neil Appleby Outstanding Teacher Educator Award and the SUNY President's and Chancellor's Awards for Excellence in Teaching. Dorit is co-editor of the two Content-Based Instruction volumes in the TESOL Case Studies series (with JoAnn Crandall).

Mary Lou McCloskey is Director of Teacher Development and Curriculum Design for Educo in Atlanta, Georgia. A former teacher in primary and secondary multilingual, multicultural classrooms, she works internationally as an author and consultant with teachers, teacher educators, and departments and ministries of education. She has written widely on aspects of teaching school-age English learners and has co-authored five programs for school-age learners.

Lindsay Miller is an Associate Professor in the Department of English and Communication and Associate Dean (Administration) in the Faculty of Humanities and Social Sciences at City University of Hong Kong. He is the co-author of *Establishing Self-Access: From Theory to Practice*: CUP (with D. Gardner), and *Second Language Listening: Theory to Practice*: CUP (with J. Flowerdew).

Tim Murphey (Ph.D., Université de Neuchâtel, Switzerland) is series editor for TESOL's *Professional Development in Language Education* series. He is presently professor in applied linguistics at Dokkyo University in Japan and a visiting professor in Hawaii Pacific University's MA TESL program. He has authored *Group Dynamics in the Language Classroom*: CUP (with Zoltán Dörnyei), *Music & Song*: OUP, and *Language Hungry!*: Helbling Languages.

Phil Quirke is Director of Madinat Zayed College, Higher Colleges of Technology, UAE. He has been in educational management for more than fifteen years and has published extensively on teacher development. Phil was also the section editor for the first three volumes of the Out of the Box section of the *Essential Teacher*.

Donna Sobel is an Associate Professor in the Special Education program at the University of Colorado at Denver & Health Sciences Center. She serves as a Site Professor at one of UCDHSC's professional development schools. Dr. Sobel's concerns about the attitudes that teachers hold regarding issues of diversity, including persons with disabilities, has led to a series of investigations of teachers' beliefs toward addressing the educational needs of learners from diverse backgrounds and with diverse needs.

Stephen Stoynoff is a professor of English and director of the MA TESL program at Minnesota State University, Mankato, where he teaches courses in research methods, second language assessment, and second language literacy development. He is coauthor (with Carol Chapelle) of *ESOL Tests and Testing* (TESOL, 2005) and was editor of *TESOL Journal* from 1998 to 2003.

Sheryl V. Taylor is an Associate Professor of Second Languages/Cultures in the Reading and Writing Program in the School of Education at University of Colorado (Denver). She teaches multicultural education, second language acquisition, and bilingual education/ESL. She regularly coaches professional teachers in Denver area schools to support English language learners in general education classrooms. Her research examines teachers' cognition and practice about addressing the needs of students from diverse backgrounds and abilities.

Barbara Thornton is an educational development consultant based in Sao Paulo, Brazil. Before becoming a freelance consultant, she was director of the MA TESOL and Applied Linguistics at the University of Leicester, UK. Barbara has worked with teachers and teacher educators in more than 20 countries on five continents.

Nadia Ahmed Touba is an associate professor at Alexandria University in Egypt. She is presently working on developing national performance standards for pre-service teachers in Egypt with the Faculties of Education Reform unit in a USAID-funded project, Education Reform Project. The FOER unit works in partnership with Michigan State University and the University of Pittsburgh.

Salah Troudi is a lecturer of TESOL and language education at the University of Exeter, UK. He is the director of the Doctorate of Education in TESOL programme in Dubai, and his research interests include teacher education, critical applied linguistics, critical pedagogy, language policy, and curriculum and syllabus design. He has published a number of articles in the area of teacher education.

Qiu Yaode is an associate professor in Department of English Education at Capital Normal University in Beijing, China. He has been teaching English to a wide variety of students for more than 32 years. He is especially keen on the methods of teaching young learners ages 3 to 12.

Jean Young is the Head of the English Language Centre at City University of Hong Kong. Her previous posts include Co-ordinator, Teacher Training at the Language Institute of the University of Waikato, New Zealand, and Deputy Director, British Council English Language Centre, Hong Kong. Her research interests include learner autonomy, teacher development, and the evaluation of teaching.

AUTHOR AND SUBJECT INDEX